A Selected Bibliography on Modern French History 1600 to the Present

COMPILED and EDITED by
JOHN BOWDITCH
AND
RAYMOND GREW
ASSISTED by ROGER GEIGER

Xerox University Microfilms
Ann Arbor, Michigan
1974

PHOTOLITHOPRINTED BY CUSHING - MALLOY, INC.
ANN ARBOR, MICHIGAN, UNITED STATES OF AMERICA
1974

CONTENTS

Part I. BOOKS

INTRODUCTION

This bibliography is intended primarily to assist those responsible for building a balanced collection on the history of France in college and university libraries. Throughout modern history, France has been among the most populous, powerful, and influential of Western nations. Understandably, the historical literature reflects this preeminence. Rich in controversy and methodological sophistication, the writings on French history range from works of grand synthesis to microscopic studies; and formal scholarship is supplemented by lively memoirs from every period and important collections of sources. Nor is the intimate concern with French history limited to Frenchmen, for perhaps no other nation has been so thoroughly studied and written about in other countries. As this bibliography suggests, particularly in the twelve hundred American doctoral dissertations cited in Part II, fascination with the history of France has been especially strong in the United States.

Major research collections are comprised of tens of thousands of volumes and even well-established libraries often find it difficult to maintain a comprehensive and balanced collection. For new or recently expanded universities, the challenge of building the kind of collection required for effective teaching can seem prohibitively demanding in expertise, time, and money. A library that contained all the works listed here would, we believe, be sufficient to sustain advanced undergraduates in studying in some depth the major topics of French history, to support term papers of high quality, and to enable beginning graduate students to meet most of the requirements for work at the master's level. Major university libraries, of course, already have a great deal that is included here and much that is not; for them this bibliography can serve as a useful checklist for additional acquisitions. Graduate students specializing in French history may take this list as one statement of the works they need to be aware of. Researchers should find the list of doctoral dissertations accepted by American universities especially valuable, for their more systematic use would both facilitate new investigations and help to avoid unnecessary repetition of the efforts already made by others.

Principles of Selection: This bibliography has been limited to works dealing with the period since 1600 on the grounds that national boundaries have less meaning prior to that date, that the conventions of historiography treat "modern history" as starting roughly from that time, and that the great majority of American students and scholars

vii

have stressed this later period. We have tried to include the classic works from which modern scholarship begins, even if they have been in part superseded, on the basis that familiarity with them is an important part of one's historical education. While necessarily selective, we have sought to include the monographs that represent the best scholarship on important topics, that exemplify diverse historical methods, and that should hold wide interest for serious students. We have given preference to titles in English, including translations, on the assumption that few historical works suffer so much as fiction from the inevitable losses in translation. Still, a high proportion of American students can read French, and no library ignores works available only in a foreign language. Most of the titles included here are formally works of history, although some were written by scholars who consider themselves anthropologists, geographers, economists, demographers, or political scientists.

On the other hand, we have not attempted to cover the important contributions to historical understanding that clearly fall within other disciplines. Nor, with rare exceptions, have we included the large and costly collections of source materials essential to the doctoral candidate and research scholar. We have left out those works, like the histories of civilization in which the French pioneered, that deal with several countries, on the assumption that libraries purchase such books without regard to an interest in France. We have also omitted atlases, bibliographical guides, biographical dictionaries, and other general books that belong in any library. Even more restrictive in our choice of primary sources, we kept the needs of a small college or new university library in mind and tried to list just enough to give the student a chance to begin that independent research that is the greatest excitement of historical study. Our initial target was a list of some one thousand titles; by painful cutting, we have not exceeded that by much. Inevitably, many choices were simply arbitrary.

Knowing that libraries but rarely have extensive collections of doctoral dissertations, however, here we used an opposite selection principle. All dissertations primarily about France which have been presented as dissertations in history are included along with many of those in the social sciences. Some of the still greater number written in fields such as literature, history of art, and music that seemed likely to be of general interest to historians are also listed.

Principles of Organization: As the Contents indicates, both the published works and the dissertations are listed in seven sections. Six of these cover specific chronological periods while the initial, general section also contains works that pertain to two or more of these periods. Each section has been further broken into the following sub-sections: General and Miscellaneous; chronological subdivisions (e.g. French Revolution, 1789-1794); Government, Administration, Education, Military; Social and Economic; Regional Studies; Intellectual and Cultural; Religion; Memoirs and Contemporary Writings. Since no title

DOCTORAL DISSERTATIONS AND OUT-OF-PRINT BOOKS ON FRENCH HISTORY

SPECIAL OFFER ORDER FORM

PLEASE SHIP THE FOLLOWING DOCTORAL DISSERTATION(S) AND/OR OUT-OF-PRINT BOOK(S) IN THE FORMAT(S) AS INDICATED TO THE SHIPPING ADDRESS GIVEN. If you order 100 or more dissertations and/or out-of-print books in any format before October 1, 1974, you are entitled to a 10% savings on the cost of these publications purchased individually. If you order 25 or more dissertations and/or out-of-print books before that date, you are entitled to a 5% savings.

TO ORDER:

1. Fill-in the order number, author's last name, and title of a selected dissertation or out-of-print book.
2. Check the format desired —

    H = electrostatically-produced book form with a hard cover.
    X = electrostatically-produced book form with a paper cover.
    M = 35mm positive microfilm.

3. Enter the appropriate price for each dissertation or out-of-print book selected. Dissertation prices are as follows: H = $13.50; X = $11.00; M = $5.00. Out-of-print book prices are as listed in the catalog.
4. Figure the total amount owed on the reverse side of this form.
5. Finally, please provide the shipping and billing information, purchase order number, and signature and date called for on the reverse side of this form. If you are entitled to a tax exemption certificate and have not filed one with Xerox University Microfilms, include one with your order so you will not be charged tax.

ORDER NUMBER	AUTHOR'S LAST NAME	FIRST 3 TO 5 WORDS OF TITLE	QTY.	FORMAT DESIRED			AMOUNT
				H	X	M	

ORDER NUMBER	AUTHOR'S LAST NAME	FIRST 3 TO 5 WORDS OF TITLE	QTY.	FORMAT DESIRED		AMOUNT
				H	X M	

	SUBTOTAL
	SUBTOTAL FROM PAGE 1
	LESS 10% (if you order 100 or more titles prior to Oct. 1, 1974)*
	LESS 5% (if you order 25 or more titles prior to Oct. 1, 1974)*
Tax Exemption No. _____ or Tax	
ADD SHIPPING AND HANDLING — 25¢ per electrostatic copy — 10¢ per microfilm copy	
TOTAL	

*To be eligible for the special savings offer, orders must be postmarked prior to Oct. 1, 1974, and this order form must accompany your order.

SHIP TO: _____

Address _____

City _____ State _____ Zip _____

Attention _____

BILL TO (if different) _____

Address _____

City _____ State _____ Zip _____

Attention _____

Signature _____ Purchase Order No. _____ Date _____

Printed in U.S.A.   DI-3135-DM

Subtotal

is listed more than once, those seeking works on a specific topic will want to check in several categories.

Studies of politics and diplomacy, along with histories of particular events, will generally be found in their appropriate chronological sub-sections. When they overlap a second chronological category by a few years, they have usually been placed in the earlier of the two appropriate categories. If they cover a time-span substantially greater than that of these sub-sections, they were included among the general and miscellaneous works which did not fit any of the specific categories. Additional sub-sections were added to accommodate the extensive literature on the Enlightenment in the eighteenth century and on socialism and the labor movement in the later periods. Works on the parliamentary activities of socialist parties, however, were normally placed in the chronological sub-sections (with other studies of political activity). Similarly, studies of legislation and decision-making were usually placed in these sub-sections, leaving the section on government and administration for works on the functions of government, including those on education and the military.

Other Guides: Librarians and scholars using this bibliography will also need to consult the appropriate sections of the American Historical Association's *Guide to Historical Literature* (both the 1931 and 1965 editions, which differ in scope and content). Although it is now being rapidly outdated, the French bibliography *La Recherche historique en France du 1940 à 1965* published under the auspices of the Centre national de la recherche scientifique, Paris, 1965, covering the works of historians published from 1946 to 1965, includes several thousand titles and a guide to French archives and research organizations. For current literature there is the annual *Bibliographie d'histoire de France,* which lists both published books and articles from several hundred French and foreign, including American journals; the issues of the *American Historical Review* and the *Journal of Modern History,* that provide reviews of most works comparable to those selected for this bibliography; and *French Historical Studies* which provides more comprehensive listings but does not review individual titles.

Libraries should acquire the debates of the parliamentary assemblies. For the early period one must in most cases depend on microfilm copies: for the period from 1789 to 1868 the debates appeared in the semi-official *Le Moniteur universel* and for most of the years from 1789 to 1838 in the *Archives parlementaires,* published later with supplementary notes by French scholars; for the years after 1868 there is the *Journal officiel de la République française.* The published volumes of the French census which, like those of the United States census, are mines of information on much more than demography are now also rare and expensive. Fortunately, a large part of these data is becoming available in machine-readable form and accessible to scholars anywhere through the École pratique des hauts-études in Paris and the Institute for Social Research at The University of Michigan.

After the parliamentary debates, libraries should acquire and continue to keep current at least a few of the major French historical journals and reviews (which go back to the seventeenth century) and newspapers (from the eighteenth century). A selected list of the most important of these follows the introduction.

Acknowledgments: In preparing the bibliography we were assisted in the initial gathering of titles by two University of Michigan graduate students Nancy Q. Crockett and Sanford J. Gutman, and the final draft is largely the work of our colleague Roger Geiger. Sections of the bibliography were reviewed by Professors Lionel Rothkrug, John Rule, David Bien, Father de Berthier de Sauvigny, David Pinkney, Claude Fohlen, Philip Bankwitz, and John Cairns — all of whom proved more successful in suggesting additions than deletions in the areas of their specialties. None of them is responsible for egregious omissions or errors. Mrs. Bonnie Davis and her efficient staff at Xerox University Microfilms carried out the laborious work of collecting the titles of dissertations for our review, prepared the index and converted our boxes of bibliographic cards into a presentable book.

John Bowditch
Raymond Grew

BASIC JOURNALS AND NEWSPAPERS

PROFESSIONAL JOURNALS
  Annales: économies, sociétés, civilisations
  Annales de la révolution française
  French Historical Studies
  Revue d'histoire moderne et
    contemporaine
  Revue historique

REVIEWS OF OPINION
(with date of first publication)
  La Gazette de France, 1631
  Journal des Savants, 1665
  Mercure de France, 1672
  Revue de Paris, 1829
  Revue des deux mondes, 1829
  L'Illustration, 1843
  La Revue socialiste, 1885
  La Revue politique et parlementaire,
    1894
  Esprit, 1932
  La Nef, 1944
  Les Temps modernes, 1945
  Le Nouvel observateur, 1950
  Preuves, 1951

NEWSPAPERS
Pre-Revolution (1760-1789)
  Courrier de l'Europe
  Gazette de France
  Journal de Paris
  Mercure de France
Revolution (1789-1799)
  L'Ami du peuple
  Journal de la République française
  Journal des débats
  Le Moniteur universel
  Le Patriote français
Napoleon (1799-1814)
  Gazette de France
  Journal des débats
  Le Moniteur universel
Restoration (1814-1830)
  Le Constitutionnel
  Le Globe
  Journal des débats
  Le Moniteur universel
  La Quotidienne

July Monarchy (1830-1847)
  Journal des débats
  Le Moniteur universel
  Le National
  Le Presse
  La Reforme
  Le Siècle
Second Republic (1848-1851)
  L'Assemblée nationale
  Journal des débats
  Le Moniteur universel
  Le National
  La Réforme
  Le Représentani du peuple
  Le Siècle
Second Empire (1852-1870)
  Le Constitutionnel
  Le Figaro
  Journal des débats
  Le Moniteur universel
  Le Siècle
  L'Univers
Third Republic (1870-1890)
  Le XIXe Siècle
  Le Figaro
  Journal des débats
  La République française
  Le Temps
  L'Univers
Third Republic (1890-1918)
  L'Aurore
  La Croix
  Le Figaro
  L'Humanité
  La République française
  Le Temps
Third Republic (1919-1939)
  L'Action française
  Le Figaro
  L'Humanité
  Le Populaire
  Le Temps
Contemporary Period (1940 to present)
  Combat
  Le Figaro
  L'Humanité
  Le Monde

ORDERING INFORMATION

Books: Many of the books listed on pages 1-56 are available through Xerox University Microfilms' Out-of-Print Book Program. Those currently for sale in microfilm and full-size xerographic form are indicated at the end of the entries by OP order numbers and prices. The prices listed are for xerographic copies with a standard 65-lb. paper cover; cloth bindings (with author and title stamped in gold on the spine) are an additional $2.50 per volume. Thirty-five mm. positive microfilm copies may also be ordered. Prices may be calculated the following way from xerographic prices listed:

Xerographic	Microfilm
$6-15	$ 5
20	7
25	8
30	10
35	12
40	14
45	15

Books lacking OP numbers may still be in print and available from the publisher. (Paperback editions are noted by publisher in parentheses at the end of some entries.) Other books may be out-of-print but not currently available from Xerox University Microfilms. On request, we will acquire OP titles. Please write for further information.

Dissertations: Many of the dissertations listed on pages 57-112 are also available in xerographic and 35mm. positive microfilm copies. These are indicated by order number and citation to an abstract in *Dissertation Abstracts International.* Microfilm is $5.00 and paperbound xerographic copies are $11.00 per title regardless of length. Cloth binding is $2.50 additional per volume. Xerographic copies are about 2/3 the page size of the original and are bound in a standard 65-lb. paper cover unless otherwise specified. Finished copy has printing on one side of the page only.

Orders.

Orders must include author, title, and order number along with type of reproduction and binding desired. Individuals must send check or money order with their orders. Institutions will be billed when their orders are shipped; they should order on their standard purchase order form, being sure to include the purchase order number and tax exemption number. Shipping charges and taxes, where applicable, are additional. Shipping and billing name and address must be indicated.

Orders should be mailed directly to:

Xerox University Microfilms
300 North Zeeb Road
Ann Arbor, Michigan 48106

In Canada
Xerox Education Group — Canada
35 Mobile Drive
Toronto, Ontario M4A 1H5,
Canada

In Europe & throughout the Eastern Hemisphere
University Microfilms Limited
St. John's Road, Tylers Green
Penn, Buckinghamshire HP10 8HR,
England

Publications and Services

DISSERTATION RELATED PUBLICATIONS AND SERVICES AVAILABLE THROUGH XEROX UNIVERSITY MICROFILMS

Xerox University Microfilms publishes the doctoral dissertations accepted by almost all accredited, degree-granting institutions in the United States and Canada. As a result, we have become a leading center for information on dissertation related activities.

In addition to offering copies of dissertations on microfilm or in electrostatically produced book-form, Xerox University Microfilms has developed a full range of publications and services which significantly increase the accessibility of doctoral research to those who need it. These publications and services include:

DISSERTATION ABSTRACTS INTERNATIONAL

This highly respected journal was first published in 1938 and is distributed on subscription to most research libraries worldwide. Issued monthly, DAI publishes 600-word abstracts of research findings written by the authors themselves, and at the time the dissertation is accepted. DAI has become one of the first resources which researchers consult to find descriptive information on doctoral research in their field.

AMERICAN DOCTORAL DISSERTATIONS

This annual publication is a complete listing of all doctoral dissertations accepted by American and Canadian universities during the year. It is organized within subject field by institution and author. This arrangement provides a concise overview of dissertations in a particular area, and serves as a valuable aid to scholars in bibliographic compilation.

COMPREHENSIVE DISSERTATION INDEX, 1861-1972

A 37-volume subject and author index which provides bibliographic information about more than 417,000 dissertations—virtually every one honored by accredited, degree-granting American and many Canadian institutions since doctoral programs began in 1861. CDI is the first work to assemble this mass of information into a single, definitive source. Well designed and easy-to-use, it expedites the search process so that the scholar or researcher can locate any dissertation or group of dissertations in minutes. A yearly update service publishes supplements which incorporate the more than 30,000 new dissertations accepted every year.

MAIL-ORDER DISSERTATION INFORMATION SERVICE

A unique mail-order service designed to prepare customized bibliographies of doctoral dissertations for those who request it. The computer stored data base created to compile and publish the Comprehensive Dissertation Index is used and continuously updated to make the prepared bibliographies as complete and up-to-date as possible. This service is significant in that it can provide the scholar or researcher with unprecedented interdisciplinary access to dissertations of potential significance as defined by his topic and research requirements.

SPECIAL SUBJECT BIBLIOGRAPHIES

Like this special bibliography of doctoral dissertations, Xerox University Microfilms periodically compiles and publishes special bibliographies of dissertations on subjects of topical interest. These bibliographies are sent free of charge to libraries and specialists in each area.

If you would like further information concerning any of the publications and services available through Xerox University Microfilms, please write to our Literature Services Department, 300 North Zeeb Road, Ann Arbor, Michigan 48106.

PART I: BOOKS

HISTORIES AND SPECIAL STUDIES COVERING MORE THAN ONE CENTURY

GENERAL AND MISCELLANEOUS

ADAM, Gerard. *Atlas des elections sociales en France.* Paris: Colin, 1964. 173 p.

ANDERSON, Frank Maloy, ed. *Constitutions and other select documents illustrative of the history of France, 1789-1901.* 2nd ed. New York: Russell & Russell, 1967. 693 p. (1904, ed. OP 19,034 $35.00)

BELLANGER, Claude, *et al.,* éds. *Histoire générale de la presse française.* Paris: Presses universitaires de France, 1969- .
I. Des origines à 1814, par Louis Charlet, *et al.* 1969.
II. De 1815 à 1871, par Louis Charlet, *et al.* 1970.

BOUJU, Paul M., *et al. Atlas historique de la France contemporaine, 1800-1965.* Paris: Colin, 1966. 233 p.

BOURGEOIS, Émile. *Manuel historique de politique étrangère.* 4 v. Paris: Belin, 1892-1926. (OP 64,580 $170.00)
I. Les origines, 6th ed. − $35.00
II. Les révolutions (1789-1830), 5th ed. − $45.00
III. Le temps présent (1830-78), 4th ed. − $45.00
IV. La politique mondiale (1878-1919), 3d ed. − $45.00

BOUSSARD, Jacques. *Atlas historique et culturel de la France.* Paris: Elsevier, 1957. 214 p.

BROGAN, Denis William. *The French nation, from Napoleon to Petain, 1814-1940.* New York: Harper, 1957. 328 p.

BURY, John P. T. *France, 1814-1940.* 3rd ed. London: Methuen, 1956. 348 p.

CAMPBELL, Peter. *French electoral systems and elections since 1789.* 2nd ed. London: Faber & Faber, 1965. 155 p.

CHEVALLIER, Jean Jacques. *Histoire des institutions et des régimes politiques de la France moderne, 1789-1958.* 3. ed. rev. et augm. Paris: Dalloz, 1967. 743 p.

COBBAN, Alfred. *A history of modern France.* 3 v. London: Cape, 1962-65. (Penguin)

DESCHAMPS, Hubert Jules. *Méthodes et doctrines coloniales de la France, du XVIe siècle à nos jours.* Paris: Colin, 1953. 222 p.

DUPEUX, Georges. *La société française, 1789-1960.* 3. éd. Paris: Colin, 1964. 295 p.

ESMONIN, Édmond. *Études sur la France des XVIIe et XVIIIe siècles.* Paris: Presses universitaires de France, 1964. 538 p.

FRIGUGLIETTI, James, and Kennedy, Emmet, eds. *The shaping of modern France: writings on French history since 1715.* New York: Macmillan, 1969. 633 p.

GUERARD, Albert Léon. *France: a modern history.* Ann Arbor: University of Michigan Press, 1959. 563 p.

HANOTAUX, Gabriel, éd. *Histoire de la nation française.* 15 v. Paris: Plon-Nourrit, 1920-29.

I. Introduction générale. Géographie humaine de la France, par Jean Brunhes.

II. Géographie humaine de la France. Géographie politique et géographie du travail, par Jean Brunhes et Pierre Deffontaines.

III. Histoire politique: des origines à 1515, par P. Imbart de la Tour.

IV. Histoire politique: de 1515 à 1804, par Louis Madelin.

V. Histoire politique: de 1804 à 1926, par G. Hanotaux.

VI. Histoire religieuse, par Georges Goyau.

VII. Histoire militaire et navale: des origines à la révolution, par J. Colin et F. Reboul.

VIII. Histoire militaire et navale: de la constituante à la guerre de 1914-18, par général Mangin, Franchet d'Esperey, G. Hanotaux.

IX. Histoire diplomatique, 1515-1928, par René Pinon.

X. Histoire économique et financière, par Germain Martin.

XI. Histoire des arts, par Louis Gillet.

XII. Histoire des lettres: des origines à Ronsard, par J. Bédier, et al.

XIII. Histoire des lettres: de Ronsard à nos jours, par F. Stowski.

XIV. Histoire des sciences en France: introduction, mathématiques, mécanique, astronomie, physique, chimie; par E. Picard, et al.

XV. Histoire des sciences en France: sciences biologiques, philosophie; par M. Caullery et René Lote.

HANOTAUX, Gabriel. *Histoire des colonies françaises et de l'expansion de la France dans le monde.* 6 v. Paris: Société de l'histoire nationale, 1929-32.

KNAPTON, Ernest John. *France, an interpretive history.* New York: Scribner's, 1971. 616 p.

LAVISSE, Ernest, éd. *Histoire de France contemporaine depuis la Révolution jusqu'à la paix de 1919.* 10 v. Paris: Hachette, 1920-22.

I. La révolution (1789-1792), par P. Sagnac.

II. La révolution (1792-99), par G. Pariset.

III. Le consulat et l'empire (1799-1815), par G. Pariset.

IV. La restauration (1815-30), par S. Charléty.

V. La monarchie de juillet (1830-48), par S. Charléty.

VI. La révolution de 1848—Le second empire (1848-59), par Ch. Seignobos.

VII. Le déclin de l'empire et l'établissement de la IIIe république (1859-75), par Ch. Seignobos.

VIII. L'évolution de la IIIe république (1875-1914), par Ch. Seignobos.

IX. La grande guerre, par H. Bidou, et al. Conclusion générale, par E. Lavisse.

X. Tables générales des origines à la paix de 1919.

LAVISSE, Ernest, éd. *Histoire de France depuis les origines jusqu'à la Révolution.* 9 v. in 18. Paris: Hachette, 1900-11.

I. 1. Tableau de la géographie de la France, par P. Vidal de la Blanche.

I. 2. Les origines; la Gaule indépendente et la Gaule romaine, par G. Bloch.

II. 1. Le christianisme, les barbares, Mérovingiens et Carolingiens, par C. Bayet, C. Pfister, A. Kleinclausz.

II. 2. Les premiers Capétiens (987-1137), par A. Luchaire.

III. 1. Louis VII—Philippe-Auguste—Louis VIII (1137-1226), par A. Luchaire.

III. 2. Saint-Louis—Philippe le Bel. Les derniers Capétiens directs (1226-1328), par C. V. Langlois.

IV. 1. Les premiers Valois et la guerre de cent ans (1328-1422), par A. Coville.

IV. 2. Charles VII, Louis XI et les premières années de Charles VIII (1422-92), par C. Petit-Dutaillis.

V. 1. Les guerres d'Italie, la France sous Charles VIII, Louis XII et François Ier (1492-1547), par H. Lemonnier.

V. 2. La lutte contre la maison d'Autriche, la France sous Henri II (1519-59), par H. Lemonnier.

VI. 1. La réforme et la ligue. L'édit de Nantes (1559-98), par J. H. Mariéjol.

VI. 2. Henry IV et Louis XIII (1598-1643), par J. H. Mariéjol.

VII. 1. Louis XIV. La fronde. Le roi. Colbert (1643-85), par E. Lavisse.

VII. 2. Louis XIV. La religion. Les lettres et les arts. La guerre (1643-85), par E. Lavisse.

VIII. 1. Louis XIV: la fin du règne (1685-1715), par A. de Saint-Léger, et al.

VIII. 2. Le règne de Louis XV (1715-74), par H. Carré.

IX. 1. Le règne de Louis XVI (1774-89), par H. Carré, et al.

IX. 2. Tables alphabétiques.

MANFRED, Al'bert Z. *Essais d'histoire de France du XVIIIe au XXe siècle — Recueil d'articles.* Moscou: Éditions du progrès, 1970. 623 p.

PRIESTLEY, Herbert I. *France overseas through the old regime: a study of European expansion.* New York: Appleton Century, 1939. 393 p. (OP 26,572 $25.00)

RAIN, Pierre. *La diplomatie française.* 2 v. Paris: Plon, 1945.
I. D'Henri IV à Vergennes.
II. De Mirabeau à Bonaparte.

REINHARD, Marcel, éd. *Histoire de France.* 2 v. Paris: Larousse, 1954.
I. Des origines à 1715.
II. De 1715 à 1946.

WARNER, Charles K., ed. *From the Ancien Régime to the Popular Front; essays in the history of modern France in honor of Shepard B. Clough.* New York: Columbia University Press, 1969. 211 p.

WOLF, John B. *France, 1815 to the present.* New York: Harper & Row, 1963. 518 p.

WRIGHT, Gordon. *France in modern times: 1760 to the present.* Chicago: Rand McNally, 1960. 621 p.

GOVERNMENT, ADMINISTRATION, EDUCATION, MILITARY

ARTZ, Frederick B. *The development of technical education in France, 1500-1850.* Cleveland: Society for the History of Technology, 1966. 274 p.

CARRIAS, E. *La pensée militaire française.* Paris: Presses universitaires de France, 1960. 378 p.

CHAPMAN, Brian. *Introduction to French local government.* London: Allen & Unwin, 1953. 238 p. (OP 26,920 $15.00)

CHÉNON, Émile. *Histoire générale du droit français public et privé des origines à 1815.* 2 v. Paris: Société anonyme du Recueil Sirey, 1926-29.

CHEVALIER, Louis Edouard. *Histoire de la marine française.* 5 v. Paris: Hachette, 1886-1902.
I. Depuis les débuts de la monarchie jusqu'au traité de paix de 1763.
II. Pendant la guerre de l'indépendance américaine.
III. Sous la première république.
IV. Sous le consulat et l'empire.
V. De 1815 à 1870.

CLOUGH, Shepard B. *France: a history of national economics, 1789-1939.* New York: Octagon, 1964 (c.1939). 498 p.

DUVERGER, Maurice. *Les institutions françaises.* Paris: Presses universitaires de France, 1962. 408 p.

GIRARDET, Raoul. *La société militaire dans la France contemporaine, 1815-1939.* Paris: Plon, 1953. 329 p. (OP 51,848 $20.00)

GLASSON, Ernest Desire. *Le Parlement de Paris; son rôle politique depuis le règne de Charles XII jusqu'à la Révolution.* 2 v. Paris: Hachette, 1901.

LA RONCIÈRE, Charles Bourel de. *Histoire de la marine française.* Paris: Larousse, 1934. 408p.

LEGENDRE, Pierre. *Histoire de l'administration, de 1750 à nos jours.* Paris: Presses universitaires de France, 1968. 580 p.

LIARD, Louis. *L'enseignement supérieur en France, 1789-1893.* 2 v. Paris: Colin, 1888-94.

PONTEIL, Felix. *Histoire de l'enseignement en France: les grandes étapes, 1789-1966.* Paris: Sirey, 1966. 454 p.

PROST, Antoine. *L'enseignement en France, 1800-1967.* Paris: Colin, 1968. 524 p.

SOCIAL AND ECONOMIC

ABBIATECI, A., et al. *Crimes et criminalité en France sous l'ancien régime, XVIIe-XVIIIe siècles.* Paris: Colin, 1971. 268 p.

ARIÈS, Philippe. *Centuries of childhood; a social history of family life.* Tr. by Robert Baldick. New York: Knopf, 1962. (Vintage) 447 p.

ARIÈS, Philippe. *Histoire des populations françaises et de leur attitudes devant la vie depuis le XVIIIe siècle.* Nouv. éd. Paris: Éditions de Seuil, 1971 (c.1948). 412 p.

BLOCH, Marc. *French rural history; an essay in its basic characteristics.* Berkeley: University of California Press, 1966 (orig. pub. 1931). 258 p.

CHARLIAT, Pierre J. *Trois siècles d'économie maritime française.* Paris: Rivière, 1931. 228 p.

4

COCHOIS, Paul. *Étude historique et critique de l'impôt sur le sel en France.* Paris: Giard et Brière, 1902. 187 p.

DUPLESSIS, Gérard. *Les mariages en France.* Paris: Colin, 1954. 196 p.

GOUBERT, Pierre. *L'ancien régime.* Paris: Colin, 1969- .
I. La société.

HAYEM, Juliem, éd. *Mémoires et documents pour servir à l'histoire du commerce et de l'industrie en France.* 12 v. Paris: Hachette, 1911-29.

LEVASSEUR, Émile. *Histoire du commerce de la France.* 2 v. Paris: Rousseau, 1911-12.
I. Avant 1789.
II. De 1789 à nos jours.

LEVASSEUR, Émile. *La population française: histoire de la population avant 1789 et démographie de la France comparée à celle des autres nations au XIXe siècle, précédée d'une introduction sur la statistique.* 3 v. Paris: Rousseau, 1889-92.

LOUIS, Paul. *Histoire du mouvement syndical en France.* 2. éd. 2 v. Paris: Librairie Valois, 1947-48.
I. De 1789 à 1918 (1st pub., 1910, as 1789-1910).
II. De 1918 à 1948.

MERLE, Louis. *La métairie et l'évolution agraire de la Gatine poitevine de la fin du moyen age à la Révolution.* Paris: S.E.V.P.E.N., 1958. 252 p.

MORAZÉ, Charles. *La France bourgeoise, XVIIIe-XXe siècles.* Paris: Colin, 1946. 220 p.

PINCHEMEL, Philippe. *La France.* 3. éd. 2 v. Paris: Colin, 1969-70.
I. Les conditiones naturelles et humaines.
II. Les milieux: campagnes, industrie et villes.

RANUM, Orest, and Ranum, Patricia, eds. *Popular attitudes toward birth control in pre-industrial France and England.* New York: Harper & Row, 1972.

RÉMOND, André. *Études sur la circulation marchande en France aux XVIIIe et XIXe siècles: le prix des transports marchands de la Révolution au Premier Empire.* Paris: Rivière, 1956. 112 p.

SEDILLOT, René. *Le franc: histoire d'une monnaie des origines à nos jours.* Paris: Sirey, 1953. 386 p.

SÉE, Henri Eugène. *Histoire économique de la France.* 2 v. Paris: Colin, 1948-51.

SÉE, Henri Eugène. *L'évolution commerciale et industrielle de la France sous l'ancien régime.* Paris: Girard, 1925. 396 p.

USHER, Abbot Payson. *The history of the grain trade in France, 1400-1710.* Cambridge: Harvard University Press, 1913. 405 p.

REGIONAL STUDIES

BOIS, Paul. *Les paysans de l'Ouest: des structures économiques et sociales aux options politiques depuis l'époque révolutionnaire dans la Sarthe.* Le Mans: Imprimerie M. Vilaire, 1960. 716 p.

CHEVALIER, Louis. *Les Parisiens.* Paris: Hachette, 1967. 395 p.

HIGONNET, P. L. R. *Pont-de-Montvert: social structure in a French village, 1700-1914.* Cambridge: Harvard University Press, 1971. 217 p.

HIGOUNET, Charles, éd. *Histoire de Bordeaux.* 6 v. (v. 7-8 in preparation). Bordeaux: Fédération Historique du Sud-Ouest, 1962- .
I. Bordeaux antique, par R. Etienne.
II. Bordeaux pendant le haut moyen age, par C. Higounet.
III. Bordeaux sous les rois d'Angleterre, sous la direction de Y. Renouard.
IV. Bordeaux, 1453-1715, par R. Boutruche.
V. Bordeaux au XVIIIe siècle, par F.-G. Pariset.
VI. Bordeaux au XIXe siècle, par L. Desbraves et G. Dupeux.

LACHIVER, Marcel. *La population de Meulan du XVIIe au XIXe siècle (vers 1600-1870): étude de démographie historique.* Paris: S.E.V.P.E.N., 1969. 339 p.

LEBRUN, François. *Les hommes et la mort en Anjou aux XVIIe et XVIIIe siècles.* Paris: Mouton, 1971. 562 p.

LEROY-LADURIE, Emmanuel. *Les paysans de Languedoc.* 2 v. Paris: S.E.V.P.E.N., 1966.

RAMBAUD, Placide, and Vincienne, Monique. *Les transformations d'une société rurale: La Maurienne, 1561-1962.* Paris: Colin, 1964. 280 p.

WOLFF, Philippe, ed. *Histoire du Languedoc.* Toulouse: Privat, 1967. 540 p.

INTELLECTUAL AND CULTURAL

BARRIÈRE, Pierre. *La vie intellectuelle en France: du XVIe siècle a l'époque contemporaine.* Paris: Michel, 1961. 635 p.

BLOMFIELD, Reginald T. *History of French architecture from the death of Mazarin to the death of Louis XV.* 2 v. London: G. Bell, 1921.

BLOMFIELD, Reginald T. *History of French architecture from the reign of Charles VIII till the death of Mazarin.* 2 v. London: G. Bell, 1911.

BOLLÈME, Geneviève. *Bibliotheque bleue: litterature populaire en France du XVIe au XIXe siècle.* Paris: Julliard, 1971. 277 p.

CURTIUS, Ernst Robert. *The civilization of France.* Tr. from the German by Olive Wyon. New York: Macmillan, 1932. 247 p.

DUBY, Georges, and Mandrou, Robert. *A history of French civilization.* Tr. by James B. Atkinson. New York: Random House, 1964. 626 p.

ELBOW, Matthew H. *French corporate theory, 1789-1948: a chapter in the history of ideas.* New York: Columbia University Press, 1953. 222 p. (OP 15,044 $15.00)

HAHN, Roger. *The anatomy of a scientific institution: the Paris Academy of Sciences, 1666-1803.* Berkeley: University of California Press, 1971. 433 p.

LEROY, Maxime. *History des idées sociales en France.* 3 v. Paris: Gallimard, 1946-54.
I. De Montesquieu a Robespierre.
II. De Babeuf à Tocqueville.
III. D'Auguste Comte à P.-J. Proudhon.

MANUEL, Frank E. *The prophets of Paris.*

Cambridge: Harvard University Press, 1962. 349 p. (Harper Torchbook)

PICAVET, François-Joseph. *Les idéologues; essai sur l'histoire des idées et des théories scientifiques, philosophiques, religieuses en France depuis 1789.* Paris: Alcan, 1891. 628 p. (OP 25,885 $35.00)

POTTINGER, David Thomas. *The French book trade in the Ancien Régime, 1500-1791.* Cambridge: Harvard University Press, 1958. 363 p.

SIEBURG, Friedrich. *Who are these French?* Tr. from the German by Alan Harris. New York: Macmillan, 1932. 303 p.

SIEGFRIED, André. *France, a study in nationality.* London: Oxford University Press, 1930. 122 p.

RELIGION

DANSETTE, Adrien. *Religious history of modern France.* Tr. by John Dingle. 2 v. New York: Herder & Herder, 1961.
I. From the revolution to the Third Republic.
II. Under the Third Republic.

LATREILLE, André, et al. *Histoire du catholicisme en France.* 3 v. Paris: Éditions Spes, 1957-62.
I. Des origines à la chrétienté médiévale.
II. Sous les rois très chrétiens (du XIIIe au XVIIIe siècle).
III. La periode contemporaine (du XVIIIe siècles à nos jours).

LE BRAS, Gabriel. *Introduction a l'histoire de la practique religieuse en France.* 2 v. Paris: Presses universitaires de France, 1942-45.

WEMYSS, Alice. *Les protestants du Mas-d'Azil; histoire d'une résistance, 1680-1830.* Toulouse: Privat, 1961. 399 p.

THE SEVENTEENTH CENTURY, 1600-1715

GENERAL AND MISCELLANEOUS

BITTON, Davis. *The French nobility in crisis, 1560-1640.* Stanford: Stanford University Press, 1969. 178 p.

BRAUDEL, Fernand. *The Mediterranean and the Mediterranean world at the time of Philip II.* Tr. by Siân Reynolds. v. 1. New York: Harper & Row, 1972.

CLARKE, Jack A. *Huguenot warrior: the life and the times of Henri de Rohan, 1579-1638.* The Hague: Nijhoff, 1966. 244 p.

FONT-RÉAULX, Hyacinthe de. *Riquet et le canal des deux-mers.* Paris: Delagrave, 1888. 165 p.

LEBRUN, François. *Le XVIIe siècle.* Paris: Colin, 1967. 377 p.

LEWIS, W. H. *Assault on Olympus: the rise of the House of Grammont between 1604 and 1678.* New York: Harcourt, Brace, 1958. 240 p.

MAGENDIE, Maurice. *La politesse mondaine et les théories de l'honnêteté en France, au XVIIe siecle, de 1600 à 1660.* 2 v. Paris: Alcan, 1925.

MALAND, David. *Culture and society in seventeenth-century France.* New York: Scribner's, 1970. 318 p.

MANDROU, Robert. *La France aux XVIIe et XVIIIe siècles.* 2. éd. Paris: Presses universitaires de France, 1970. 335 p.

MANDROU, Robert. *Introduction à la France moderne, 1500-1640; essai de psychologie historique.* Paris: Michel, 1961. 400 p.

MANDROU, Robert. *Magistrats et sorciers en France au XVIIe siècle.* Paris: Plon, 1968. 583 p.

MARTIN, Henri-Jean. *Livre, pouvoirs et société à Paris au XVIIe siècle (1598-1701).* 2 v. Genève: Droz, 1969.

MOUSNIER, Roland. *État et société sous François I et pendant le gouvernement personnel de Louis XIV.* Paris: Centre de

Documentation universitaire, 1967. 340 p.

MOUSNIER, Roland. *Peasant uprisings in seventeenth-century France, Russia and China.* Tr. by Brian Pearce. New York: Harper & Row, 1970. 358 p.

MOUSNIER, Roland. *La plume, la faucille et le marteau: institutions et société en France du moyen age à la Révolution.* Paris: Presses universitaires de France, 1970. 404 p.

NEF, John U. *Industry and government in France and England, 1540-1640.* Ithaca: Cornell University Press, 1957 (c.1940). 162 p.

PAGÈS, Georges. *Naissance du grand siècle; la France de Henri IV à Louis XIV, 1598-1661.* Paris: Hachette, 1948. 221 p.

PORSHNEV, Boris Fedorovich. *Les soulèvements populaires en France en 1623 à 1648.* Paris: S.E.V.P.E.N., 1963. 679 p.

SAINT-GERMAIN, Jacques. *Samuel Bernard, le banquier des rois.* Paris: Hachette, 1960. 288 p.

SAINTOYANT, Jules François. *La colonisation française sous l'ancien régime (du XVe siècle à 1789).* 2 v. Paris: La Renaissance du Livre, 1929.

TREASURE, Geoffrey R. R. *Seventeenth century France; a study in absolutism.* London: Rivingtons, 1966. 548 p.

ZELLER, Gaston. *Aspects de la politique française sous l'ancien régime.* Paris: Presses universitaires de France, 1964. 392 p.

HENRY IV AND THE REGENCY, 1589-1624

BATIFFOL, Louis. *Marie de Medicis and the French Court in the seventeenth century.* Tr. by Mary King. Freeport, N.Y.: Books for Libraries Press, 1970 (c.1908). 314 p.

BUISSERET, David. *Sully and the growth of centralized government in France, 1598-1610.* London: Eyre & Spottiswoode, 1968. 240 p.

DURAND, Yves. *Cahiers de doléances des paroisses du bailliage de Troyes pour les États généraux de 1614.* Paris: Presses universitaires de France, 1966. 361 p.

KIERSTEAD, Raymond F. *Pomponne de Bellièvre; a study of the king's men in the age of Henry IV.* Evanston, Ill.: Northwestern University Press, 1968. 157 p.

RÉMY, Jean Charles. *Catherine de Médicis; ou, la mère de trois rois.* Lausanne: Éditions Rencontre, 1965. 207 p.

SEWARD, Desmond. *The first Bourbon: Henry IV of France and of Navarre.* London: Constable, 1971. 235 p.

RICHELIEU AND LOUIS XIII, 1624-1642

AVENEL, George, vicomte d'. *Richelieu et la monarchie absolue.* 4 v. Paris: Plon, 1884-90.

BATIFFOL, Louis. *Richelieu et le roi Louis XIII.* Paris: Calmann-Levy, 1934. 316 p.

BURCKHARDT, Carl J. *Richelieu and his age.* 3 v. London: Allen & Unwin, 1967-71.
I. Richelieu, his rise to power.
II. Assertion of power and cold war.
III. Power politics and the cardinal's death.

CHURCH, William F. *Richelieu and reason of state.* Princeton: Princeton University Press, 1972.

ERLANGER, Philippe. *Richelieu.* 3 v. Paris: Perrin, 1967-70.
I. L'ambitieux (Am. ed.: Richelieu, the thrust for power. Tr. by Patricia Wolf. New York: Stein & Day, 1968).
II. Le révolutionnaire.
III. Le dictateur.

FAGNIEZ, Gustav Charles. *Le père Joseph et Richelieu.* 2 v. Paris: Hachette, 1894.

FEDERN, Karl. *Richelieu.* London: Allen & Unwin, 1928. 253 p.

FOISIL, Madeline. *La révolte des nu-pieds et les révoltes normandes de 1639.* Paris: Presses universitaires de France, 1970. 369 p.

HANOTAUX, Gabriel, and A. de Caumont, duc de la Force. *Histoire du Cardinal Richelieu.* 6 v. Paris: Société de l'histoire nationale, 1932-47.

HAUSER, Henri. *La pensée et l'action économique du Cardinal Richelieu.* Paris: Presses universitaires de France, 1944. 194 p.

LIUBLINSKAIA, Aleksandra D. *French absolutism: the crucial phase, 1620-29.* Tr. by Brian Pearce. London: Cambridge University Press, 1968. 349 p.

SALMON, J. H. M. *Cardinal de Retz: the anatomy of a conspirator.* New York: Macmillan, 1970. 447 p.

TAPIÉ, Victor Lucien. *La France de Louis XIII et de Richelieu.* Paris: Flammarion, 1952. 561 p.

THUAU, Étienne. *Raison d'état et pensée politique à l'époque de Richelieu.* Paris: Colin, 1966. 477 p.

TREASURE, Geoffrey R. R. *Cardinal Richelieu and the development of absolutism.* New York: St. Martin's, 1972. 316 p.

MAZARIN, 1642-1661

CHERUEL, Pierre Adolphe. *Histoire de France pendant la minorité de Louis XIV.* 4 v. Paris: Hachette, 1879-80.

CHERUEL, Pierre Adolphe. *Histoire de France sous la ministère de Mazarin, 1651-61.* 3 v. Paris: Hachette, 1882.

DETHAN, Georges. *Mazarin et ses amis: étude sur la jeunesse du cardinal d'après ses papiers conservés aux Quai d'Orsay, suivie d'un choix de lettres inédites.* Paris: Berger-Levrault, 1968. 368 p.

DOOLIN, Paul Rice. *The Fronde.* Cambridge: Harvard University Press, 1935. 181 p.

FEDERN, Karl. *Mazarin, 1602-61.* Tr. par P.-A. Degon. Paris: Payot, 1934. 595 p.

GRAND-MESNIL, Marie Noelle. *Mazarin, La Fronde et la presse, 1647-49.* Paris: Colin, 1967. 307 p.

KNACHEL, Philip A. *England and the Fronde: the impact of the English Civil War and Revolution on France.* Ithaca: Cornell University Press, 1967. 312 p.

KOSSMANN, Ernst H. *La Fronde.* Leiden: Universitaire Pers Leiden, 1954. 275 p. (OP 41,852 $15.00)

MOOTE, Alanson Lloyd. *The revolt of the judges: the Parlement of Paris and the Fronde, 1643-52.* Princeton: Princeton University Press, 1972. 407 p.

LOUIS XIV, 1661-1715

BROCHER, Henri. *A la cour de Louis XIV: le rang et l'étiquette sous l'ancien régime.* Paris: Alcan, 1934. 154 p.

DEDIEU, Joseph. *Le rôle politique des protestants français, 1685 à 1715.* Paris: Bloud & Gay, 1920. 362 p.

ERLANGER, Philippe. *Louis XIV.* Tr. by Stephen Cox. London: Weidenfeld & Nicolson, 1970. 412 p.

ERLANGER, Philippe. *Monsieur, frère de Louis XIV.* Paris: Hachette, 1970. 320 p.

GAXOTTE, Pierre. *The age of Louis XIV.* Tr. by Michael Shaw. New York: Macmillan, 1970. 346 p.

GOUBERT, Pierre. *Louis XIV and twenty million Frenchmen.* Tr. by Anne Carter. New York: Pantheon, 1970. 350 p.

HALÉVY, Daniel. *Vauban.* Paris: Grasset, 1923. 205 p.

KING, James Edward. *Science and rationalism in the government of Louis XIV, 1661-83.* Baltimore: John Hopkins Press, 1949. 337 p. (OP 12,002 $20.00)

LACOUR-GAYET, Georges. *L'éducation politique de Louis XIV.* 2. éd. Paris: Hachette, 1923. 358 p.

LAIR, Jules Auguste. *Nicolas Foucquet, procureur général, surintendant des finances, ministre d'état de Louis XIV.* 2 v. Paris: Plon-Nourrit, 1890.

LANGLOIS, Marcel. *Madame de Maintenon.* Paris: Plon, 1932. 291 p.

LEWIS, Warren Hamilton. *The splendid century: life in the France of Louis XIV.* New York: Anchor, 1957 (c.1953). 304 p.

PICAVET, Camille Georges. *La diplomatie française au temps de Louis XIV, 1661-1715: institutions, moeurs et coutumes.* Paris: Alcan, 1930. 339 p.

ROTHKRUG, Lionel. *Opposition to Louis XIV: the political and social origins of the French Enlightenment.* Princeton: Princeton University Press, 1965. 533 p.

RULE, John C., ed. *Louis XIV and the craft of kingship.* Columbus: Ohio State University Press, 1969. 478 p.

VAST, Henri, éd. *Les grands traités du règne de Louis XIV.* 3 v. Paris: Picard, 1893-99.

VOLTAIRE, François Marie Arouet de. *The age of Louis XIV.* Tr. by Martyn Pollack. New York: Dutton, 1961. 475 p.

WOLF, John B. *Louis XIV.* New York: Norton, 1968. 678 p.

ZIEGLER, Gilette, ed. *At the court of Versailles: eye witness reports from the reign of Louis XIV.* Tr. by Simon W. Taylor. New York: Dutton, 1966. 402 p.

GOVERNMENT, ADMINISTRATION, EDUCATION, MILITARY

ANDRÉ, Louis. *Michel Le Tellier et Louvois.* 2. éd. Paris: Colin, 1943. 709 p. (OP 54,818 $35.00)

BAMFORD, Paul Walden. *Fighting ships and prisons: the Mediterranean galleys and France in the age of Louis XIV.* Minneapolis: University of Minnesota Press, 1973. 412 p.

BAMFORD, Paul Walden. *Forests and French sea power, 1660-1789.* Toronto: University of Toronto Press, 1956. 240 p.

CHARMEIL, Jean Paul. *Les trésoriers de France à l'époque de la Fronde: contribution à l'histoire de l'administration financière sous l'ancien régime.* Paris: Picard, 1964. 592 p.

CLÉMENT, Pierre. *Histoire de Colbert et de son administration.* 3. éd. 2 v. Paris: Perrin, 1892.

CORVISIER, André. *L'armée française de la fin du XVIIe siècle au ministère Choiseul: le soldat.* 2 v. Paris: Presses universitaires de France, 1964.

DURAND, Georges. *États et institutions, XVIe-XVIIe siècles.* Paris: Colin, 1969. 312 p.

ESMONIN, Edmond. *La taille en Normandie au temps de Colbert, 1661-83.* Paris: Hachette, 1913. 552 p.

GIRARD, Georges Antoine. *Le service militaire en France à la fin du règne de Louis XIV: racolage et milice (1701-15).* Paris: Plon-Nourrit, 1922. 336 p.

HINCKER, François. *Les francais devant l'impôt sous l'ancien régime.* Paris: Flammarion, 1971. 186 p.

LACOUR-GAYET, Georges. *La marine militaire de la France sous les règnes de Louis XIII et Louis XIV.* 1 v. Paris: Champion, 1911.

LUÇAY, Charles Helion Marie le Gendre, comte de. *Des origines du pouvoir ministériel en France: les Secrétaires d'État, depuis leur institution jusqu'à la mort de Louis XV.* Paris: Librairie de la Société Bibliographique, 1881. 647 p.

MARION, Marcel. *Dictionnaire des institutions de la France aux XVIIe et XVIIIe siècles.* Paris: Picard, 1923. 564 p.

MILNE, Pierre. *L'impôt des Aides sous l'ancien régime, 1360-1791.* Paris: Rousseau, 1908. 262 p.

MOUSNIER, Roland. *État et société en France au XVIIe et XVIIIe siècles.* Paris: Centre de Documentation Universitaire, 1968- .
I. Le gouvernement et les corps.

MOUSNIER, Roland. *La vénalité des offices sous Henry IV et Louis XIII.* 2. éd. Paris: Presses universitaires de France, 1971. 726 p.

RANUM, Orest. *Richelieu and the councillors of Louis XIII; a study of the secretaries of state and superintendants of finance in the ministry of Richelieu, 1635-42.* New York: Oxford University Press, 1963. 211 p.

ROBIN, Pierre. *La compagnie des secrétaires du roi, 1351-1791.* Paris: Recueil Sirey, 1933. 124 p.

SHENNAN, Joseph Hugh. *The Parlement of Paris.* Ithaca: Cornell University Press, 1968. 359 p.

SNYDERS, George. *La pédagogie en France aux XVIIe et XVIIIe siècles.* Paris: Presses universitaires de France, 1965. 459 p.

SOCIAL AND ECONOMIC

BOISSONADE, Prosper. *Colbert, le triomphe de l'étatisme, la fondation de la suprématie industrielle de la France, la dictature du travail (1661-83).* Paris: Rivière, 1932. 392 p.

BOISSONADE, Prosper. *Le socialisme d'état: l'industrie et les classes industrielles en France pendant les deux premiers siècles de l'ère moderne (1453-1661).* Paris: Champion, 1927. 380 p.

CARR, John Laurence. *Life in France under Louis XIV.* New York: Putnam, 1966. 176 p. (Capricorn)

COLE, Charles Woolsey. *French mercantilism, 1683-1700.* New York: Columbia University Press, 1943. 354 p.

COLE, Charles Woolsey. *Colbert and a century of French mercantilism.* 2 v. New York: Columbia University Press, 1939.

COORNAERT, Émile. *Les campagnonnages en France, du moyen âge à nos jours.* Paris: Éditions ouvrieres, 1966. 435 p.

COORNAERT, Émile. *Les corporations en France avant 1789.* 2. éd. Paris: Les Éditions ouvrieres, 1968 (orig. pub. 1941). 316 p.

ERLANGER, Philippe. *La vie quotidienne sous Henri IV.* Paris: Hachette, 1958. 256 p.

ESTIVALS, Robert. *Le dépôt légal sous l'ancien régime de 1537 à 1791.* Paris: Rivière, 1961. 141 p.

FAGNIEZ, Gustav Charles. *L'économie sociale de la France sous Henri IV, 1589-1610.* Paris: Hachette, 1897. 428 p.

FAGNIEZ, Gustav Charles. *La femme et la société française dans la première moitié du XVIIe siècle.* Paris: J. Gamber, 1929. 397 p.

GOUBERT, Pierre. *Familles marchandes sous l'ancien régime: les Danse et les Motte de Beauvais.* Paris: S.E.V.P.E.N., 1959. 192 p.

HARSIN, Paul. *Crédit public et banque d'état en France du XVIe au XVIIIe siècle.* Paris: Droz, 1933. 221 p.

HUNT, David. *Parents and children in history: the psychology of family life in early modern France.* New York: Basic Books, 1970. 226 p.

KUNSTLER, Charles. *La vie quotidienne sous Louis XIV.* Paris: Hachette, 1950. 348 p.

LEVRON, Jacques. *Daily life at Versailles in the seventeenth and eighteenth centuries.* Tr. by C. E. Engel. New York: Macmillan, 1968. 239 p.

LODGE, Eleanor. *Sully, Colbert, Turgot: a chapter in French economic history.* Port Washington, N.Y.: Kennikat Press, 1970 (c.1931). 263 p.

LUETHY, Herbert. *La banque protestante en France de la révocation de l'Édit de Nantes à la Révolution.* 2 v. Paris: S.E.V.P.E.N., 1959-61.

MAGNE, Émile. *La vie quotidienne au temps de Louis XIII.* Paris: Hachette, 1942. 253 p.

MANDROU, Robert. *Classes et luttes de classes en France au debut du XVIIe siècle.* Messina: G. d'Anna, 1965. 125 p.

MARTIN SAINT-LEON, Etienne. *Histoire des corporations de métiers depuis leurs origines jusqu'à leur suppression en 1791.* 4. ed. Paris: Presses universitaires de France, 1941. 576 p.

MONGRÉDIEN, Georges. *La vie quotidienne sous Louis XIV.* Paris: Hachette, 1948. 250 p.

PICARD, Roger. *Les salons littéraires et la société français, 1610-1789.* New York: Brentano's, 1943. 361 p.

PRICE, Jacob. *France and the Chesapeake: a history of the French tobacco monopoly, 1674-1791, and of its relationship to the British and American tobacco trades.* 2 v. Ann Arbor: University of Michigan Press, 1973.

ROUPNEL, Gaston. *La ville et la campagne au XVIIe siecle; études sur les populations du pays dijonnais.* Paris: Colin, 1955 (c.1922). 357 p.

SAGNAC, Philippe. *La formation de la société française moderne.* 2 v. Paris: Presses universitaires de France, 1945-46.
I. La société et la monarchie absolue (1661-1715)
II. La révolution des idées et des moeurs et le déclin de l'ancien régime (1715-88).

SCOVILLE, Warren Chandler. *The persecution of the Huguenots and the French economic development, 1680-1720.* Berkeley: University of California Press, 1960. 497 p.

VENARD, Marc. *Bourgeois et paysans au XVIIe siècle; recherche sur le rôle des bourgeois parisiens dans la vie agricole au sud de Paris au XVIIe siècle.* Paris: S.E.V.P.E.N., 1957. 126 p.

REGIONAL STUDIES

BAEHREL, René. *Une croissance: la Basse-Provence rurale, fin XVIe siècle-1789; essai d'économie historique statistique.* Paris: S.E.V.P.E.N., 1961. 842 p.

BERNARD, Leon. *The emerging city: Paris in the age of Louis XIV.* Durham: Duke University Press, 1970. 326 p.

COSTE, Jean Paul. *La ville d'Aix en 1695; structure urbaine et société.* 2 v. Aix-en-Provence: Presses universitaires, 1970.

DEYON, Pierre. *Amiens, capitale provinciale: étude sur la société urbaine au XVIIe siècle.* Paris: Mouton, 1967. 608 p.

FORD, Franklin L. *Strasbourg in transition, 1648-1789.* Cambridge: Harvard University Press, 1958. 321 p.

GOUBERT, Pierre. *Cent mille provinciaux au XVIIe siècle; Beauvais et la Beauvaisis de 1600 à 1730.* Paris: Flammarion, 1968. 439 p.

LIVET, Georges. *L'intendance d'Alsace sous Louis XIV, 1648-1715.* Paris: Les Belles Lettres, 1956. 1084 p.

MOUSNIER, Roland. *Paris au XVIIe siècle.* Paris: Centre de Documentation universitaire, 1961. 350 p.

RANUM, Orest. *Paris in the age of absolutism.* New York: Wiley, 1968. 316 p.

RÉBILLON, Armand. *Les états de Bretagne de 1661 à 1789: leur organization — l'évolution de leur pouvoirs — leur administration financière.* Paris: Picard, 1932. 825 p.

ROUSSET, Camille Félix Michel. *Histoire de Louvois et de son administration politique et militaire.* 4 v. Paris: Didier, 1862-63.

INTELLECTUAL AND CULTURAL

ADAM, Antoine. *Grandeur and illusion: French literature and society, 1600-1715.* New York: Basic Books, 1972 311 p.

ALBERTINI, Rudolf von. *Das politische Denken in Frankreich zur Zeit Richelieus.* Marburg: Simons, 1951. 220 p.

ASCOLI, Georges. *La Grande-Brétagne devant l'opinion française au XVIIe siècle.* 2 v. Paris: J. Gamber, 1930.

BÉNICHOU, Paul. *Man and ethics; studies in French classicism.* Tr. by Elizabeth Hughes. New York: Anchor, 1971. 266 p.

BOISGUILBERT, Pierre Le Pesant, sieur de. *Pierre de Boisguilbert ou la naissance de l'économie politique.* 2 v. Paris: Institut national d'études démographiques, 1966. I. Études. Biographie. Correspondence. Bibliographies. II. Oeuvres manuscrites et imprimées.

BOLLÈME, Geneviève. *Les almanacs populaires aux XVIIe et XVIIIe siècles: essai d'histoire sociale.* Paris: Mouton, 1969. 147 p.

BRUNSCHVICG, Leon. *Pascal.* Paris: Rieder, 1936. 86 p.

CHEVALIER, Jacques. *Descartes.* Nouv. ed. Paris: Plon, 1957 (orig. pub. 1921). 374 p.

CHINARD, Gilbert. *L'Amérique et le rêve exotique dans la littérature française au XVIIe et XVIIIe siècles.* Paris: Droz, 1934. 454 p.

DOMMANGET, Maurice. *Le curé Meslier, athée, communiste et révolutionnaire sous Louis XIV.* Paris: Julliard, 1965. 549 p.

FOUCAULT, Michel. *Madness and civilization: history of insanity in the Age of Reason.* Tr. by Richard Howard. New York: Pantheon, 1965. 299 p. (New American Library)

GILLET, Louis. *La peinture, XVIIe et XVIIIe siècles.* Paris: H. Laurens, 1913. 508 p.

HARSIN, Paul. *Les doctrines monétaires et financières en France du XVIe au XVIIIe siècles.* Paris: Alcan, 1928. 326 p.

KIRKINEN, Heikki. *Les origines de la conception moderne de l'homme-machine: le probleme de l'âme en France à la fin du règne de Louis XIV (1670-1715).* Helsinki: n.p., 1960. 518 p.

LABROUSSE, Elizabeth. *Pierre Bayle.* 2 v. La Haye: Nijhoff, 1963-64.

LEVI, Anthony. *French moralists: the theory of the passions, 1585-1649.* Oxford: Clarendon Press, 1964. 362 p.

MESNARD, Jean. *Pascal: his life and works.* Tr. by G. S. Fraser. London: Harvill Press, 1952. 210 p.

ORNSTEIN, Martha. *The role of scientific societies in the seventeenth century.* 3rd ed. Hamden, Conn.: Archon Books, 1963 (c.1938). 308 p.

PALMER, John Leslie. *Molière.* New York: B. Blom, 1970 (c.1930). 518 p.

ROBERTS, Hazel Van Dyke. *Boisguillebert; economist of the reign of Louis XIV.* New York: Columbia University Press, 1935. 378 p.

ROBINSON, Howard. *Bayle the sceptic.* New York: Columbia University Press, 1931. 334 p.

SÉE, Henri Eugène. *Les idées politiques en France au XVIIe siècle.* Paris: Hachette, 1923. 371 p.

SOULEYMAN, Elizabeth V. *The vision of world peace in seventeenth and eighteenth century France.* New York: Putnam's, 1941. 232 p. (OP 23,643 $15.00).

SPINK, John S. *French free thought from Gassendi to Voltaire.* London: University of London, Athalone Press, 1960. 345 p.

STANKIEWICZ, W. J. *Politics and religion in seventeenth-century France: a study of political ideas from the monarchomachs to Bayle, as reflected in the toleration controversy.* Berkeley: University of California Press, 1960. 269 p.

RELIGION

ABERCROMBIE, Nigel. *Origins of Jansenism.* Oxford: Clarendon Press, 1936. 341 p. (OP 17,179 $20.00)

ARMSTRONG, Brian G. *Calvinism and the Amyaut heresy: protestant scholasticism and humanism in seventeenth-century France.* Madison: University of Wisconsin Press, 1969. 330 p.

BLET, Pierre. *Le clergé de France et la monarchie: étude sur les Assemblées générales du clergé de 1615 à 1666.* 2 v. Rome: Librairie éditrice de l'Université grégorienne, 1959.

BUSSON, Henri. *La pensée religieuse française de Charron à Pascal.* Paris: Vrin, 1933. 664 p.

COSTE, Pierre. *Le grand saint du grand siècle, Monsieur Vincent.* 2. éd. 3 v. Paris: Desclée de Brouwer, 1934.

FERTÉ, Jeanne. *La vie religieuse dans les campagnes parisiennes, 1622-95.* Paris: Vrin, 1962. 453 p.

LAPORTE, Jean Marie. *La doctrine de Port Royal.* 2 v. Paris: Vrin, 1951-52 (orig. pub. 1923).
I. La loi morale.
II. La pratique des sacrements.

MARTIMORT, Aimé Georges. *Le gallicanisme de Bossuet.* Paris: Editions du Cerf, 1953. 791 p.

MARTIN, Victor. *Le gallicanisme et la réforme catholique; essai historique sur l'introduction en France des décrets du Concile de Trente, 1563-1615.* Paris: Picard, 1919. 415 p.

MARTIN, Victor. *Le gallicanisme politique et le clergé de France.* Paris: Université de Strasburg — Institut de Droit canonique, 1929. 337 p.

ORCIBAL, Jean. *Louis XIV et les protestants: "la cabale des accomodeurs de religion," la caisse des conversions, la révocation de l'Édit de Nantes.* Paris: Vrin, 1951. 192 p.

ORCIBAL, Jean. *Saint-Cyran et le jansénisme.* Paris: Éditions du Seuil, 1961. 191 p.

REX, W. *Essays on Pierre Bayle and religious controversy.* The Hague: Nijhoff, 1965. 271p.

SAINTE-BEUVE, Charles Augustin. *Port Royal.* 10 v. in 7. Paris: "La Connaissance," 1926-32.

SCHMITT, Thérès Jean. *L'organisation ecclésiastique et la pratique religieuse dans l'Archidiaconé d'Autun de 1650 a 1750.* Autun: Société d'Imprimerie L. Marcelin, 1957. 371 p.

TAVENEAUX, Réné, éd. *Jansénisme et politique.* Paris: Colin, 1965. 258 p.

TAVENEAUX, Réné. *Le Jansénisme en Lorraine, 1640-1789.* Paris: Vrin, 1960. 759 p.

MEMOIRS AND CONTEMPORARY WRITINGS

ARGENSON, René Louis de Voyer, marquis d'. *Journal et mémoires du Marquis D'Argenson.* 9 v. Paris: Renouard, 1859-67.

CHOISY, François Timoléon de. *Mémoires de l'abbé de Choisey: mémoires pour servir a l'histoire de Louis XIV.* Ed. par Georges Mongrédien. Paris: Mercure de France, 1966. 412 p.

COLBERT, Jean Baptiste. *Lettres, instructions et mémoires de Colbert.* Pierre Clement, éd. 7 v. Paris: Imprimérie impériale, 1861-73.

DURAND, Yves; Labatut, J.-P.; and Mousnier, Roland, éds. *Problèmes de stratification sociale: deux cahiers de la noblesse pour les États généraux de 1649-51.* Paris: Presses universitaires de France, 1965. 184 p.

L'ESTOILE, Pierre de. *The Paris of Henry of Navarre, as seen by Pierre de L'Estoile: selections from his memoires-journaux.* Ed. and tr. by N. L. Roelker. Cambridge: Harvard University Press, 1958. 321 p.

LOUIS XIV. *Memoires for the instruction of the Dauphin.* Introd., tr., and notes by Paul Sonnino. New York: Free Press, 1970. 281 p.

MAZARIN, Jules, Cardinal. *Lettres du Cardinal Mazarin pendant son ministère.* 9 v. Paris: Imprimérie nationale, 1872-1906. (OP 22,754 v. 1—$45.00; v. 2—$45.00; v. 3—$45.00; v. 4—$45.00; v. 5—$45.00; v. 6—$40.00; v. 7—$45.00; v. 8—$45.00; v. 9—$45.00. Total $400.00)

MICHAUD, Joseph François, éd. *Nouvelle collection des mémoires pour servir à l'histoire de France depuis le XIIIe siècle jusqu'à la fin du XVIIIe siècle.* . . . 2nd series (10 v.) and 3rd series (10 v.). Paris: Éditeur du Commentaire Analytique du Code Civil, 1836-39.

MONTCHAL, Charles de. *Mémoires de monseigneur de Montchal, archevêque de Toulouse, contenant des particularitez de la vie et du ministère du Cardinal de Richelieu.* 2 v. in 1. Rotterdam: pour Gaspar Fritsch (fictitious imprint), 1718. 750 p.

MOUSNIER, Roland, éd. *Lettres et mémoires adressés au chancelier Séguier, 1633-49.* 2 v. Paris: Presses universitaires de France, 1964.

QUINCY, Joseph Sevin, comte de. *Mémoires de chevalier de Quincy.* 3 v. Paris: Renouard, 1898-1901.

RICHELIEU, Armand Jean du Plessis, cardinal, duc de. *Mémoires du cardinal de Richelieu.* 10 v. Paris: Renouard, 1907-31.

RICHELIEU, Armand Jean du Plessis, cardinal, duc de. *Political testament; the significant chapters and supporting selections.* Tr. and ed. by Henry B. Hill. Madison: University of Wisconsin Press, 1961. 128 p.

SAINT-SIMON, Louis de Rouvroy, duc de. *Historical memoires of duc de Saint-Simon; a shortened version.* 3 v. Ed. and tr. by Lucy Norton. London: H. Hamilton, 1967-72.

SÉVIGNÉ, Marie (de Rabutin-Chantal), marquise de. *Lettres.* Texte établi et annoté par Gerard-Gailly. 3 v. Paris: Gallimard, 1953-57.

VAUBAN, Sébastien Le Prestre de. *Projet d'une dixme royale.* Paris: Alcan, 1933. 295 p.

THE EIGHTEENTH CENTURY, 1715-1789

GENERAL AND MISCELLANEOUS

DAKIN, Douglas. *Turgot and the Ancien Régime in France.* London: Methuen, 1939. 361 p.

DODWELL, Henry H. *Dupleix and Clive: the beginning of empire.* London: Methuen, 1920. 277 p.

ÉGRET, Jean. *Louis XV et l'opposition parlementaire, 1715-74.* Paris: Colin, 1970. 246 p.

ÉGRET, Jean. *La pré-révolution française, 1787-88.* Paris: Presses universitaires de France, 1962. 400 p.

FAURE, Edgar. *La disgrace de Turgot.* Paris: Gallimard, 1961. 610 p.

GAXOTTE, Pierre. *Le siècle de Louis XV.* Nouv. éd. Paris: Fayard, 1958 (c.1933). 492 p.

GODECHOT, Jacques. *France and the Atlantic Revolution of the eighteenth century, 1770-79.* Tr. by Herbert Rowen. New York: Free Press, 1965. 279 p.

GOOCH, George Peabody. *Louis XV: the monarchy in decline.* New York: Longmans, Green, 1956. 285 p.

GOTTSCHALK, Louis R. *Lafayette between the American and the French Revolutions, 1783-89.* Chicago: University of Chicago Press, 1950. 461 p.

HALL, Thadd E. *France and the eighteenth-century Corsican question.* New York: New York University Press, 1971. 255 p.

HERR, Richard. *Tocqueville and the old regime.* Princeton: Princeton University Press, 1962. 142 p.

HYDE, Harford Montgomery. *John Law.* London: Home & Van Thal, 1948. 200 p.

HYSLOP, Beatrice F. *L'Apanage de Philippe-Égalité, duç d'Orléans, 1785-91.* Paris: Société d'Études robespierristes, 1965. 452 p.

LACOMBE, Bernard Mercier de. *La résistance janséniste et parlementaire au temps de Louis XV: l'abbé Nigon de Berty, 1702-72.* Paris: Société du grand Armorial de France, 1948. 279 p.

LACOUR-GAYET, Robert. *Calonne; financier, reformateur, contre-révolutionnaire, 1734-1802.* Paris: Hachette, 1963. 510 p.

LECLERCQ, Henri. *Histoire de la régence pendant la minorité de Louis XV.* 3 v. Paris: Champion, 1922.

LIGOU, Daniel. *Montauban à la fin de l'ancien régime et au débuts de la révolution, 1787-94.* Paris: Rivière, 1958. 719 p.

LOUGH, John. *An introduction to eighteenth-century France.* London: Longmans, 1960. 349 p. (McKay)

MAXWELL, Constantia E. *The English traveller in France, 1698-1815.* London: G. Routledge & Sons, 1932. 301 p.

SAGNAC, Philippe. *La fin de l'ancien régime et la révolution américaine, 1763-89.* 3. éd. rev. et augm. 1 v. Paris: Presses universitaires de France, 1952.

TAINE, Hippolyte Adolphe. *The ancient regime.* Gloucester, Mass.: Peter Smith, 1962 (1st pub. 1876). 421 p.

TOCQUEVILLE, Alexis Charles Henri de. *The old regime and the French Revolution.* Tr. by Stuart Gilbert. New York: Doubleday, 1955 (1st pub. 1856). 300 p. (Anchor)

WADDINGTON, Richard. *Louis XV et la renversement des alliances; préliminaires de la guerre de sept ans, 1754-56.* Paris:

Firmin-Didot, 1896. 533 p.

WILSON, Arthur McCandless. *French foreign policy during the administration of Cardinal Fleury, 1726-43.* Cambridge: Harvard University Press, 1936. 433 p.

GOVERNMENT, ADMINISTRATION, EDUCATION, MILITARY

ANCHEL, Robert. *Crimes et châtiments au XVIIIe siècle.* Paris: Perrin, 1933. 237 p.

ANTOINE, Michel. *Le Conseil du Roi sous le règne de Louis XV.* Genève: Droz, 1970. 666 p.

ARDASHEV, Pavel Nikolaevich. *Les intendants de province sous Louis XVI.* Tr. du russe par Louis Jousserandot. Paris: Alcan, 1909. 487 p.

BICKART, Roger. *Les parlements et la notion de souveraineté nationale au XVIIIe siècle.* Paris: Alcan, 1932. 285 p.

BISSON DE BARTHELÉMY, Paul. *Les Joly de Fleury: procureurs généraux au Parlement de Paris au XVIIIe siècle.* Paris: Société d'édition d'Enseignement supérieur, 1964. 324p.

BLOCH, Camille. *L'assistance et l'état en France à la veille de la révolution, 1764-90.* Paris: Picard, 1908. 504 p. (OP 53,373 $30.00)

BLUCHE, François. *Les magistrats du Parlement de Paris au XVIIIe siècle, 1715-71.* Paris: Les Belles Lettres, 1960. 462 p.

CARRÉ, Henri. *La fin des parlements (1788-90).* Paris: Hachette, 1912. 382 p.

FLAMMERMONT, Jules, éd. *Remonstrances du Parlement de Paris au XVIIIe siècle.* 3 v. Paris: Imprimerie Nationale, 1888-98.

GRUDER, Vivian R. *The royal provincial intendants: a governing elite in eighteenth-century France.* Ithaca: Cornell University Press, 1968. 293 p.

KENNETT, Lee. *The French armies in the Seven Years War: a study in military organization and administration.* Durham: Duke University Press, 1967. 165 p.

LACOUR-GAYET, Georges. *La marine*

militaire de la France sous le règne de Louis XV. Paris: Champion, 1902. 571 p.

LACOUR-GAYET, Georges. La marine militaire de la France sous le règne de Louis XVI. Paris: Champion, 1905. 719 p.

LARDÉ, Georges. La capitation dans les pays de taille personnelle. Paris: Imprimerie de Bonvalot-Jouve, 1906. 480 p.

LÉONARD, Émile-G. L'armée et ses problèmes au XVIIIe siècle. Paris: Plon, 1958. 360 p.

McCLOY, Shelby T. Government assistance in eighteenth-century France. Durham: Duke University Press, 1946. 496 p. (OP 2,000,427 $30.00)

MARION, Marcel. Les impôts directs sous l'ancien régime, principalement au XVIIIe siècle. Paris: Connély, 1910. 434 p.

MARION, Marcel. Machault d'Arnouville: étude sur l'histoire du contrôle général des finances de 1749 à 1754. Paris: Hachette, 1891. 462 p.

MATTHEWS, George Tennyson. The Royal General Farms in eighteenth-century France. New York: Columbia University Press, 1958. 318 p.

MENTION, Leon. Le Comte de Saint-Germain et ses réformes (1775-77), d'après les archives du Dépôt de la Guerre. Paris: Clavel, 1884. 323 p.

OZANAM, Denise. Claude Baudard de Saint-James: Trésorier générale de la Marine et Brasseur d'affaires (1738-87). Genève: Droz, 1969. 214 p.

PIETRI, François. La réforme de l'état au XVIIIe siècle. Paris: Les Éditions de France, 1935. 309 p.

QUIMBY, Robert S. The background of Napoleonic warfare: the theory of military tactics in eighteenth-century France. New York: AMS Press, 1968 (c.1957). 385 p.

TUETEY, Louis. Les officiers sous l'ancien régime; nobles et roturiers. Paris: Plon, 1908. 407 p.

VILLAIN, Jean. Le recouvrement des impôts directs sous l'ancien régime. Paris: Rivière, 1952. 321 p.

SOCIAL AND ECONOMIC

BARBER, Elinor G. The bourgeoisie in eighteenth-century France. Princeton: Princeton University Press, 1955. 165 p.

BEIK, Paul. A judgement of the old regime; being a judgement of Provence of French economic and fiscal policies at the close of the Seven Years War. New York: Columbia University Press, 1944. 290 p.

BOSHER, J. F. French finances, 1770-95: from business to bureaucracy. New York: Cambridge University Press, 1970. 369 p.

BOSHER, J. F. The single duty project; a study of the movement for a French customs union in the eighteenth century. London: University of London, Athlone Press, 1964. 215 p.

BOUCHARY, Jean. Les manieurs d'argent à Paris à la fin du XVIIIe siècle. 3 v. in 1. Paris: Rivière, 1939-43.

BOURDE, André J. Agronomie et agronomes en France au XVIIIe siècle. 3 v. Paris: S.E.V.P.E.N., 1967.

CARRÉ, Henri Pierre. La noblesse de France et l'opinion public au XVIIIe siècle. Paris: Champion, 1920. 650 p.

DAUMARD, Adeline, and Furet, François. Structures et relations sociales à Paris au milieu du XVIIIe siècle. Paris: Colin, 1961. 97 p.

FORD, Franklin L. Robe and sword: the regrouping of the French aristocracy after Louis XIV. Cambridge: Harvard University Press, 1953. 280 p. (Harper Torchbook)

FORSTER, Robert. The House of Saulx-Tavanes: Versailles and Burgundy, 1700-1830. Baltimore: Johns Hopkins University Press, 1971. 277 p.

GROETHUYSEN, Bernard. The bourgeois: Catholicism vs. capitalism in eighteenth-century France. Tr. from the French ed. of 1927. New York: Holt, Rinehart & Winston, 1968. 268 p.

KAPLOW, Jeffry. *The names of kings: The Parisian laboring poor in the eighteenth century.* New York: Basic Books, 1972. 222 p.

LABROUSSE, Camille Ernest. *La crise de l'économie francaise à la fin de l'ancien régime et au début de la révolution.* Paris: Presses universitaires de France, 1944. 664 p.

LABROUSSE, Camille Ernest. *Esquisse du mouvement des prix et des revenus en France au XVIIIe siècle.* 2 v. Paris: Dalloz, 1933.

LEVASSEUR, Émile. *Histoire des classes ouvrières et de l'industrie en France avant 1789.* 2. éd. 2 v. Paris: A. Rousseau, 1900-01 (orig. ed. 1859).

MARION, Marcel. *Histoire financière de la France depuis 1715.* 6 v. Paris: Rousseau, 1914-31.

MORINEAU, Michel. *Les faux-semblants d'un démarrage économique; agriculture et démographie en France au XVIIIe siècle.* Paris: Colin, 1971. 388 p.

MOUSNIER, Roland. *Société française de 1770 à 1789.* Paris: Centre de Documentation universitaire, 1970. 196 p.

SÉE, Henri Eugène. *Economic and social conditions in France during the eighteenth century.* Tr. by Edwin H. Zeydel. New York: Cooper Square, 1968 (c.1927). 245 p.

SOBOUL, Albert. *La France à la veille de la révolution.* Nouv. éd. Paris: Société d'Éditions d'Enseignement supérieur, 1966- .
I. Économie et société.

SOBOUL, Albert. *La société française dans la seconde moitié du XVIIIe siècle: structures sociales, cultures et modes de vie.* Paris: Centre de Documentation universitaire, 1969. 232 p.

REGIONAL STUDIES

AGULHON, Maurice. *Pénitents et francmaçons de l'ancienne Provence.* Paris: Fayard, 1968. 452 p.

AGULHON, Maurice. *La sociabilité méridionale: confrèries et associations dans la vie collective en Provence orientale à la fin du XVIIIe siècle.* 2 v. Aix-en-Provence: La Pensée universitaire, 1966. 878 p.

CHAUSSINARD-NOGARET, Guy. *Les financiers de Languedoc au XVIIIe siècle.* Paris: S.E.V.P.E.N., 1970. 370 p.

ÉGRET, Jean. *Le parlement de Dauphiné et les affaires publiques dans la deuxième moitié du XVIIIe siècle.* 2 v. Paris: Arthaud, 1942.
I. L'opposition parlementaire, (1756-75).
II. Le Parlement et la révolution dauphinoise, (1775-90).

FORSTER, Robert. *The nobility of Toulouse in the eighteenth century: a social and economic study.* New York: Octagon, 1971 (c.1960). 212 p.

FREVILLE, Henri. *L'Intendance de Bretagne, 1689-1790: essai sur l'histoire d'une intendance en pays d'états au XVIIIe siècle.* 3 v. Rennes: Plihon, 1953.

GEBHART, Monique, and Mercadier, Claude. *L'Octroi de Toulouse à la veille de la révolution.* Paris: Bibliothèque Nationale, 1967. 176 p.

HUFTON, Olwen H. *Bayeux in the late eighteenth century: a social study.* New York: Oxford University Press, 1967. 317 p.

LE MOY, A. *Le Parlement de Bretagne et le pouvoir au XVIIIe siècle.* Angers: Imprimerie de Burdin, 1909. 605 p.

MARTIN, Gaston. *Nantes au XVIIIe siècle.* 2 v. Toulouse: Lion; Nantes: Durance, 1928-31.
I. L'administration de Gerard Mellier (1709-20-29).
II. L'ère des négiers (1714-74).

MEYER, Jean. *La noblesse bretonne au XVIIIe siècle.* 2 v. Paris: S.E.V.P.E.N., 1966.

POITRINEAU, Abel. *La vie rurale en Basse-Auvergne au XVIIIe siècle (1726-89).* 2 v. Paris: Presses universitaires de France, 1965.

SAINT-JACOB, Pierre de. *Les paysans de la Bourgogne du nord au dernier siècle de l'ancien regime.* Dijon: Bernigand et Privat, 1960. 643 p.

SHEPPARD, Thomas F. *Loumarin in the eighteenth century: a study of a French village.* Baltimore: John Hopkins Press, 1971. 248 p.

ZINK, Annie. *Azereix: la vie d'une communauté rurale à la fin du XVIIIe siècle.* Paris: S.E.V.P.E.N., 1969. 323 p.

INTELLECTUAL AND CULTURAL*

ACOMB, Frances D. *Anglophobia in France, 1763-89.* Durham: Duke University Press, 1950. 167 p. (OP 2,000,704 $10.00)

ALASSEUR, Claude. *La Comédie française au XVIIIe siècle: étude économique.* Paris: Mouton, 1967. 206 p.

ALDRIDGE, A. O. *Franklin and his French contemporaries.* New York: New York University Press, 1957. 260 p.

ATKINSON, Geoffrey, and Keller, Abraham C. *Prelude to Enlightenment: French literature, 1690-1740.* London: Allen & Unwin, 1971. 221 p.

ATKINSON, Geoffrey. *Les relations de voyages du XVIIe siècle et l'évolution des idées; contribution a l'étude de la formation de l'esprit du XVIIIe siècle.* Paris: Champion, 1924. 220 p.

BONNO, G. *La constitution britannique devant l'opinion française de Montesquieu à Bonaparte.* Paris: Champion, 1931. 317 p.

BOURDE, André J. *The influence of England on the French agronomes, 1750-1789.* Cambridge: The University Press, 1953. 249 p.

CROCKER, Lester G. *An age of crisis; man and the world in eighteenth-century French thought.* Baltimore: Johns Hopkins Press, 1959. 496 p.

DARNTON, Robert. *Mesmerism and the end of the Enlightenment in France.* Cambridge: Harvard University Press, 1968. 218 p.

---

*See next section for the French Enlightenment.

EHRARD, Jean. *L'idée de nature en France dans la première moitié du XVIIIe siecle.* 2 v. Paris: S.E.V.P.E.N., 1963. 863 p.

HERMANN-MASCARD, Nicole. *La censure des livres à Paris à la fin de l'ancien régime (1750-1789).* Paris: Presses universitaires de France, 1968. 148 p.

HUBERT, René. *Les sciences sociales dans l'Encyclopédie; la philosophie de l'histoire et la problème des origines sociales.* Paris: Alcan, 1923. 368 p.

LIVRE et société dans la France du XVIIIe siècle. 2 v. Paris: Mouton, 1965-70.

McCLOY, Shelby T. *The humanitarian movement in eighteenth-century France.* Lexington: University of Kentucky Press, 1957. 274 p.

MCKIE, Douglas. *Antoine Lavoisier: scientist, economist, social reformer.* New York: Schuman, 1952. 440 p.

MARTIN, Kingsley. *French liberal thought in the eighteenth century; a study of political ideas from Bayle to Condorcet.* New York: Harper & Row, 1962 (orig. pub. 1929). 313 p.

MAUZI, Robert. *L'idée du bonheur dans la littérature et la pensée françaises au XVIIIe siècle.* 2. éd. Paris: Colin, 1965. 725 p.

MORNET, Daniel. *French thought in the eighteenth century.* Tr. by L. M. Levin. New York: Prentice-Hall, 1929. 336 p.

MORNET, Daniel. *Les origines intellectuelles de la révolution française, 1715-87.* 6. éd. Paris: Colin, 1967 (c.1933). 552 p.

MORNET, Daniel. *Romanticisme en France au XVIIIe siècle.* Paris: Librairie Hachette, 1912. 286 p. (OP 12,961 $15.00)

MORNET, Daniel. *Les sciences de la nature en France au XVIIIe siècle: un chapitre de l'histoire des idées.* Paris: Colin, 1911. 290 p. (OP 60,297 $20.00)

MOUSNIER, Roland. *Progrès scientifique et technique au XVIIIe siècle.* Paris: Plon, 1958. 451 p.

NIKLAUS, Robert. *A literary history of France: the eighteenth century, 1715-89.* New York: Barnes & Noble, 1970. 435 p.

18

SÉE, Henri Eugène. *Les idées politiques en France au XVIIIe siècle.* Paris: Hachette, 1920. 264 p.

SMITH, Edwin Burrows. *Jean-Sylvain Bailly: astronomer, mystic, revolutionary, 1736-1793.* Philadelphia: American Philosophical Society, Transactions, new series v. 44, pt. 4, 1954. p. 427-538.

TRÉNARD, Louis. *Lyon, de l'Encyclopédie au préromanticisme; histoire sociale des idées.* 2 v. Grenoble: Imprimerie Allier, 1958. 821 p.

WADE, Ira O. *The clandestine organization and diffusion of philosophic ideas in France from 1700-50.* Princeton: Princeton University Press, 1938. 329 p.

WADE, Ira O. *The intellectual origins of the French Enlightenment.* Princeton: Princeton University Press, 1971. 678 p.

WEULERSSE, Georges. *Le mouvement physiocratique en France de 1756 à 1770.* 2 v. New York: Johnson Reprint Corp., 1968 (orig. pub. 1910).

WEULERSSE, Georges. *La physiocratie à la fin du règne de Louis XV, 1770-74.* Paris: Presses universitaires de France, 1959. 238 p.

WEULERSSE, Georges. *La physiocratie sous les ministères de Turgot et de Necker, 1774-81.* Paris: Presses universitaires de France, 1950. 374 p.

INTELLECTUAL AND CULTURAL — THE FRENCH ENLIGHTENMENT

ALTHUSSER, Louis. *Montesquieu: la politique et l'histoire.* Paris: Presses universitaires de France, 1959. 119 p.

BECKER, Carl L. *Heavenly City of the eighteenth-century philosophers.* New Haven: Yale University Press, 1932. 168 p.

BESTERMAN, Theodor. *Voltaire.* New York: Harcourt, Brace, 1969. 637 p.

BLANCHARD, William H. *Rousseau and the spirit of revolt: a psychological study.* Ann Arbor: University of Michigan Press, 1967. 300 p.

CARCASSONE, Élie. *Montesquieu et le*

problème de la constitution française au XVIIIe siècle. Paris: Presses universitaires de France, 1927. 736 p.

CARRÉ, Jean Raoul. *Reflexions sur l'anti-Pascal de Voltaire.* Paris: Alcan, 1935. 120 p.

CASSIRER, Ernst. *The philosophy of the Enlightenment.* Tr. by F. C. A. Koelln and J. P. Pettegrove. Princeton: Princeton University Press, 1951. 366 p.

CASSIRER, Ernst. *The question of Jean-Jacques Rousseau.* Tr. and ed. by Peter Gay. Bloomington: Indiana University Press, 1963. 129 p.

CROCKER, Lester G. *Jean-Jacques Rousseau.* New York: Macmillan, 1968- I. The quest (1712-58).

CROCKER, Lester G. *Nature and culture; ethical thought in the French Enlightenment.* Baltimore: Johns Hopkins Press, 1963. 540 p.

DERATHE, Robert. *Rousseau et la science politique de son temps.* 2. éd. Paris: J. Vrin, 1970 (c.1958). 473 p.

DUCROS, Louis. *Les encyclopédistes.* Genève: Slatkine Reprints, 1967 (c.1900). 376 p.

GAY, Peter. *The Enlightenment: an interpretation.* 2 v. New York: Knopf, 1966-69.
I. The rise of modern paganism. (Random House)
II. The science of freedom.

GAY, Peter. *The party of humanity; essays in the French Enlightenment.* New York: Knopf, 1964. 289 p. (Norton)

GAY, Peter. *Voltaire's politics: the poet as realist.* Princeton: Princeton University Press, 1959. 417 p. (Vintage)

GRIMSLEY, R. *Jean d'Alembert, 1717-83.* Oxford: Clarendon Press, 1963. 316 p.

GRIMSLEY, R. *Jean-Jacques Rousseau; a study in self-awareness.* 2nd ed. Cardiff: University of Wales Press, 1969. 338 p.

HANKINS, Thomas L. *Jean d'Alembert: science and the Enlightenment.* Oxford: Clarendon Press, 1970. 260 p.

HERTZBURG, Arthur. *The French Enlightenment and the Jews.* New York: Columbia University Press, 1968. 420 p.

KNIGHT, Isabel F. *The geometric spirit: the abbe de Condillac and the French Enlightenment.* New Haven: Yale University Press, 1968. 321 p.

LANSON, Gustave. *Voltaire.* Tr. by Robert A. Wagoner. New York: Wiley, 1966. 258 p. (Fr. ed., 1906, OP 56,379 $15.00)

MARSAK, Leonard Mendes. *Bernard de Fontenelle: the idea of science in the French Enlightenment.* Philadelphia: American Philosophical Society, Transactions, new series v. 49, pt. 7, 1959. 64 p.

MASTERS, Roger. *The political philosophy of Rousseau.* Princeton: Princeton University Press, 1968. 464 p.

PROUST, Jacques. *Diderot et l'Encyclopédie.* Paris: Colin, 1962. 621 p.

ROCKWOOD, Raymond O., ed. *Carl Becker's Heavenly City revisited.* Ithaca: Cornell University Press, 1958. 227 p.

SCHAPIRO, Jacob Salwyn. *Condorcet and the rise of liberalism.* New York: Octagon, 1963 (c.1934). 311 p.

SHACKLETON, Robert. *Montesquieu; a critical biography.* London: Oxford University Press, 1961. 432 p.

SHKLAR, Judith N. *Men and citizens: a study of Rousseau's social theory.* New York: Cambridge University Press, 1969. 245 p.

SMITH, David Warner. *Helvétius: a study in persecution.* Oxford: Clarendon Press, 1965. 248 p.

VARTANIAN, Aram. *Diderot and Descartes; a study of scientific naturalism in the Enlightenment.* Princeton: Princeton University Press, 1953. 336 p. (OP 2,000,885 $20.00)

VYVERBERG, Henry. *Historical Pessimism in the French Enlightenment.* Cambridge: Harvard University Press, 1958. 253 p.

WADE, Ira O. *The intellectual development of Voltaire.* Princeton: Princeton University Press, 1969. 807 p.

WILSON, Arthur McCandless. *Diderot.* 2 v. New York: Oxford University Press, 1957-72.

RELIGION

BIEN, David D. *The Calas affair: persecution, toleration and heresy in eighteenth-century Toulouse.* Princeton: Princeton University Press, 1960. 199 p. (OP 61,955 $15.00)

CHEVALLIER, Pierre. *Loménie de Brienne et l'ordre monastique, 1766-89.* 2 v. Paris: Vrin, 1959-60.

DEDIEU, Joseph. *Histoire politique des protestants français, 1715-94.* 2 v. Paris: Gabalda, 1925.

HARDY, Georges. *Le Cardinal de Fleury et le mouvement janséniste.* Paris: Champion, 1925. 360 p.

McMANNERS, John. *French ecclesiastical society under the Ancien Regime; a study of Angers in the eighteenth century.* Manchester: Manchester University Press, 1960. 416 p.

PALMER, Robert R. *Catholics and unbelievers in eighteenth-century France.* Princeton: Princeton University Press, 1939. 236 p.

PRECLIN, Edmond. *Les Jansénistes du XVIIIe siècle et la constitution civile du clergé; la développement du richerisme, sa propagation dans le bas clergé, 1713-91.* Paris: Gamber, 1929. 578 p.

SICARD, Augustin. *L'ancien clergé de France.* 5e éd. rev. et augm. 3 v. Paris: Lecoffre, 1912.
I. Les évêques avant la révolution.

MEMOIRS AND CONTEMPORARY WRITINGS

BARBIER, Edmund Jean François. *Chronique de la régence et du règne de Louis XV (1718-1763); ou, Journal de Barbier.* 8 v. Paris: Charpentier, 1857-58.

BOULAINVILLIERS, Henri, comte de. *Mémoires présentés à Monseigneur le duc d'Orleans; contenant les moyens de rendre ce royaume très-puissant et d'augmenter considérablement les revenus du roi et du peuple.* 2 v. in 1. La Haye: n.p., 1727.

DAIRE, Eugène, éd. *Économistes financiers du XVIIIe siècle.* Paris: Guillaumin, 1843. 1008 p.

LUYNES, Charles Philippe d'Albert, duc de. *Mémoires du Duc de Luynes sur la cour de Louis XV, 1735-58.* 17 v. Paris: Didot, 1860-65.

MARAIS, Mathieu. *Journal et mémoires . . . sur la régence et le règne de Louis XV, 1715-37.* 4 v. Paris: Didot, 1863-68.

RESTIF DE LA BRETONNE, Nicolas Edme. *La vie de mon père.* Intro. et notes de Maurice Boisson. Paris: Éditions Bossard, 1924 (orig. pub. 1779). 289 p.

RICHELIEU, Louis François Armand de Plessis, duc de. *Mémoires authentiques du maréchal de Richelieu (1725-57).* Pub. par A. de Boislisle. Paris: Société de l'Histoire de France, 1918. [cxiv] 259 p.

SOULAVIE, Jean Louis Giraud. *Mémoires historiques et politiques du règne de Louis XVI.* 6 v. Paris: Treutell et Wurtz, 1801.

TURGOT, Anne Robert Jacques. *Oeuvres de Turgot et documents le concernant, avec biographie et notes par Gustave Schelle.* 5 v. Paris: Alcan, 1913-23. (OP 50,955 v. 1—$35.00; v. 4—$40.00. Total $75.00)

YOUNG, Arthur. *Travels in France during the years 1787, 1788 and 1789.* Cambridge: The University Press, 1929. 428 p.

THE REVOLUTION AND THE NAPOLEONIC EMPIRE, 1789-1815

GENERAL AND MISCELLANEOUS

ACTON, John Emrich, baron. *Lectures on the French Revolution.* New York: Noonday Press, 1959 (c.1910). 379 p.

AULARD, François Victor Alphonse. *The French Revolution: a political history, 1789-1804.* Tr. by Bernard Miall from the French of the third ed. 4 v. New York: Russell & Russell, 1965 (orig. French ed., 1901).
I. The Revolution under the monarchy, 1789-92.
II. The democratic republic, 1792-95.
III. The revolutionary government, 1793-97.
IV. The bourgeois republic and the Consulate, 1797-1804.

BEIK, Paul H. *The French Revolution seen from the right; social theories in motion, 1789-1799.* Philadelphia: American Philosophical Society, 1956. 122 p.

BIRO, S. *The German policy of Revolutionary France: a study in French diplomacy during the war of the first coalition, 1792-97.* 2 v. Cambridge: Harvard University Press, 1957.

BRINTON, Crane. *The lives of Tallyrand.*

New York: Norton, 1936. 316 p.

CARLYLE, Thomas. *The French Revolution.* New York: Modern Library, 1934 (orig. pub. 1837). 748 p.

CHUQUET, Arthur Maxime. *Les guerres de la révolution.* 11 v. Paris: Plon-Nourrit, 1886-96.

COBB, Richard. *Reactions to the French Revolution.* New York: Oxford University Press, 1972. 310 p.

COBBAN, Alfred. *Aspects of the French Revolution.* New York: Norton, 1970. 328 p.

COBBAN, Alfred, ed. *The debate of the French Revolution, 1789-1800.* 2nd ed. New York: Barnes & Noble, 1961 (c.1950). 495 p.

COCHIN, Augustin. *La crise de l'histoire révolutionnaire; Taine et M. Aulard.* Paris: Champion, 1909. 103 p.

COOPER, Duff. *Tallyrand.* Stanford: Stanford University Press, 1967 (c.1932). 399 p.

EISENSTEIN, Elizabeth L. *The first pro-*

fessional revolutionist, Filippo Michele Buonarroti, (1767-1837); a biographical essay. Cambridge: Harvard University Press, 1959. 205 p.

FARMER, Paul. *France reviews its revolutionary origins: social politics and historical opinion in the Third Republic.* New York: Octagon, 1963. 174 p.

FUGIER, André. *La révolution française et l'empire napoléonien.* Paris: Hachette, 1954. 422 p.

FURET, François, and Richet, Denis. *The French Revolution.* Tr. by Stephen Hardman. London: Weidenfeld & Nicolson, 1970. 416 p.

GAXOTTE, Pierre. *The French Revolution.* Tr. by Walter Alison Phillips. New York: Scribner's, 1932. 416 p. (OP 2776 $25.00)

GERSHOY, Leo. *The French Revolution and Napoleon.* New York: Appleton, Century, Crofts, 1964 (first pub. 1933). 584 p.

GODECHOT, Jacques. *The Counter-Revolution, 1789-1804: doctrines and events.* Tr. by Salvator Attansio. New York: Fertig, 1971. 405 p.

GODECHOT, Jacques. *La grande nation; l'expansion révolutionnaire de la France dans le monde de 1789 à 1799.* 2 v. Paris: Aubrier, 1956.

GOODWIN, Albert. *The French Revolution.* 2nd ed. London: Hutchinson's University Library, 1956. 192 p. (Harper Torchbook)

JAURÈS, Jean Léon. *Histoire socialiste de la révolution française.* Édition revue et annotée par Albert Soboul. 6 v. Paris: Éditions Sociales, 1968-72 (orig. pub. 1901-04).

JOMINI, Henri. *Histoire critique et militaire des guerres de la révolution.* 4 v. Bruxelles: Petit, 1840-42. (1820-24 ed. OP 60,484 v. 1—$20.00; v. 2—$20.00; v. 3—$25.00. Total $65.00)

KAPLOW, Jeffry. *New perspectives on the French Revolution: readings in historical sociology.* New York: Wiley, 1965. 354 p.

LACOUR-GAYET, Georges. *Tallyrand, 1754-1838.* 3 v. Paris: Payot, 1928-31.

LEFEBVRE, Georges. *The French Revolution.* Tr. by John Hall Stewart & James Friguglietti. 2 v. New York: Columbia University Press, 1962-64.
I. From its origins to 1793.
II. From 1793 to 1799.

LEFEBVRE, Georges. *Études sur la révolution française.* 2. ed. Paris: Presses universitaires de France, 1963. 443 p.

LÉVY-SCHNEIDER, Léon. *Le conventionnel Jeanbon Saint-André, membre du Comité de salut public, organisateur de la marine de la Terreur, 1749-1813.* 2 v. Paris: Alcan, 1901.

MADELIN, Louis. *Fouché, 1759-1829.* Paris: Plon, 1955. 396 p.

MADELIN, Louis. *Tallyrand: a vivid biography of the amoral, unscrupulous and fascinating French statesman.* Tr. by Rosalie Feltenstein. New York: Roy Publishers, 1948. 320 p.

MAHAN, Alfred Thayer. *The influence of sea power on the French Revolution and Empire, 1793-1812.* 14th ed. 2 v. Boston: Little, Brown, 1918. (9th ed, 1898, OP 19,471 v. 1—$25.00; v. 2—$25.00. Total $50.00)

MAY, Gita. *Madame Roland and the age of revolution.* New York: Columbia University Press, 1970. 360 p.

MICHELET, Jules. *History of the French Revolution.* Tr. by Charles Cooks. Ed. by Gordon Wright. Chicago: University of Chicago Press, 1967. 476 p.

PATRICK, Alison. *The men of the first French Republic; political alignments in the National Convention of 1792.* Baltimore: Johns Hopkins University Press, 1972. 407 p.

REINHARD, Marcel. *La grand Carnot.* 2 v. Paris: Hachette, 1950-52.

SOBOUL, Albert. *La civilisation et la révolution française.* Paris: Arthaud, 1970-
I. La crise de l'ancien régime.

SOBOUL, Albert. *La Première République, 1792-1804.* Paris: Calman-Lévy, 1968. 365 p.

SOBOUL, Albert. *La révolution française.* 2 v. Paris: Gallimard, 1964.

SOREL, Albert. *L'Europe et la révolution française.* 8 v. Paris: Plon-Nourrit, 1885-1904. (Vol. I tr. as: *Europe and the French Revolution: The political traditions of the Old Regime.* London: Collins, 1969. 606 p.).

STEWART, John Hall. *A documentary survey of the French Revolution.* New York: Macmillan, 1951. 818 p.

TAINE, Hippolyte Adolphe. *The French Revolution.* Tr. by John Durand. 3 v. Gloucester, Mass.: Peter Smith, 1962 (reprint of 1878-1885 ed.).

THIERS, Adolphe. *History of the French Revolution.* 4 v. New York: Appleton, 1854.

THOMPSON, James Matthew, ed. *English witnesses of the French Revolution.* Oxford: Clarendon Press, 1938. 267 p.

THE REVOLUTION, 1789-1794

AULARD, François Victor Alphonse. *Le culte de la raison et le culte de l'être suprême, (1793-1794).* Paris: Alcan, 1892. 371 p. (OP 27,701 $20.00)

BRUUN, Geoffrey. *Saint-Just, apostle of the Terror.* Boston: Houghton Mifflin, 1932. 168 p.

CARON, Pierre. *Les massacres de septembre.* Paris: En vente à la Maison du Livre Français, 1935. 559 p.

CARON, Pierre. *La première terreur, 1792.* Paris: Presses universitaires de France, 1950-
I. Les missions du Conseil exécutif provisoire et de la Commune de Paris.

ÉGRET, Jean. *La révolution des notables: Mounier et les monarchiens, 1789.* Paris: Colin, 1950. 244 p.

GERSHOY, Leo. *Bertrand Barère, a reluctant terrorist.* Princeton: Princeton University Press, 1962. 459 p.

GODECHOT, Jacques. *The taking of the Bastille, July 14th, 1789.* Tr. by Jean Stewart. New York: Scribner's, 1970. 368 p.

GOOCH, Robert Kent. *Parliamentary government in France: revolutionary origins, 1789-91.* Ithaca: Cornell University Press, 1960. 253 p.

GOTTSCHALK, Louis, and Maddox, Margaret. *Lafayette in the French Revolution: through the October Days.* Chicago: University of Chicago Press, 1969. 414 p.

GOTTSCHALK, Louis. *Jean-Paul Marat; a study in radicalism.* New York: B. Blom, 1966 (c.1927). 221 p.

HYSLOP, Beatrice F. *French nationalism in 1789 according to the general cahiers.* New York: Octagon, 1968 (c.1934). 343 p.

HYSLOP, Beatrice F. *A guide to the general cahiers of 1789, with the texts of unedited cahiers.* New York: Octagon, 1968 (c.1936). 484 p.

KERR, Wilfred Branton. *The reign of terror, 1793-94; the experiment of the democratic republic and the rise of the bourgeoisie.* Toronto: University of Toronto Press, 1927. 499 p.

LEFEBVRE, Georges. *La grande peur de 1789.* Nouv. éd. Paris: Colin, 1971 (orig. pub. 1932). 280 p.

LEFEBVRE, Georges. *The coming of the French Revolution, 1789.* Tr. by R. R. Palmer. New York: Random House, 1957 (first Fr. ed. 1939). 233 p. (Princeton)

MADELIN, Louis. *Danton.* Tr. by Lady Mary Loyd. New York: Knopf, 1921. 378 p.

MATHIEZ, Albert. *Études Robespierristes.* 2 v. Paris: Colin, 1917-18.

MATHIEZ, Albert. *The fall of Robespierre and other essays.* (Tr. of *Autour de Robespierre,* 1927). New York: A. M. Kelly, 1968. 249 p.

MATHIEZ, Albert. *The French Revolution.* Tr. by Catherine A. Phillips. New York: Grosset & Dunlap, 1964. 259 p. (Universal Library)

MATHIEZ, Albert. *Girondins et Montagnards.* Paris: Firmin-Didot, 1930. 305 p.

MATHIEZ, Albert. *Les origines des cultes révolutionnaires, 1789-92.* Paris: Société Nouvelle de Librarie, 1904. 150 p.

MICHON, Georges. *Robespierre et la guerre révolutionnaire, 1791-92.* Paris: Rivière, 1937. 138 p.

PALMER, Robert R. *Twelve who ruled; the year of the Terror in the French Revolution.* Princeton: Princeton University Press, 1959 (c.1941). 417 p. (Atheneum) (1941 ed. OP 16,880 $25.00)

ROBERTS, John M., ed. *French Revolution documents.* New York: Barnes & Noble, 1966-
I. 1787-92.

ROGERS, Cornwall Burnham. *The spirit of revolution in 1789: a study of public opinion as revealed in political songs and other popular literature at the beginning of the French Revolution.* Princeton: Princeton University Press, 1949. 363 p.

SALVEMINI, Gaetano. *The French Revolution, 1788-92.* Tr. from the Italian by I. M. Rawson. London: Cape, 1954. 343 p. (Norton)

SHEPARD, William Finley. *Price control and the Reign of Terror; France, 1793-95.* Berkeley: University of California Press, 1953. 139 p.

SIRICH, John Black. *Revolutionary committees in the departments of France, 1793-94.* New York: Fertig, 1971 (c.1943). 238 p.

SOBOUL, Albert. *Paysans, sans-culottes et jacobins.* Paris: Clavreuil, 1966. 386 p.

SOBOUL, Albert. *The Parisian sans-culottes and the French Revolution, 1793-94.* Tr. by Gwynne Lewis. Oxford: Clarendon Press, 1964. 280 p.

SYDENHAM, M. J. *The Girondins.* London: University of London, Athlone Press, 1961. 252 p.

TERNAUX, Louis Mortimer. *Histoire de la Terreur, 1792-94.* 8 v. Paris: Levy, 1866-81.

THOMPSON, James Matthew. *Robespierre.* 2 v. New York: Fertig, 1968 (c.1935). (1935 ed. OP 49,354 v. 1—$20.00; v. 2—$20.00. Total $40.00)
I. From the birth of Robespierre to the death of Louis XVI.
II. From the death of Louis XVI to the death of Robespierre.

TÖNNESON, Kare D. *La defaite des sans-culottes; mouvements populaires et réaction bourgeoise en l'an III.* Oslo: Presses universitaires, 1959. 456 p.

WALLON, Henri Alexandre. *Histoire du Tribunal révolutionnaire de Paris, avec le journal de ses actes.* 6 v. Paris: Hachette, 1880-82.

WALTER, Gérard. *Histoire des Jacobins.* Paris: Somogy, 1946. 380 p.

WALTER, Gérard. *Robespierre.* Éd. définitive. 2 v. Paris: Gallimard, 1961 (first pub. 1936-46).

THE REVOLUTION, 1794-1799

DEJOINT, Georges. *La politique économique du directoire.* Paris: Rivière, 1951. 280 p.

GUYOT, Raymond. *La Directoire et la paix de l'Europe, des traités de Bâle à la deuxième coalition (1795-99).* Paris: Alcan, 1911. 956 p.

LEFEBVRE, Georges. *The Thermidorians and the Directory; two phases of the French Revolution.* Tr. by Robert Baldick. New York: Random House, 1964. 461 p.

MATHIEZ, Albert. *After Robespierre: the Thermidorian reaction.* Tr. by Catherine A. Phillips. New York: Grosset & Dunlap, 1965 (c.1931). 259 p. (Universal Library)

MITCHELL, Harvey. *The underground war against revolutionary France; the missions of William Wickham, 1794-1800.* Oxford: Clarendon Press, 1965. 286 p.

REINHARD, Marcel. *La France du Directoire.* 2 v. Paris: Centre de Documentation universitaire, 1956.

THOMSON, David. *The Babeuf plot; the making of a republican legend.* London: K. Paul, 1947. 112 p. (OP 56,988 $10.00)

WILKINSON, Spenser. *The rise of General Bonaparte*. Oxford: Clarendon Press, 1930. 179 p.

WOLOCH, Isser. *Jacobin legacy: the democratic movement under the Directory*. Princeton: Princeton University Press, 1970. 455 p.

THE CONSULATE AND THE EMPIRE, 1799-1815

BAINVILLE, Jacques. *Napoleon*. Tr. Hamish Miles. Boston: Little, Brown, 1933. 418 p.

BUTTERFIELD, Herbert. *The peace tactics of Napoleon, 1806-08*. Cambridge: The University Press, 1929. 395 p.

CHANDLER, David G. *The campaigns of Napoleon*. New York: Macmillan, 1966. 1172 p.

CHUQUET, Arthur Maxime. *La jeunesse de Napoléon*. 3 v. Paris: Colin, 1897-99.

COLIN, Jean Lambert Alphonse. *L'éducation militaire de Napoléon*. Paris: Chapelot, 1900. 507 p. (OP 46,527 $30.00)

CONNELLY, Owen. *The gentle Bonaparte: a biography of Joseph, Napoleon's elder brother*. New York: Macmillan, 1968. 335 p.

CONNELLY, Owen. *Napoleon's satellite kingdoms*. New York: Free Press, 1965. 387 p.

DEUTCH, Harold Charles. *The genesis of Napoleonic imperialism*. Cambridge: Harvard University Press, 1938. 460 p. (OP 54,916 $25.00)

DRIAULT, Édouard. *Napoléon et l'Europe*. 5 v. Paris: Alcan, 1910-27.
La politique extérieure du premier consul, 1800-1803.
Austerlitz, la fin du Saint-empire (1804-1806).
Tilsit, France et Russie sous le premier empire, la question de Pologne (1806-1809)
Le grand empire (1809-1812)
La chute de l'empire; la légende de Napoléon (1812-1815). (OP 45, 447 $25.00)

ESPOSITO, Vincent Joseph, and Elting, John Robert. *A military history and atlas of the Napoleonic Wars*. New York: Praeger, 1964. n.p. 2 v.

FOURNIER, August. *Napoleon I*. Tr. by Annie E. Adams. 2 v. New York: Holt, 1911.

GEER, Walter. *Napoleon and his family: the story of a Corsican clan*. 3 v. London: Allen & Unwin, 1928-29.
I. Corsica- Madrid, 1769-1809.
II. Madrid—Moscow, 1809-13.
III. Moscow—St. Helena, 1813-21.

GEOFFROY DE GRANDMAISON, Charles. *L'Espagne et Napoléon*. 3 v. Paris: Plon-Nourrit, 1908-31.

GEYL, Pieter. *Napoleon, for and against*. Tr. from the Dutch by Olive Renier. London: Cape, 1964 (c.1949). 477 p. (Yale)

GODECHOT, Jacques. *Napoléon*. Paris: Michel, 1969. 447 p.

HOLTMAN, Robert B. *Napoleonic propaganda*. Baton Rouge: Louisiana State University Press, 1950. 272 p.

HOLTMAN, Robert B. *The Napoleonic revolution*. Philadelphia: Lippincott, 1967. 225 p.

KIRCHEISEN, Friedrich Max. *Napoleon*. Tr. Henry St. Lawrence. New York: Harcourt, 1932. 761 p.

KNAPTON, Ernest John. *Empress Josephine*. Cambridge: Harvard University Press, 1963. 359 p.

KORNGOLD, Ralph. *The last years of Napoleon: his captivity on St. Helena*. New York: Harcourt, Brace, 1959. 429 p.

LACHOUQUE, Henry. *Napoleon's battles: a history of his campaigns*. Tr. by Roy Monkom. New York: Dutton, 1967. 479 p.

LEFEBVRE, Georges. *Napoleon*. 2 v. New York: Columbia University Press, 1969 (first Fr. ed. 1935-36).
I. From 18 Brumaire to Tilsit, 1799-1807. Tr. by H. F. Stockhold.
II. From Tilsit to Waterloo, 1807-15. Tr. by J. E. Anderson.

MacDONELL, Archibald Gordon. *Napoleon and his marshalls.* London: Macmillan, 1934. 368 p.

MARKHAM, Felix. *Napoleon.* London: Weidenfeld & Nicolson, 1963. 292 p. (New American Library)

MASSON, Frédéric. *Napoléon et sa famille.* 13 v. Paris: Ollendorff, 1900-19.

MOWAT, Robert Balmain. *The diplomacy of Napoleon.* London: Arnold, 1924. 315 p. (OP 56,702 $20.00)

OMAN, Sir Charles William. *Studies in the Napoleonic Wars.* London: Methuen, 1929. 284 p. (OP 25,253 $20.00)

PONTEIL, Felix. *La chute de Napoléon I et la crise française de 1814-15.* Paris: Aubier, Éditions montagne, 1943. 350 p.

ROSE, John Holland. *The life of Napoleon I.* 2 v. London: Bell, 1924 (c.1901).

SÉGUR, Philippe Paul, comte de. *La campagne de Russie.* 2 v. Paris: Hachette, 1960. (Abridged translation by J. David Townsend as *Napoleon's Russian campaign.* Boston: Houghton Mifflin, 1958. 306 p.).

TARLÉ, Evgenii V. *Le blocus continental et le royaume d'Italie; la situation économique de l'Italie sous Napoléon I d'après des documents inédits.* Paris: Alcan, 1928. 377 p.

TARLÉ, Evgenii V. *Napoleon's invasion of Russia, 1812.* New York: Oxford University Press, 1942. 422 p.

THIERS, Adolphe. *History of the Consulate and the Empire of France under Napoleon.* Tr. by D. F. Campbell and J. Stebbing. 20 v. in 10. London: Colburn, 1845-62. (French ed. OP 63,231 v. 1—$30.00; v. 2—$23.20; v. 3—$30.00; v. 4—$35.00; v. 5—$25.00; v. 6—$30.00; v. 7—$35.00; v. 8—$35.00; v. 9—$35.00; v. 10—$30.00; v. 11—$25.00; v. 12—$40.00; v. 13—$30.00; v. 14—$35.00; v. 15—$35.00; v. 16—$35.00; v. 17—$45.00; v. 18—$35.00; v. 19—$35.00; v. 20—$45.00; v. 21—$35.00. Total $705.00)

THOMPSON, James Matthew. *Napoleon Bonaparte, his rise and fall.* Oxford: Blackwell, 1952. 411 p.

VANDAL, Albert. *L'avènement de Bonaparte.* 2 v. Paris: Plon-Nourrit, 1902-07.

GOVERNMENT, ADMINISTRATION, EDUCATION, MILITARY

BARNARD, Howard Clive. *Education and the French Revolution.* London: Cambridge University Press, 1969. 267 p.

BRISSET, Jacqueline. *L'adoption de la communauté comme régime légal dans le code civil.* Paris: Presses universitaires de France, 1967. 92 p.

CHASSIN, Charles Louis, and Hennet, L. *Les volontaires nationaux pendant la révolution.* 3 v. Paris: Cerf, 1899-1906.

COBB, Richard C. *Les armées révolutionnaires, instrument de la Terreur dans les départements, avril 1793-floréal an II.* 2 v. Paris: Mouton, 1961-63.

DURAND, Charles. *Études sur le Conseil d'État napoléonien.* v. 1. Paris: Presses universitaires de France, 1949.

FESTY, Octave. *Les délits ruraux et leur répression sous la révolution et le Consulat.* Paris: Rivière, 1956. 198 p.

GARAUD, Marcel. *Histoire générale du droit privée française de 1789 à 1804.* 2 v. Paris: Sirey, 1953-58. I. La révolution et l'égalite civile. II. La révolution et la propriété foncière.

GODECHOT, Jacques. *Les institutions de la France sous la révolution et l'empire.* 2. éd. rev. Paris: Presses universitaires de France, 1968. 789 p.

GODECHOT, Jacques Léon. *Les commissaires aux armées sous le Directoire.* 2 v. Paris: Fustier, 1937.

GODFREY, James L. *Revolutionary justice: a study of the organization, personnel, and the procedures of the Paris Tribunal, 1793-95.* Chapel Hill: University of North Carolina Press, 1951. 166 p.

GONTARD, Maurice. *L'enseignement primaire en France de la révolution à la loi Guizot, (1789-1833).* Paris: Éditions Les Belles Lettres, 1959. 576 p.

HAMPSON, Norman. *La marine en l'an II; mobilisation de la flotte de l'océan, 1793-94.* Paris: Rivière, 1959. 276 p.

HARTMANN, Louis. *Les officiers de l'armée royale et la révolution.* Paris: Alcan, 1910. 540 p. (OP 57,880 $30.00)

HAUTERIVE, Ernest d'. *Napoléon et sa police.* Paris: Flammarion, 1944. 344 p.

LATREILLE, Albert. *L'oeuvre militaire de la révolution: l'armée et la nation à la fin de l'ancien régime; les derniers ministres de la guerre de la monarchie.* Paris: Chapelot, 1914. 460 p.

PHIPPS, Ramsay Weston. *The armies of the first French republic and the rise of the marshals of Napoleon I.* 5 v. London: Oxford University Press, 1926-39.

POISSON, Charles. *Les fournisseurs aux armées sous la révolution française: le directoire des achats (1792-93).* Paris: Margraff, 1932. 366 p.

PONTEIL, Felix. *Napoléon I et l'organisation autoritaire de la France.* Paris: Colin, 1956. 222 p.

SAVANT, Jean. *Les préfets de Napoléon.* Paris: Hachette, 1958. 331 p.

SELIGMAN, Edmund. *La justice en France pendant la révolution.* 2 v. Paris: Plon-Nourrit, 1901-13.

SOBOUL, Albert. *Les soldats de l'an II.* Paris: Club française du Livre, 1959. 297 p.

VIGNERY, J. Robert. *The French Revolution and the schools: educational policies of the Mountain, 1792-94.* Madison: Madison State Historical Society, 1965. 208 p.

WILKINSON, Spenser. *The French army before Napoleon.* Oxford: Clarendon Press, 1915. 151 p. (OP 30,379 $10.00)

SOCIAL AND ECONOMIC

AULARD, Francois Victor Alphonse. *La révolution française et le régime féodal.* Paris: Alcan, 1919. 286 p.

BALLOT, Charles. *L'introduction du machinisme dans l'industrie française.* Paris: Rieder, 1923. 575 p. (OP 50,770 $30.00)

BOULOISEAU, Marc. *Étude de l'émigration et de la vente des biens des émigrés, (1792-1830).* Paris: Imprimerie nationale, 1963. 179 p.

BRINTON, Clarence Crane. *The Jacobins: an essay in the new history.* New York: Russell & Russell, 1961 (c.1930). 319 p.

CHABERT, A. *Essai sur les mouvements des prix et des revenus en France de 1798 à 1820.* 2 v. Paris: Librairie de Médicis, 1945-49.

COBB, Richard C. *Terreur et subsistances, 1793-95.* Paris: Clavreuil, 1965. 396 p.

COBB, Richard C. *The police and the people: French popular protest, 1789-1820.* Oxford: Clarendon Press, 1970. 393 p.

COBBAN, Alfred. *The social interpretation of the French Revolution.* Cambridge: The University Press, 1964. 178 p.

FESTY, Octave. *L'agriculture pendant la révolution française: les conditions de production et de récolte des céréales: Étude d'histoire économique, 1789-95.* Paris: Gallimard, 1947. 463 p.

FESTY, Octave. *L'agriculture française sous le Consulat.* Paris: Académie Napoléon, 1952. 287 p.

GREER, Donald. *The incidence of the emigration during the French Revolution.* Cambridge: Harvard University Press, 1951. 173 p.

GREER, Donald. *The incidence of the Terror during the French Revolution; a statistical interpretation.* Gloucester, Mass.: Peter Smith, 1966 (c.1935). 196 p.

GUERIN, Daniel. *La lutte de classes sous la première république; bourgeois et "bras nus," 1793-97.* Nouv. éd. rev. 2 v. Paris: Gallimard, 1968 (first pub. 1946).

HAMPSON, Norman. *A social history of the French Revolution.* London: Routledge & K. Paul, 1963. 278 p. (University of Toronto Press)

HARRIS, Seymour E. *The assignats.* New York: AMS Press, 1969 (c.1930). 293 p.

HECKSCHER, Eli Filip. *The continental system; an economic interpretation.* Ed. by Harald Westergaard. Gloucester, Mass.: Peter Smith, 1964 (c.1922). 420 p. (1922 ed. OP 4378 $25.00)

JOUVENAL, Bertrand de. *Napoléon et l'économie dirigée, le blocus continental.* Bruxelles: Les Éditions de la Toison d'Or, 1942. 417 p.

LEVASSEUR, Émile. *Histoire des classes ouvrières et de l'industrie en France de 1789 à 1870.* 2 v. Paris: Rousseau, 1903-04.

MATHIEZ, Albert. *La vie chère et le mouvement social sous la Terreur.* Paris: Payot, 1927. 620 p.

MELVIN, Frank E. *Napoleon's navigation system: a study of trade control during the continental blocade.* New York: Appleton, 1919. 449 p.

NUSSBAUM, Frederick Louis. *Commercial policy in the French Revolution; a study of the career of G. J. A. Ducher.* [Washington, D.C.: n.p., 1923] 388 p. (OP 35,765 $20.00)

ROBIQUET, Jean. *Daily life in the French Revolution.* Tr. by James Kirkup. New York: Macmillan, 1965. 246 p.

RUDÉ, George F. E. *The crowd in the French Revolution.* Oxford: Clarendon Press, 1959. 267 p.

SAGNAC, Philippe. *La legislation civile de la révolution française, 1789-1804; essai d'histoire sociale.* Glashütten im Taunus: D. Avermann, 1971 (first pub. 1898).

SOBOUL, Albert. *La France à la veille de la révolution.* Nouv. éd. Paris: Société d'Éditions d'enseignement supérieur, 1966-
I. Économie et société.

VIENNET, Odette. *Napoléon et l'industrie française: la crise de 1810-11.* Paris: Plon, 1947. 342 p.

WILLIAMS, Gwyn A. *Artisans and sans-culottes: popular movements in France and Britain during the French Revolution.* London: Edward Arnold, 1968. 128 p.

REGIONAL STUDIES

BRACE, Richard Munthe. *Bordeaux and the Gironde, 1789-94.* New York: Russell & Russell, 1968 (c.1947). 279 p.

CLEMENDOT, Pierre. *Le Département de la Meurthe à l'époque du Directoire.* Raon-l'Étape, Vosges: Imprimerie Fetzer, 1966. 502 p.

DESCHUYTTER, Joseph. *La Révolution française en province: l'esprit public dans le Nord en 1791, ou le mythe de l'élan populaire.* Gap: Imprimerie Louis-Jean, 1971. 182 p.

FAUCHEUX, Marcel. *L'insurrection vendéene de 1793: aspects économiques et sociaux.* Paris: Imprimerie nationale, 1964. 412 p.

KAPLOW, Jeffry. *Elbeuf during the Revolutionary period: history and social structure.* Baltimore: Johns Hopkins Press, 1964. 278 p.

LEFEBVRE, Georges. *Cherbourg à la fin de l'ancien régime et au début de la révolution.* Caen: n.p., 1965. 295 p.

LEFEBVRE, Georges. *Études orléanaises.* 2 v. (Commission d'histoire économique et sociale de la Révolution, Mémoires et documents, no. 15). Paris: Bibliotheque Nationale, 1962-63.
I. Contribution à l'étude des structures sociales à la fin du XVIIIe siècle.
II. Subsistances et maximum (1789-An IV).

LEFEBVRE, Georges. *Les paysans du nord pendant la révolution.* 2 v. Bari: Editore Laterza, 1959 (c.1924). (1924 ed. OP 54,739 $45.00)

REINHARD, Marcel. *Le département de la Sarthe sous le régime directorial.* [Saint-Brieuc: Les Presses bretonnes, 1936] 657 p.

REINHARD, Marcel. *Nouvelle histoire de Paris: la révolution, 1789-99.* Paris: Hachette, 1971.

ROBIN, Régine. *La société française en 1789: Sémur-en-Auxois.* Paris: Plon, 1970. 522 p.

SENTOU, Jean. *Fortunes et groups sociaux à Toulouse sous la révolution (1789-99):*

essai d'histoire statistique. Toulouse:
Édouard Privat, 1969. 496 p.

TILLY, Charles. *The Vendée.* Cambridge:
Harvard University Press, 1964. 373 p.
(Wiley)

INTELLECTUAL AND CULTURAL

BALDENSPERGER, Fernand. *Le mouvement des idées dans l'émigration française
(1789-1815).* 2 v. Paris: Plon-Nourrit,
1924. (OP 53,572 $40.00)
I. Les expériences du présent.– $20.00
II. Prophètes du passé; théories de
l'avenir.– $20.00

BELIN, Jean. *La logique d'une idée-force;
l'idée d'utilité sociale et la révolution
française, (1789-92).* Paris: Hermann,
1939. 635 p.

BOUISSOUNOUSSE, Janine. *Condorcet; le
philosophe dans la révolution.* Paris:
Hachette, 1962. 319 p.

CARLSON, Marvin A. *The theater of the
French Revolution.* Ithaca: Cornell University Press, 1966. 328 p.

COCHIN, Augustin. *Les sociétés de pensée
et la démocratie; études d'histoire révolutionnaire.* Paris: Plon-Nourrit, 1921.
300 p.

CROSLAND, Maurice. *The society of
Arcueil: a view of French science at the
time of Napoleon I.* London: Heinemann,
1967. 514 p.

DOWD, David. *Pageant-master of the
Republic: Jacques-Louis David and the
French Revolution.* Lincoln: University
of Nebraska Press, 1948. 205 p.
(OP 24,983 $12.25)

FAYET, Joseph. *La révolution française et
la science, 1789-95.* Paris: Rivière, 1960.
498 p.

HENDERSON, Ernest Flagg. *Symbol and
satire in the French Revolution.* New
York: Putnam's, 1912. 456 p.

LEITH, James A. *The idea of art as propaganda in France, 1750-99: a study in the
history of ideas.* Toronto: University of
Toronto Press, 1965. 184 p.

McDONALD, Joan. *Rousseau and the
French Revolution, 1762-91.* New York:
Oxford University Press, 1965. 190 p.

PARKER, Harold Talbot. *The cult of antiq-
uity and the French revolutionaries; a
study in the development of the revolutionary spirit.* New York: Octagon, 1965
(c.1937). 225 p.

RELIGION

AULARD, François Victor Alphonse.
Christianity and the French Revolution.
Tr. by Lady Fraser. New York: Fertig,
1966 (c.1927). 164 p.

CONSTANT, Gustave Léon. *L'église de
France sous le consulat et l'empire, 1800-
14.* Paris: Gabalda, 1928. 393 p.

DEBIDOUR, Antonin. *Histoire des rapports
de l'église et de l'état en France de 1789 à
1870.* Paris: Alcan, 1898. 740 p.

JETTE, Marie Henry. *France religieuse sous
la révolution et de l'empire, prises de vue.*
Nouv. éd. Paris: Casterman, 1958. 292 p.

LA GORCE, Pierre de. *Histoire religieuse de
la révolution française.* 5 v. Paris: Plon-
Nourrit, 1912-23.

LATREILLE, André. *L'Église catholique et
la révolution française, 1775-1815.* 2 v.
Paris: Hachette, 1946-50.
I. Le pontificat de Pie VI et la crise
française (1775-99).
II. L'ère napoléonienne et la crise
européenne (1800-15).

LEFLON, Jean. *La crise révolutionnaire,
1789-1846.* (Histoire de l'Église depuis
l'origines jusqu'a nos jours, T. 20). Paris:
Bloud & Gay, 1949. 524 p.

McMANNERS, John. *The French Revolution and the Church.* London: S.P.C.K.
for the Church Historical Society, 1969.
161 p.

MARKOV, Walter. *Die Freiheiten des
Priesters Roux.* Berlin: Akademie-Verlag,
1967. 430 p.

PHILLIPS, Charles Stanley. *The Church in
France, 1789-1848; a study in revival.*
New York: Russell & Russell, 1966
(c.1929). 315 p.

PLONGERON, Bernard. *Conscience religieuse en révolution: regards sur l'historiographie religieuse de la révolution française.* Paris: Éditions A. & J. Picard, 1969. 352 p.

POLAND, Burdette C. *French Protestantism and the French Revolution; a study in church and state, thought and religion, 1685-1815.* Princeton: Princeton University Press, 1957. 315 p. (OP 2,000,887 $20.00)

ROBERT, Daniel. *Les églises reformées en France, 1800-30.* Paris: Presses universitaires de France, 1961. 632 p.

MEMOIRS AND CONTEMPORARY WRITINGS

AULARD, François Victor Alphonse. *La société des jacobins. Recueil de documents pour l'histoire du club des jacobins de Paris, 1789-94.* 6 v. Paris: Librairie Jouaust, 1889-97. (OP 27,588 $235.00)
I. 1789-1790.—$35.00
II. Janvier à juillet.—$35.00
III. Juillet 1791 à juin 1792.—$40.00
IV. Juin 1792 à janvier 1793.—$40.00
V. Janvier 1793 à mars 1794.—$40.00
VI. Mars à novembre 1794.—$45.00

BARÈRE DE VIEUZAC, Bertrand. *Memoirs of Bertrand Barère, Chairman of the Committee of Public Safety during the Revolution.* 4 v. London: H. S. Nichols, 1896.

BARRAS, Paul François Jean Nicolas, vicomte de. *Memoirs of Barras, member of the Directorate.* Tr. by C. E. Roche. Ed. by George Duruy. 4 v. New York: Harper, 1895-96.

BUONARROTI, Filippo Michele. *Buonarroti's history of Babeuf's conspiracy for equality.* Tr. by Bronterre [pseud.]. London: H. Hetherington, 1836. 454 p. (OP 1045 $25.00)

BURKE, Edmund. *Reflections on the Revolution in France.* Harmondsworth: Penguin, 1969. (1890 ed. OP 47,284 $30.00)

CARNOT, Hippolyte. *Mémoires sur Carnot, par son fils.* 2 v. Paris: Pagnarre, 1861-63.

CAULAINCOURT, Armand Augustin Louis, marquis de. *With Napoleon in Russia: the memoirs of General de Caulaincourt, duke of Vicenza.* Tr. by George Libraire. New York: Grosset & Dunlap, 1959 (abridged English ed., c.1935). 422p. (Universal Library)

CAULAINCOURT, Armand Augustin Louis, marquis de. *No peace with Napoleon! Concluding the Memoirs of General de Caulaincourt, duke of Vicenza.* Tr. by George Libraire. New York: Morrow, 1936. 286 p.

FOUCHÉ, Joseph, duc d'Otrante. *The memoirs of Joseph Fouché, duke of Otranto, minister of the general police of France.* Tr. from the French. 2 v. London: Printed for C. Knight, n.d.

LA FAYETTE, Marie Joseph, marquis de. *Mémoires, correspondance et manuscrits du général La Fayette.* 12 v. in 6. Bruxelles: Société Belge de Librarie, 1837-39.
I-III. Révolution d'Amerique.
IV-IX. Révolution française.
X. Première Restauration et cent jours.
XI. Seconde Restauration.
XII. Révolution de 1830.

LAS CASES, Emmanuel, comte de. *Mémorial de Sainte Hélène. Journal of the private life and conversations of the Emperor Napoleon at Saint Helena.* 8 pts. in 4 v. London: Colburn, 1823.

MIRABEAU, Honoré Gabriel Riquette, comte de. *Memoirs of Mirabeau: biographical, literary, and political.* 4 v. London: Churton, 1835-36.

MOLLIEN, François Nicholas, comte. *Mémoires d'un ministre du trésor public, 1780-1815.* 4 v. Paris: Fournier, 1845.

NAPOLÉON I. *Correspondance de Napoléon I; publiée par ordre de l'empereur Napoléon III.* 32 v. Paris: Plon, 1858-70.

NAPOLEON I. *Letters and Documents.* Selected and tr. by J. E. Howard. New York: Oxford University Press, 1961-
I. The rise to power.

NAPOLEON I. *The mind of Napoleon: a selection of his written and spoken words.* Ed. and tr. by J. Christopher Herold. New York: Columbia University Press, 1955. 322 p.

PASQUIER, Etienne Denis. *A history of my time: memoirs of Chancellor Pasquier.* Tr. by Charles E. Roche. 3 v. New York: Scribner's, 1893-94.

REYNAUD DE MONTLOSIER, François Dominique, comte de. *Souvenirs d'un émigré, 1791-98.* Paris: Hachette, 1951. 302 p.

ROBESPIERRE, Maximilien. *Oeuvres complètes de Maximilien Robespierre.* 10 v. Paris: Société des Études robespierristes, 1910-67.

ROLAND DE LA PLATIÈRE, Marie Jean. *The private memoirs of Madame Roland.* Ed. by Edward G. Johnson. 2. ed. Chicago: McClurg, 1901. 381 p.

SAINT-JUST, Louis Antoine de. *Discours et rapports.* Introduction et notes par Albert Soboul. Paris: Éditions sociales, 1957. 222 p.

STAEL-HOLSTEIN, Anne Louie Germaine (Necker), baronne de. *Considerations on the principal events of the French Revolution.* Tr. from the French. 2 v. New York: James Eastburn, 1818.

STAEL-HOLSTEIN, Anne Louie Germaine (Necker), baronne de. *Ten years exile, or memoirs of that interesting period of the life of Baroness de Stael-Holstein.* Fontwell: Centaur Press, 1968 (first pub. 1812). 434 p.

TALLYRAND-PÉRIGORD, Charles Maurice de, prince de Bénévent. *Memoirs of the Prince de Tallyrand.* 5 v. New York: Putnam's, 1891-92. (OP 27,840 v. 1—$25.00; v. 2—$25.00; v. 3—$20.00; v. 4—$20.00; v. 5—$25.00. Total $115.00)

THE NINETEENTH CENTURY, 1815-1870

GENERAL AND MISCELLANEOUS

BEAU DE LOMÉNIE, Emmanuel. *Les responsibilités des dynasties bourgeoises.* 3 v. Paris: Denoel, 1943-54.
I. De Bonaparte à Mac-Mahon.
II. De Mac-Mahon à Poincaré.
III. Sous la IIIe République; la guerre et l'immédiat après-guerre (1914-24).

DUVEAU, Georges. *De 1848 à nos jours.* (Tome IV, Histoire du peuple français, L. H. Parias, ed.) Paris: Nouvelle Librairie de France, 1952.

JULIEN, Charles-André. *Histoire de l'Algérie contemporaine.* Paris: Presses universitaires de France, 1964.
I. La conquete et les debuts de la colonisation, 1827-1871.

MARTIN, Claude. *Histoire de l'Algérie française, 1830-62.* Paris: Éditions de 4 Fils Aymon, 1963. 508 p.

PLAMANETZ, John. *Revolutionary movements in France, 1815-71.* London: Longmans, 1952. 184 p. (OP 17,678 $15.00)

REMOND, René. *The right wing in France from 1815 to DeGaulle.* Tr. by James M. Laux. Philadelphia: University of Pennsylvania Press, 1969. 465 p.

WEILL, Georges. *Histoire du parti républicain en France, 1814-70.* 2. éd. Paris: Alcan, 1928. 431 p.

ZELDIN, Theodore, ed. *Conflicts in French society: anticlericalism, education and morals in the nineteenth century.* London: Allen & Unwin, 1970. 236 p.

THE RESTORATION, 1815-1830

ARTZ, Frederick B. *France under the Bourbon Restoration, 1814-1930.* New York: Russell & Russell, 1963 (c. 1931). 443 p.

BASTID, Paul. *Institutions politiques de la monarchie parlementaire française, 1814-48.* Paris: Recueil Sirey, 1954. 425 p.

BEACH, Vincent W. *Charles X of France: his life and times.* Boulder, Colo.: Pruett, 1971. 488 p.

BERTIER DE SAUVIGNY, Guillaume de. *The Bourbon restoration.* Tr. by Lynn Case. Philadelphia: University of Pennsylvania Press, 1966. 499 p.

COX, Cynthia. *Tallyrand's successor: the life of Armand Emmanuel du Plessis, duc de Richelieu, 1766-1822.* London: Barker. 1959. 224 p.

DUVERGIER DE HAURANNE, Prosper Léon. *Histoire du gouvernement parlementaire en France, 1814-48, [i.e. 1830].* 10 v. Paris: Lévy, 1857-71.

GAIN, André. *La restauration et les biens des émigrés; la legislation concernant les biens nationaux de seconde origine et son application dans l'Est de la France, 1814-32.* 2 v. Nancy: Société d'Impressions typographiques, 1929.

HUDSON, Nora Eileen. *Ultra-Royalism and the French Restoration.* Cambridge: Harvard University Press, 1936. 209 p. (OP 31,017 $15.00)

LANGERON, Roger. *Un conseiller secret de Louis XVIII; Royer-Collard.* Paris: Hachette, 1956. 253 p.

LANGERON, Roger. *Decazes, ministre du roi.* Paris: Hachette, 1960. 299 p.

LEDRÉ, Charles. *La presse à l'assaut de la monarchie, 1815-48.* Paris: Colin, 1960. 269 p.

LUCAS-DUBRETON, Jean. *Le culte de Napoléon, 1815-48.* Paris: Michel, 1960. 468 p.

LUCAS-DUBRETON, Jean. *The restoration and the July Monarchy.* Tr. by E. F. Buckley. New York: Putnam's, 1929. 380 p.

OECHSLIN, Jean Jacques. *Le mouvement ultraroyaliste sous la Restauration; son idéologie et son action politique, 1814-30.* Paris: Librairie générale de droit et de jurisprudence, 1960. 218 p.

PONTEIL, Félix. *La monarchie parlementaire, 1815-1848.* Paris: Colin, 1949. 224 p.

POUTHAS, Charles H. *Guizot pendant la restauration; préparation de l'homme d'Etat, 1814-30.* Paris: Plon-Nourrit, 1923. 497 p.

RESNICK, Daniel P. *The white terror and the political reaction after Waterloo.* Cambridge: Harvard University Press, 1966. 152 p.

SPITZER, Alan Barrie. *Old hatreds and young hopes: the French Carbonari against the Bourbon Restoration.* Cambridge: Harvard University Press, 1971. 334 p.

TOLEDANO, André Daniel. *La vie de famille sous la restauration et la monarchie de juillet.* Paris: Michel, 1943. 254 p. (OP 60, 286 $15.00)

THE JULY MONARCHY, 1830-1848

ALLISON, John M. S. *Thiers and the French monarchy.* Boston: Houghton Mifflin, 1926. 379 p. (OP 39, 097 $25.00)

BLANC, Louis. *The history of ten years, 1830-40.* Tr. by Walter Kelly. 2 v. New York: A.M. Kelly, 1969 (reprint of 1845 ed.).

COMITÉ Français des Sciences Historiques. *1830: études sur les mouvements liberaux et nationaux de 1830.* Paris: Rieder, 1932. 226 p.

HOWARTH, T. E. B. *Citizen-King: the life of Louis-Philippe, King of the French.* London: Eyre & Spottiswoode, 1961. 358 p.

JOHNSON, Douglas W. J. *Guizot: aspects of French history, 1787-1874.* London: Routledge & K. Paul, 1963. 469 p.

KENT, Sherman. *Electoral procedure under Louis Philippe.* New Haven: Yale University Press, 1937. 264 p. (OP 24,131 $15.00)

LHOMME, Jean. *La grande bourgeoisie au pouvoir, 1830-80; essai sur l'histoire sociale de la France.* Paris: Presses universitaires de France, 1960. 378 p.

MALO, Henri. *Thiers, 1797-1877.* Paris: Payot, 1932. 597 p.

PINKNEY, David H. *The French Revolution of 1830.* Princeton: Princeton University Press, 1972. 397 p.

TCHERNOFF, J. *Le parti républicain sous la monarchie de juillet: formation et évolution de la doctrine republicaine.* Paris: Pedone, 1901. 496 p.

THUREAU-DANGIN, Paul Marie Pierre. *Histoire de la monarchie de juillet.* 2. éd. 7 v. Paris: Plon-Nourrit, 1888-92.

TUDESQ, André-Jean. *Les grands notables en France, 1840-49: étude historique d'une psychologie sociale.* 2 v. Paris: Presses universitaires de France, 1964.

VIGIER, Philippe. *La monarchie de juillet.* Paris: Presses universitaires de France. 1962. 128 p.

THE REVOLUTION OF 1848 AND THE SECOND REPUBLIC, 1848-1852

AGOULT, Marie Catherine, comtesse d' (pseud. Daniel Stern). *Histoire de la révolution de 1848.* 2. éd. 2 v. Paris: Charpentier, 1862.

BASTID, Paul. *Doctrines et institutions politiques de la seconde république.* 2 v. Paris: Hachette, 1945.

BLANC, Louis. *Histoire de la révolution de 1848.* 2 v. Paris: Lacroix, Verboeckhoven, 1871.

CRÉMIEUX, Albert. *La révolution de février; étude critique sur les journées des 21, 22, 23 et 24 février, 1848.* Paris: Lyon Imprimeries réunies, 1912. 535 p.

DAUTRY, Jean. *1848 et la Deuxième République.* 2. éd., rev. Paris: Editions Sociales, 1957. 338 p.

DELUNA, Frederick A. *The French Republic under Cavaignac, 1848.* Princeton: Princeton University Press, 1969. 451 p.

DUVEAU, Georges. *1848, the making of a revolution.* Tr. by Anne Carter. New York: Pantheon Books, 1967. 254 p. (Vintage).

GARNIER-PAGÈS, Louis Antoine. *Histoire de la révolution de 1848.* 11 v. Paris: Pagnerre, 1861-72.

GIRARD, Louis. *La seconde république, 1848-51.* Paris: Calmann-Lévy, 1969. 318 p.

GUICHEN, Eugène, vicomte de. *Les grandes questions européennes et la diplomatie des puissances sous la seconde république française.* 2 v. Paris: V. Attinger, 1925-29.

GUILLEMIN, Henri. *Le coup d'État du 2 décembre.* Paris: Gallimard, 1951. 478 p.

McKAY, Donald C. *The national workshops; a study in the French Revolution of 1848.* Cambridge: Harvard University Press, 1933. 191 p.

PIMIENTA, Robert. *La propagande bonapartiste en 1848.* Paris: Société d'Histoire de la Révolution de 1848, 1911. 128 p.

PRICE, Roger. *The French Second Republic: a social history.* London: Batsford, 1972. 386 p.

QUENTIN-BAUCHART, Pierre. *La crise sociale de 1848: les origins de la révolution de février.* Paris: Hachette, 1920. 326 p.

RENARD, Georges François. *La République de 1848 (1848-52).* (Tome IX, Histoire socialiste (1789-1900), Jean Jaurès, éd.) Paris: Rouff, 1907. 384 p.

SCHNERB, Robert. *Ledru-Rollin.* Paris: Presses universitaires de France, 1948. 75 p.

TÉNOT, Eugène. *Paris en décembre, 1851; étude historique sur le coup d'État.* 2. éd. Paris: Le Chevalier, 1868. 216 p.

TÉNOT, Eugène. *La province en décembre, 1851; étude historique sur le coup d'État.* 2. éd. Paris: Le Chevalier, 1870. 228 p.

TUDESQ, André-Jean. *L'élection présidentielle de Louis Napoléon Bonaparte, 10 decembre 1848.* Paris: Colin, 1965. 271 p.

VICTOR, Pierre. *Histoire de la République de 1848.* 2 v. Paris: Plon, 1878.

THE SECOND EMPIRE, 1852-1870

ARMENGAUD, André. *L'opinion publique en France et la crise nationale allemande en 1866.* Paris: Société les Belles Lettres, 1962. 119 p.

BELLESSORT, André. *La société française sous Napoléon III.* Paris: Perrin, 1932. 353 p.

BELLET, Roger. *Presse et journalisme sous le Second Empire.* Paris: Colin, 1967. 326 p.

BOON, Hendrik N. *Rêve et réalité dans l'oeuvre économique et sociale de Napoléon III.* La Haye: Nijhoff, 1936. 176 p.

BURY, John P. T. *Gambetta and national defense: a republican dictatorship in France.* London: Longmans, Green, 1936. 341 p.

BURY, John P. T. *Napoleon III and the Second Empire.* New York: Harper & Row, 1964. 199 p.

CASE, Lynn Marshall. *French opinion on war and diplomacy during the Second Empire.* Philadelphia: University of Pennsylvania Press, 1954. 339 p.

CASE, Lynn M., and Spencer, Warren. *The United States and France: Civil War diplomacy.* Philadelphia: University of Pennsylvania Press, 1970. 747 p.

CHAPMAN, Joan Margaret, and Chapman, Brian. *The life and times of Baron Haussmann: Paris in the Second Empire.* London: Weidenfeld & Nicolson, 1957. 262 p.

DANSETTE, Adrien. *Histoire du Second Empire.* Paris: Hachette, 1961- . I. Louis-Napoléon à la conquête de pouvoir.

DESMAREST, Jacques. *Évolution de la France contemporaine: La France de 1870.* Paris: Hachette, 1970. 424 p.

EULER, Heinrich. *Napoleon III, in seiner Zeit.* Wurzburg: Ploetz, 1961- I. Der Aufstieg.

FARAT, Honoré. *Persigny, un ministre de Napoléon III, 1808-72.* Paris: Hachette, 1957. 320 p.

FLETCHER, Willard A. *The mission of Vincent Benedetti to Berlin, 1864-70.* The Hague: Nijhoff, 1965. 303 p.

GIRARD, Louis. *La politique des travaux publics du Second Empire.* Paris: Colin, 1952. 415 p.

GIRARD, Louis, éd. *Les élections de 1869.* Paris: Société d'Histoire de la Révolution de 1848, 1960. 214 p.

GOOCH, Brison D. *The new Bonapartist generals in the Crimean War; distrust and decision making in the Anglo-French Alliance.* The Hague: Nijhoff, 1959. 289 p.

GOOCH, George Peabody. *The Second Empire.* London: Longmans, 1960. 324 p.

GUÉRARD, Albert Leon. *Napoleon III.* Cambridge: Harvard University Press, 1943. 338 p. (OP 37, 073 $20.00)

GUICHEN, Eugène, vicomte de. *La guerre de Crimée, 1854-56, et l'attitude des puissances européennes: étude d'histoire diplomatique.* Paris: Éditions A. Pedone, 1936. 382 p.

GUILLEMIN, Henri. *Les origines de la Commune.* 3 v. Paris: Gallimard, 1956-60. I. Cette curieuse guerre de 1870: Thiers, Trochu, Bazaine. II. L'héroique défense de Paris, 1870-71. III. La capitulation.

GUIRAL, Pierre. *Prévost-Paradol, (1829-70): Pensée et action d'un libéral sous le second empire.* Paris: Presses universitaires de France, 1955. 842 p.

HOWARD, Michael. *The Franco-Prussian War; the German invasion of France, 1870-71.* New York: Macmillan, 1961. 512 p. (Free Press)

KRANZBERG, Melvin. *The siege of Paris, 1870-71; a political and social history.* Ithaca: Cornell University Press, 1950. 213 p.

KULSTEIN, Daniel I. *Napoleon III and the working class: a study in government propaganda under the Second Empire.* Los Angeles: Ward Ritchie Press, 1969. 250 p.

LA GORCE, Pierre de. *Histoire du second empire.* 7 v. Paris: Plon, 1894-1905.

MAURAIN, Jean. *Un bourgeois francais du XIXe siècle: Baroche, ministre de Napoléon III.* Paris: Alcan, 1936. 526 p.

ONCKEN, Hermann. *Napoleon III and the Rhine; the origin of the war of 1870-71.* Tr. by Edwin Zeydel. New York: Knopf, 1928. 209 p.

34

PAYNE, Howard C. *The police state of Louis Napoleon Bonaparte, 1851-60.* Seattle: University of Washington Press, 1966. 340 p.

PICARD, Roger. *Le romantisme sociale.* Paris: Brentano's, 1944. 437 p.

PINKNEY, David H. *Napoleon III and the rebuilding of Paris.* Princeton: Princeton University Press, 1958. 245 p.

POTTINGER, E. Ann. *Napoleon III and the German crisis, 1865-66.* Cambridge: Harvard University Press, 1966. 238 p.

SCHNERB, Robert. *Rouher et le second empire.* Paris: Colin, 1949. 351 p.

SIMPSON, Frederick Arthur. *Louis Napoleon and the recovery of France.* London: Longmans, 1951 (c.1923). 400 p.

SIMPSON, Frederick Arthur. *The rise of Louis Napoleon.* London: Longmans, 1950 (c.1925). 384 p.

TCHERNOFF, J. *Histoire politique contemporaine: Le parti républicain au coup d'État et sous le second empire.* Paris: Pedone, 1906. 676 p.

THOMPSON, James M. *Louis Napoleon and the Second Empire.* Oxford: Blackwell, 1954. (Norton)

TOUCHARD, Jean. *La gloire de Béranger.* 2 v. Paris: Colin, 1968.

WILLIAMS, Roger. *The world of Napoleon III, 1851-70.* New York: Free Press, 1965. 288 p. (Originally pub. as *Gaslight and Shadows,* c.1957.)

ZELDIN, Theodore. *Emile Ollivier and the liberal empire of Napoleon III.* New York: Oxford University Press, 1963. 248 p.

ZELDIN, Theodore. *The political system of Napoleon III.* London: Macmillan, 1958. 195 p. (Norton)

GOVERNMENT, ADMINISTRATION, EDUCATION, MILITARY

CHALMIN, Pierre. *L'officier français de 1815 à 1870.* Paris: Rivière, 1957. 408 p.

COLLINS, Irene. *The government and the newspaper press in France, 1814-81.* London: Oxford University Press, 1959. 201 p.

DUVEAU, Georges. *Les instituteurs.* Paris: Éditions du Seuil, 1957. 190 p.

GERBOD, Paul. *La condition universitaire en France au XIXe siècle.* Paris: Presses universitaires de France, 1965. 720 p.

GERBOD, Paul. *La vie quotidienne dans les lycées et collèges au XIXe siècle.* Paris: Hachette, 1968. 272 p.

GIRARD, Louis. *La Garde nationale, 1814-71.* Paris: Plon, 1964. 338 p.

GIRARD, Louis; Gossez, R.; and Prost, Antoine. *Les conseillers généraux en 1870: étude statistique d'un personnel politique.* Paris: Presses universitaires de France, 1967. 211 p.

GIRARDET, Raoul, *et al. L'armée et la Seconde République.* Paris: Societe d'histoire de la Revolution de 1848, 1955. 160 p.

PONTEIL, Félix. *Les institutions de la France de 1814 à 1870.* Paris: Presses universitaires de France, 1966. 489 p.

RICHARDSON, Nicholas J. *The French prefectoral corps: 1814-30.* Cambridge: Cambridge University Press, 1966. 263 p.

SCHNAPPER, Bernard. *Le remplacement militaire en France: quelques aspects politiques, économiques et sociaux du recrutement au XIXe siècle.* Paris: S.E.V.P.E.N., 1968.

TUDESQ, André-Jean. *Les conseillers généraux en France au temps de Guizot, 1840-48.* Paris: Colin, 1967. 294 p.

SOCIAL AND ECONOMIC

ALLEM, Maurice (pseud. of Maurice Allemand). *La vie quotidienne sous le Second Empire.* Paris: Hachette, 1948. 287 p.

ARMENGAUD, André. *La population française au XIXe siècle.* Paris: Presses universitaires de France, 1971. 121 p.

BIGO, Robert. *Les banques françaises au cours du XIXe siècle.* Paris: Receuil Sirey, 1947. 304 p.

BOUVIER, Jean. *Naissance d'une banque: le Crédit Lyonnais.* Paris: Flammarion, 1968. 382 p.

BOUVIER, Jean; Furet, François; and Gillet, Marcel. *Le mouvement du profit en France au XIXe siècle: materiaux et études.* Paris: Mouton, 1965. 465 p.

BURNAND, Robert. *La vie quotidienne en France en 1830.* Paris: Hachette, 1943. 255 p.

CAMERON, Rondo E. *France and the economic development of Europe, 1800-1914; conquests of peace and seeds of war.* Chicago: Rand McNally, 1966 (c.1961). 347 p.

CAMP, Wesley Douglass. *Marriage and the family in France since the revolution; an essay in the history of population.* New York: Bookman Association, 1961. 203 p.

CHEVALIER, Louis, éd. *Le choléra, la première épidémie du XIXe siècle.* Paris: Société d'Histoire de la Revolution de 1848, 1958. 188 p.

CHEVALIER, Louis. *Laboring classes and dangerous classes: Paris during the first half of the nineteenth century.* Tr. by Frank Jellinek. New York: Fertig, 1972.

DAUMARD, Adeline. *Les bourgeois de Paris au XIXe siècle.* Paris: Flammarion, 1970. 382 p.

DUNHAM, Arthur L. *The Anglo-French treaty of commerce of 1860 and the progress of the industrial revolution in France.* Ann Arbor: University of Michigan Press, 1930. 409 p.

DUNHAM, Arthur L. *The industrial revolution in France, 1815-48.* New York: Exposition Press, 1955. 516 p.

EPSZTEIN, Léon. *L'économie et la morale aux débuts du capitalisme industriel en France et en Grande-Bretagne.* Paris: Colin, 1966. 351 p.

FOHLEN, Claude. *L'industrie textile au temps du Second Empire.* Paris: Plon, 1956. 534 p.

GILLE, Bertrand. *La banque et le crédit en France de 1815 à 1848.* Paris: Presses universitaires de France, 1959. 380 p.

GILLE, Bertrand. *Histoire de la Maison Rothschild.* 2 v. Geneve: Droz, 1965-67. I. Des origines à 1848. II. 1848-70.

GILLE, Bertrand. *Les origines de la grande industrie métallurgique en France.* Paris: Domat-Montchrestien, 1947. 212 p.

GILLE, Bertrand. *Recherches sur la formation de la grand enterprise capitaliste, 1815-48.* Paris: S.E.V.P.E.N., 1959. 164 p.

GILLE, Bertrand. *La sidérurgie française au XIXe siècle.* Geneve: Droz, 1968. 317 p.

HAMMER, Karl. *Jakob Ignaz Hittorff: Ein pariser Baumeister, 1792-1867.* Stuttgart: Anton Hiersemann, 1968. 386 p.

LABROUSSE, Charles E., éd. *Aspects de la crise et la dépression de l'économie française au milieu du XIXe siècle (1846-51).* Paris: Société d'Histoire de la Révolution de 1848, 1956. 360 p.

LANDES, David S. *Bankers and Pashas: international finance and economic imperialism in Egypt.* Cambridge: Harvard University Press, 1958. 354 p.

PALMADE, Guy. *French capitalism in the nineteenth century.* Tr. by Graeme M. Holmes. Newton Abbot: David & Charles, 1972. 256 p.

PONTEIL, Félix. *Les classes bourgeoises et l'avènement de la démocratie, 1815-1914.* Paris: Éditions Michel, 1968. 573 p.

POUTHAS, Charles H. *La population française pendant la première moitié du XIXe siècle.* Paris: Presses universitaires de France, 1956. 225 p.

RAMON, Gabriel. *Histoire de la Banque de France.* Paris: Grasset, 1929. 501 p.

RENOUARD, Dominique. *Les transports de marchandises par fer, route et eau, depuis 1850.* Paris: Colin, 1960. 125 p.

VIDALENC, Jean. *La société française de 1815 à 1848; Vol. I, le peuple des campagnes.* Paris: Rivière, 1970. 401 p.

WEILL, Georges. *Histoire du mouvement social en France, 1852-1910.* Paris: Alcan, 1911. 531 p.

SOCIALISM AND THE LABOR MOVEMENT

AGUET, J.-P. *Les grèves sous la monarchie de juillet, 1830-47: contribution a l'étude du mouvement ouvrier français.* Genève: Droz, 1954. 406 p.

ANSART, Pierre. *Naissance de l'anarchisme: esquisse d'un explication sociologique du Proudhonisme.* Paris: Presses universitaires de France, 1970. 263 p.

ARMAND, Felix. *Fourier.* 2 v. Paris: Éditions Sociales Internationales, 1937.

BERNSTEIN, Samuel. *Blanqui.* Paris: François Maspero, 1970. 360 p.

BRUHAT, Jean. *Histoire du mouvement ouvrier français.* Paris: Éditions sociales, 1952.
I. Des origines à la révolte des canuts.

DOLLÉANS, Édouard, and Dehove Gérard. *Histoire du travail en France; mouvement ouvrier et législation sociale.* 3. éd. 2 v. Paris: Domat-Montchrestien, 1953-55.
I. Des origines à 1919.
II. De 1919 à nos jours.

DOMMANGET, Maurice. *Les idées politiques et sociales d'Auguste Blanqui.* Paris: Rivière, 1957. 429 p.

DUVEAU, Georges. *La vie ouvrière en France sous le Second Empire.* Paris: Gallimard, 1946. 605 p. (OP 61,562 $35.00)

EVANS, David O. *Le socialisme romantique: Pierre Leroux et ses contemporains.* Paris: Rivière, 1948. 260 p.

FESTY, Octave. *Le mouvement ouvrier au début de la monarchie de juillet, 1830-34.* Paris: Cornély, 1908. 360 p.

GOSSEZ, Remi. *Les ouvriers de Paris; Livre I: l'organization (1848-51).* Paris: Société d'Histoire de la Révolution de 1848, 1967. 442 p.

HOFFMAN, Robert L. *Revolutionary justice: the social and political theories of*

P.-J. Proudhon. Chicago: University of Illinois Press, 1972. 480 p.

LABROUSSE, Charles E. *Le mouvement ouvrier et les théories sociales en France de 1815 à 1848.* Paris: Centre de Documentation Universitaire, 1954. 226 p.

L'HUILLIER, Fernand. *Le lutte ouvrière à la fin du Second Empire.* Paris: Colin, 1957. 81 p.

LOUBERE, Leo. *Louis Blanc; his life and his contribution to the rise of French Jacobin-socialism.* Evanston Ill.: Northwestern University Press, 1961. 256 p.

PRUDHOMMEAUX, Jules. *Icarie et son fondateur, Étienne Cabet; contribution à l'étude du socialisme expérimental.* Paris: Cornély, 1907. 688 p.

RIASNOVSKY, Nicholas V. *The teaching of Charles Fourier.* Berkeley: University of California Press, 1969. 256 p.

RITTER, A. *The political thought of Pierre-Joseph Proudhon.* Princeton: Princeton University Press, 1969. 256 p.

SPITZER, Alan Barrie. *The revolutionary theories of Louis August Blanqui.* New York: Columbia University Press, 1957. 208 p.

TREMPÉ, Roland. *Les mineurs de Carmaux, 1848-1914.* 2 v. Paris: Les Éditions ouvrières, 1971.

WOODCOCK, George. *Pierre-Joseph Proudhon, a biography.* London: Routledge & Paul, 1956. 291 p.

REGIONAL STUDIES

AGULHON, Maurice. *La République au village; les populations du Var de la Révolution à la Seconde République (1815-1851).* Paris: Plon, 1970. 546 p.

AGULHON, Maurice. *La vie sociale en Provence intérieure au lendemain de la Révolution.* Paris: Société des Études robespierristes, 1970. 531 p.

AGULHON, Maurice. *Une ville ouvrière au temps du socialisme utopique; Toulon, de 1815 à 1851.* Paris: Mouton, 1970. 368 p.

ARMENGAUD, André. *Les populations de l'Est-Aquitain au début de l'époque contemporaine; recherches sur une région moins developée (vers 1845-vers 1871).* Paris: Mouton, 1961. 589 p.

BERNARD, Philippe. *Économie et sociologie de la Seine-et-Marne, 1850-1950.* Paris: Colin, 1953. 303 p.

BOIS, Paul. *Paysans de l'ouest; des structures économiques et sociales aux options politiques depuis l'époque révolutionnaire dans la Sarthe.* Le Mans: Vilaire, 1960. 716 p.

CHEVALIER, Louis. *La formation de la population parisienne au XIXe siècle.* Paris: Presses universitaires de France, 1950. 312 p.

DUPEUX, Georges. *Aspects de l'histoire politique du Loire-et-Cher, 1848-1914.* Paris: Mouton, 1962. 631 p.

DUTACQ, F. *Histoire politique de Lyon pendant la Révolution de 1848.* Paris: Société d'Histoire de la Revolution de 1848, 1910. 450 p.

GARAVEL, Joseph. *Les paysans de Morette: un siècle de vie rurale dans une commune de Dauphiné.* Paris: Colin, 1948. 124 p.

GREENBERG, Louis M. *Sisters of liberty: Marseilles, Lyon, Paris and the reaction to a centralized state, 1868-71.* Cambridge: Harvard University Press, 1971. 391 p.

HIGGS, David. *Ultraroyalism in Toulouse from its origins to the Revolution of 1830.* Baltimore: Johns Hopkins University Press, 1973. 223 p.

IBARROLA, Jésus. *Structure sociale et fortune mobilière et immobilière à Grenoble en 1847.* Paris: Mouton, 1965. 124 p.

IBARROLA, Jésus. *Structure sociale et fortune dans la compagne proche de Grenoble en 1847.* Paris: Mouton, 1966. 153 p.

IBARROLA, Jésus. *Structures d'une population active de type traditionnel: Grenoble 1848.* Paris: Mouton, 1968. 126 p.

LEONARD, Charlene Marie. *Lyon transformed: public works of the Second Empire, 1853-64.* Berkeley: University of California Press, 1961. 160 p.

LEUILLOT, Paul. *L'Alsace au début du XIXe siècle; essais d'histoire politique, économique et religieuse, 1815-30.* 3 v. Paris: S.E.V.P.E.N., 1959-60.
I. La vie politique.
II. Les transformations économiques.
III. L'Alsace au debut du XIXe siècle.

PIERRARD, Pierre. *La vie ouvrière à Lille sous le second empire.* Paris: Bloud & Gay, 1965. 532 p.

RUDE, Fernand. *L'insurrection lyonnaise de novembre 1831; le mouvement ouvrier à Lyon de 1827 à 1832.* Paris: Editions Anthropos, 1969. 785 p.

SINGER-KÉREL, Jeanne. *La coût de la vie à Paris de 1840 à 1954.* Paris: Colin, 1961. 560 p.

THABAULT, Roger. *Education and change in a village community: Mazières-en-Gâtine, 1848-1914.* Tr. by Peter Tregear. New York: Schocken, 1971. 270 p.

THUILLIER, Guy. *Aspects de l'économie nivernaise au XIXe siècle.* Paris: Colin, 1966. 555 p.

VIDALENC, Jean. *Le département de l'Eure sous la monarchie constitutionelle, 1814-48.* Paris: Rivière, 1952. 700 p.

VIGIER, Philippe. *La Second République dans la région Alpine: étude politique et sociale.* 2 v. Paris: Presses universitaires de France, 1963.

INTELLECTUAL AND CULTURAL

BAGGE, Dominique. *Les idées politiques en France sous la Restauration.* Paris: Presses universitaires de France, 1952. 462 p.

BASTID, Paul. *Benjamin Constant et sa doctrine.* 2 v. Paris: Colin, 1966.

BAYLE, Francis. *Les idées politiques de Joseph de Maistre.* Paris: Domat Montchrestien, 1945. 168 p.

BEAU DE LOMÉNIE, Emmanuel. *La carrière politique de Chateaubriand de 1814 à 1830.* 2 v. Paris: Plon, 1929.

BOURGIN, Hubert. *Victor Considérant, son oeuvre.* Paris: Société d'Histoire de la Révolution de 1848, 1909. 128 p.

CARTER, Alfred E. *The idea of decadence in French literature, 1830-1900.* Toronto: University of Toronto Press, 1958. 154 p.

CHARLTON, Donald G. *Positivist thought in France during the Second Empire, 1852-70.* Oxford: Clarendon Press, 1959. 251 p.

CHARLTON, Donald G. *Secular religions in France, 1815-70.* New York: Oxford University Press, 1963. 249 p.

CUVILLIER, Armand. *Hommes et idéologies de 1840.* Paris: Rivière, 1956. 250 p.

DERRÉ, Jean René. *Lamennais, ses amis et le mouvement des idées à l'époque romantique (1824-34).* Paris: Klincksieck, 1962. 763 p.

EVANS, David Owen. *Social romanticism in France, 1830-48.* Oxford: Clarendon Press, 1951. 149 p.

GARGAN, Edward. *Alexis de Tocqueville: the critical years, 1848-51.* Washington, D.C.: Catholic University of America Press, 1955. 324 p. (OP 13,367 $20.00)

GEORGE, Albert Joseph. *The development of French Romanticism: the impact of the industrial revolution on literature.* New York: Syracuse University Press, 1955. 193 p.

GRAÑA, César. *Bohemian versus bourgeois; French society and the French man of letters in the nineteenth century.* New York: Basic Books, 1964. 220 p. (Harper Torchbook title: *Modernity and its discontents.*)

GUÉRARD, Albert Leon. *Reflections on the Napoleonic legend.* New York: Scribner's, 1924. 276 p.

GUYON, Bernard. *La pensée politique et sociale de Balzac.* 3. éd. Paris: Colin, 1969. 864 p.

HARPAZ, Éphraïm. *L'école liberale sous la Restauration; le Mercure et la Minerva, 1817-20.* Genève: Droz, 1968. 424 p.

IGGERS, Georg G. *The cult of authority; the political philosophy of the Saint-Simonians, a chapter in the intellectual history of totalitarianism.* The Hague: Nijhoff, 1958. 210 p.

LA LOMBARDIÈRE, Jacqueline de. *Les idées de Benjamin Constant.* Paris: Au Commerce des Idées, 1928. 143 p.

LEROY, Alfred. *Civilisation française du XIXe siècle.* Tournai, Belgium: Casterman, 1962. 434 p.

LIVELY, Jack. *The social and political thought of Alexis de Tocqueville.* Oxford: Clarendon Press, 1962. 263 p.

MANUEL, Frank E. *The new world of Henry Saint-Simon.* Cambridge: Harvard University Press, 1956. 433 p.

MAYER, Jacob Peter. *Alexis de Tocqueville; a biographical study in political science.* Gloucester, Mass.: Peter Smith, 1966 (c.1960, 1940). 144 p.

MELLON, Stanley. *The political uses of history; a study of historians in the French Restoration.* Stanford: Stanford University Press, 1958. 226 p. (OP 27,128 $15.00)

MURET, Charlotte (Touzalin). *French royalist doctrines since the Revolution.* New York: Columbia University Press, 1933. 326 p.

RUDE, Fernand. *Stendhal et la pensée sociale de son temps.* Paris: Plon, 1967. 318 p.

SOLTAU, Roger. *French political thought in the nineteenth century.* New York: Russell & Russell, 1959 (c.1931). 500 p.

SWART, Koenraad W. *The sense of decadence in nineteenth-century France.* The Hague: Nijhoff, 1964. 272 p.

TRIOMPHE, Robert. *Joseph de Maistre: étude sur la vie et sur la doctrine d'un matérialiste mystique.* Genève: Droz, 1968. 654 p.

VANIER, Henriette. *La mode et ses métiers: frivolités et luttes de classes, 1830-70.* Paris: Colin, 1960. 280 p.

WEILL, Georges. *Histoire de l'idée laique en France au XIXe siècle.* Nouv. ed. Paris: Alcan, 1929. 376 p.

WEINER, Dora B. *Raspail, scientist and reformer.* New York: Columbia University Press, 1968. 336 p.

RELIGION

BOULARD, Fernand. *An introduction to religious sociology: pioneer work in France.* Tr. by M. J. Jackson. London: Darton, Longman & Todd, 1960. 166 p.

DUROSELLE, Jean Baptiste. *Les débuts du catholicisme social en France, 1822-70.* Paris: Presses universitaires de France, 1951. 787 p.

GUILLEMIN, Henri. *Histoire des catholiques français au XIXe siècle, 1815-1905.* Genève: Éditions du Milieu du Monde, 1947. 392 p.

LECANUET, Édouard. *Montalembert.* 3 v. Paris: Poussielgue, 1900-09.
I. Sa jeunesse (1810-36).
II. La liberté d'enseignement (1835-50).
III. L'église et le second empire.

MAURAIN, Jean. *La politique ecclésiastique du Second Empire de 1852 à 1869.* Paris: Alcan, 1930. 989 p. (OP 37,114 $55.00)

MOODY, Joseph N. *The church as enemy: anticlericalism in nineteenth century French literature.* Washington, D.C.: Corpus Books, 1968. 305 p.

PHILLIPS, Charles Stanley. *The Church in France, 1848-1907.* New York: Macmillan, 1936. 341 p.

SPENCER, Philip Herbert. *Politics of belief in nineteenth-century France: Lacordaire, Michon, Veuillot.* London: Faber & Faber, 1954. 284 p. (OP 59,024 $15.00)

STEARNS, Peter N. *Priest and revolutionary: Lammenais and the dilemma of French Catholicism.* New York: Harper & Row, 1967. 209 p.

THUREAU-DANGIN, Paul Marie Pierre. *L'église et l'état sous la monarchie de juillet.* Paris: Plon, 1880. 497 p.

VIDLER, Alexander Roper. *Prophecy and papacy; a study of Lamennais, the Church and the revolution.* London: SCM Press, 1954. 300 p.

WEILL, Georges. *Histoire du catholicisme libéral en France, 1828-1908.* Paris: Alcan, 1909. 312 p.

MEMOIRS AND CONTEMPORARY WRITINGS

ALTON-SHÉE, Edmond de Le Lignères, comte d'. *Mes mémoires (1826-48).* 2 v. Paris: Librarie internationale, 1869.

BARROT, Odilon. *Mémoires posthumes d'Odilon Barrot.* 4 v. Paris: Charpentier, 1875-76.

BROGLIE, Jacques Victor Albert, duc de. *Mémoires du duc de Broglie.* 2 v. Paris: Calmann-Lévy, 1938-41.

CASTELLANE, Esprit Victor, comte de. *Journal du maréchal de Castellane, 1804-62.* 5 v. Paris: Plon, 1895-97.

CAUSSIDIÈRE, Marc. *Mémoires de Caussidière, ex-préfet de police et représentant du peuple.* 2 v. Paris: Levy, 1849.

CHATEAUBRIAND, François Auguste René, vicomte de. *Mémoires d'outre-tombe.* Édition du Centenaire, 2. éd. 4 v. Paris: Flammarion, 1964.

COMTE, Auguste. *The positive philosophy of Auguste Comte.* Freely trans. and condensed by Harriet Martineau. 2 v. New York: Appleton, 1853-54 (orig. French ed., 6 v., 1830-42.) (1896 London ed. OP 10,451 v. 1—$25.00; v. 2—$20.00; v. 3—$25.00. Total $70.00) (1858 New York ed. OP 19,156 $45.00)

COMTE, Auguste. *System of positive polity.* 4 v. New York: B. Franklin, 1968 (orig. pub., 1851-54). (1875-78 London ed. OP 59,079 v. 1—$35.00; v. 2—$25.00; v. 3—$35.00; v. 4—$45.00. Total $140.00)

DURUY, Victor. *Notes et souvenirs, 1811-94.* 2 v. Paris: Hachette, 1901.

FALLOUX, Alfred Pierre, comte de. *Mémoires d'un royaliste.* 3 v. Paris: Perrin, 1925-26.

FLEURY, Émile Felix, comte. *Souvenirs du général comte Fleury, (1837-67).* 2 v. Paris: Plon, 1897-98.

FOURIER, Charles. *Oeuvres complètes.* 6 v.
Paris: Librairie sociétaire, 1829-46.
I. Théorie des quatres mouvements et des
destinées générales.
II-V. Théorie de l'unité universelle.
VI. Le nouveau monde industriel et
sociétaire.

FRÉYCINET, Charles Louis de. *Souvenirs,
1848-93.* 2 v. Paris: Delagrave, 1912-13.

GUIZOT, François Pierre Guillaume.
*Mémoires pour servir à l'histoire de mon
temps.* 8 v. Paris: Lévy, 1858-67.

HAUSSMANN, Georges Eugène, baron.
Mémoires du baron Haussmann. 3 v.
Paris: Victor-Harvard, 1890-93.
I. Avant l'Hôtel de Ville.
II. Préfecture de la Seine.
III. Grand travaux de Paris.

HUGO, Victor. *Napoleon the Little.* Tr.
from the French. Boston: Little, Brown,
1909. 335 p.

LAFFITTE, Jacques. *Mémoires de Laffitte,
1767-1844, publiés par Paul Duchon.*
Paris: Firmin-Didot, 1932. 347 p.

LAMARTINE, Alphonse Marie Louis de.
History of the French Revolution of 1848.
Tr. from the French. London: Bohn,
1852. 572 p.

LESSEPS, vicomte Ferdinand Marie de.
Recollections of forty years. Tr. by C. B.
Pitman. 2 v. London: Chapman & Hall,
1887.

MAISTRE, Joseph de. *Considérations sur la
France.* Intro. par René Johannet &
François Vermale. Paris: Vrin, 1936.
184 p.

MAISTRE, Joseph de. *Works; selected,
translated and introduced by Jack Lively.*
New York: Macmillan, 1965. 303 p.

MARX, Karl. *The civil war in France: the
Paris Commune.* New York: International
Publishers, 1968. 142 p.

MARX, Karl. *The class struggles in France,
1848-1850.* New York: International Publishers, 1964. 161 p.

MARX, Karl. *The eighteenth Brumaire of
Louis Bonaparte.* New York: International
Publishers, 1964. 161 p.

MAUPAS, Charlemagne Émile de. *Mémoires
sur le Second Empire.* 2 v. Paris: Dentu,
1884-85.
I. La Présidence de Louis Napoléon.
II. L'Empire et ses transformations.

MELUN, Armand Marie, vicomte de.
Mémoires du vicomte Armand de Melun.
Paris: Leday, 1891.

MOLÉ, Louis Mathieu, comte. *The life and
mémoires of Count Molé, 1781-1855,* ed.
by the Marques de Noailles. 2 v. New
York: Doran, 1924.

NADAUD, Martin. *Les Mémoires de Leonard, ancien garçon maçon: précédés d'un
avant-propos et d'une biographie de Martin
Nadaud par H. Germouty.* Paris: Delagrave, 1912. 240 p.

NAPOLÉON III. *Oeuvres de Napoléon III.*
5 v. Paris: Amyot, 1856-69.

NORMANBY, Constantine Henry Phipps,
marquis of. *A year of revolution: from a
journal kept in Paris in 1848.* 2 v. London: Longmans, 1857. (OP 41,135
v. 1—$30.00; v. 2—$25.00. Total $55.00)

OLLIVIER, Émile. *Journal, 1846-69.* Texte
choisi et annoté par Theodore Zeldin et
Anne Troisier de Diaz. 2 v. Paris: Julliard,
1961.

OLLIVIER, Émile. *L'empire libéral; études,
récits, souvenirs.* 18 v. Paris: Garnier,
1895-1918.

PERSIGNY, Jean Gilbert Victor, duc de.
Mémoires du duc de Persigny. Paris: Plon,
1896. 512 p.

PROUDHON, Pierre Joseph. *What is property? An inquiry into the principle of right
and of government.* Tr. by Benjamin R.
Tucker with a biographical essay by J. A.
Langois. New York: Fertig, 1966. 457 p.

REMUSAT, Charles François Marie, comte
de. *Mémoires de ma vie (1797-1875).* 5 v.
Paris: Plon, 1958-67.

SENIOR, Nassau William. *Conversations
with distinguished persons during the second empire, 1860-63.* 2 v. London: Hurst
& Blackett, 1880.

SENIOR, Nassau William. *Conversations
with M. Thiers, M. Guizot and other distinguished persons during the second empire,
1852-60.* 2 v. London: Hurst & Blackett,
1878.

TOCQUEVILLE, Alexis Charles Henri de. *Recollections.* Tr. by George Lawrence. Ed. by J. P. Mayer & A. P. Kerr. New York: Doubleday, 1970. 333 p.

THE THIRD REPUBLIC, 1870-1940

GENERAL AND MISCELLANEOUS

L'ANNÉE politique . . . *avec un index alphabétique, une table chronologique, des notes, des documents et des pièces justificatives, par André Daniel* (pseud.), (1874-1905). 32 v. Paris: Charpentier, 1875-1906.

BAINVILLE, Jacques. *The French Republic, 1870-1935.* Tr. and intro. by Hamish Miles. London: J. Cape, 1936. (Fr. ed., 1935.) 253 p.

BAUMONT, Maurice. *L'essor industriel et l'impérialisme colonial, 1878-1904.* 2. éd. rev. Paris: Presses universitaires de France, 1949. 627 p.

BINION, Rudolph. *Defeated leaders: the political fate of Caillaux, Jouvenal and Tardieu.* New York: Columbia University Press, 1960. 425 p.

BLOCH, Roger. *Histoire du Parti Radical-Socialiste; des radicaux-socialistes d'hier aux démocrates-socialistes de demain.* Paris: Librairie générale de Droit et de Jurisprudence, 1968. 190 p.

BLOND, Georges. *Pétain, 1856-1951.* Paris: Presses de la Cité, 1966. 587 p.

BONNEFOUS, Édouard and Georges. *Histoire politique de la Troisième République (1906-40).* 7 v. 2. éd. Paris: Presses universitaires de France, 1968.

BROGAN, Denis William. *The development of modern France, 1870-1939.* Rev. ed. London: Hamilton, 1967. 775 p. (Harper Torchbook, 2 v.)

BROWN, Marvin L. *The Comte de Chambord: the Third Republic's uncompromising king.* Durham, N.C.: Duke University Press, 1968. 265 p.

BRUNSCHWIG, Henri. *French colonialism,*

1871-1914; myths and realities. Tr. by William G. Brown. New York: Praeger, 1966. 228 p.

BRUUN, Geoffrey. *Clemenceau.* Hamden, Conn.: Archon Books, 1962 (c.1943). 225 p.

CARROLL, E. Malcolm. *French public opinion and foreign affairs, 1870-1914.* Hamden, Conn.: Archon Books, 1964 (c.1931). 348 p.

CHASTENET, Jacques. *Cent ans de République.* 9 v. Paris: Talandier, 1970. (Vols. 1-7, Histoire de la Troisième République, 1952-63).
I. L'enfance de la Troisième, 1870-78.
II. La République des républicaines, 1879-93.
III. La République triomphante, 1893-1906.
IV. Jours inquiets et jours sanglantes, 1906-18.
V. Les années d'illusion, 1918-31.
VI. Déclin de la Troisième, 1931-38.
VII. Le drame final, 1938-40.
VIII. De Pétain à de Gaulle, 1940-44.
IX. Un monde nouveau, 1944-70.

CONFER, Vincent. *France and Algeria; the problem of civil and political reform, 1870-1920.* New York: Syracuse University Press, 1966. 148 p.

CONTAMINE, Henry. *La Revanche, 1871-1914.* Paris: Berger-Levrault, 1957. 280 p.

DE TARR, Francis. *The French Radical Party; from Herriot to Mendes-France.* New York: Oxford University Press, 1961. 264 p.

EARLE, Edward Mead, ed. *Modern France: Problems of the Third and Fourth Republics.* New York: Russell & Russell, 1964 (1st ed., 1951). 522 p.

ERLANGER, Philippe. *Clemenceau.* Paris:

Grasset, 1968. 659 p.

ESTIER, Claude. *La Gauche hebdomadaire,*
1914-62. Paris: Colin, 1962. 287 p.

GANIAGE, Jean. *L'Expansion coloniale de*
la France sous la Troisième République,
1871-1914. Paris: Payot, 1968. 436 p.

GIRARDET, Raoul. *Le nationalisme*
français, 1871-1914. Paris: Colin, 1966.
276 p.

GOGUEL-NYGAARD, François. *La*
politique des partis sous la Troisième
République. 3. éd. Paris: Éditions du
Seuil, 1958. 566 p.

GOGUEL-NYGAARD, François. *Géographie*
des élections françaises sous la Troisième
et la Quatrième Républiques. 2. éd. Paris:
Colin, 1970. 185 p.

GOLDBERG, Harvey. *The Life of Jean*
Jaurès. Madison: University of Wisconsin
Press, 1962. 590 p.

GRIMAL, Henri. *La décolonisation, 1919-*
63. Paris: Colin, 1965. 407 p.

HANOTAUX, Gabriel. *Contemporary*
France. V. 1 tr. by J. C. Tarver; v. 4 tr. by
E. Sparvel-Bayly. 4 v. London: Constable,
1903-09.

HAYES, Carlton Joseph Huntly. *France, a*
nation of patriots. New York: Columbia
University Press, 1930. 487 p.

JACKSON, John Hampden. *Clemenceau and*
the Third Republic. New York: Macmillan,
1948. 266 p.

KUISEL, Richard F. *Ernest Mercier: French*
technocrat. Berkeley: University of California, 1967. 184 p.

LAFUE, Pierre. *Gaston Doumergue, sa vie*
et son destin. Paris: Plon, 1933. 192 p.

MANÉVY, Raymond. *La presse de la*
Troisième République. Paris: Foret, 1955.
248 p.

MONNERVILLE, Gaston. *Clemenceau.*
Paris: Fayard, 1968. 766 p.

NETON, Alberic. *Delcassé, 1852-1923.*
Paris: Académie Diplomatique Internationale, 1967. 587 p.

OLLÉ-LAPRUNE, Jacques. *La stabilité des*
ministres sous la Troisième République,
1879-1940. Paris: Librairie générale de
Droit et de Jurisprudence, 1962. 376 p.

OSGOOD, Samuel M. *French royalism*
since 1870. 2d enl. ed. The Hague:
Nijhoff, 1970. 241 p.

OZOUF, Mona. *L'École, l'Église et la*
République, 1871-1914. Paris: Colin,
1963. 304 p.

PRIESTLEY, Herbert I. *France overseas; a*
study of modern imperialism. New York:
Appleton-Century, 1938. 463 p.

RECLUS, Maurice. *La Troisième Répub-*
lique de 1870 à 1918. Paris: Fayard,
1945. 312 p.

ROBERTS, Stephen Henry. *The history of*
French colonial policy, 1870-1925. 2 v.
London: P. S. King and Son, 1929.
(Archon) (OP 10,140 v. 1—$25.00;
v. 2—$20.00. Total $45.00)

ROTHNEY, John. *Bonapartism after Sedan.*
Ithaca: Cornell University Press, 1969.
360 p.

SHAPIRO, David, ed. *The Right in France,*
1890-1919. London: Chatto & Windus,
1962. 144 p.

SOULIER, Auguste. *L'Instabilité ministéri-*
elle sous la Troisième République (1871-
1938). Paris: Sirey, 1939. 603 p.
(OP 11,422 $35.00)

SUAREZ, Georges. *Briand; sa vie, son*
oeuvre; avec son journal et de nombreux
documents inédits. 6 vols. Paris: Plon,
1938-52. (OP 61,720 v. 2—$30.00)

TANNENBAUM, Edward R. *The Action*
française; diehard reactionaries in
twentieth-century France. New York:
Wiley, 1962. 316 p.

THOMPSON, David. *Democracy in France*
since 1870. 5th ed. New York: Oxford
University Press, 1969. 344 p.

TINT, Herbert. *The decline of French*
patriotism, 1870-1940. London:
Weidenfeld & Nicolson, 1964. 272 p.

WEBER, Eugen. *Action française: royalism*
and reaction in twentieth-century France.

Stanford: Stanford University Press, 1962. 594 p.

WORMSER, Georges. *La république de Clemenceau.* Paris: Presses universitaires de France, 1961. 522 p.

ZÉVAÈS, Alexandre Bourson. *Histoire de la Troisième République.* Nouv. éd. Paris: Éditions de la Nouvelle Revue Critique, 1946. 411 p.

ZIEBURA, Gilbert. *Léon Blum et le Parti Socialiste, 1872-1934.* Tr. de l'allemande par Jean Duplex. Paris: Colin, 1967. 405 p.

THE THIRD REPUBLIC, 1870-1900

ACOMB, Evelyn M. *The French laic laws, 1879-89, the first anti-clerical campaign of the Third French Republic.* New York: Octagon, 1967 (c.1941). 282 p.

BRABANT, Frank Herbert. *The beginning of the Third Republic in France; a history of the National Assembly (Feb.-Sept., 1871).* London: Macmillan, 1940. 555 p.

BROWN, Roger Glenn. *Fashoda reconsidered; the impact of domestic politics on French policy in Africa, 1893-98.* Baltimore: Johns Hopkins Press, 1970. 157 p.

BRUHAT, Jean; Dautry, Jean; and Terson, Émile. *La Commune de 1871.* 2. éd. Paris: Éditions Sociales, 1970. 463 p.

CAPÉRAN, Louis. *Histoire contemporaine de la laïcité française.* 3 v. Paris: Riviere, 1957-59; Paris: Nouvelles Éditions Latines, 1961.
I. La crise du 16 mai et la revanche Républicaine.
II. La révolution scolaire.
III. La laïcité en marche.

CHAPMAN, Guy. *The Dreyfus case, a reassessment.* New York: Reynal, 1955. 400 p.

CHAPMAN, Guy. *The Third Republic of France; the first phase, 1871-1894.* New York: St. Martin's, 1962. 433 p.

CHASTENET, Jacques. *Gambetta.* Paris: Fayard, 1968. 395 p.

DANSETTE, Adrien. *Les affaires de Panama.* Paris: Perrin, 1934. 301 p.

DANSETTE, Adrien. *Du Boulangisme à la révolution Dreyfusienne: le Boulangisme, 1886-90.* Paris: Librairie académique Perrin, 1938. 416 p.

DREYFUS, Robert. *Monsieur Thiers contre l'Empire, la guerre, la Commune, 1869-71.* Paris: Grasset, 1928. 351 p.

DREYFUS, Robert. *La République de Monsieur Thiers, 1871-73.* Paris: Gaillimard, 1930. 352 p.

DUPUY, Aimé. *1870-71; la guerre, la Commune et la presse.* Paris: Colin, 1959. 253 p.

EDWARDS, Stewart. *The Paris Commune, 1871.* Chicago: Quadrangle Books, 1971. 417 p.

GIESBERG, Robert I. *The Treaty of Frankfort; a study in diplomatic history, (Sept. 1870 – Sept. 1873).* Philadelphia: University of Pennsylvania Press, 1966. 329 p.

GOUAULT, Jacques. *Comment la France est devenue républicaine, les élections générales et partielles à l'Assemblée nationale, 1870-75.* Paris: Colin, 1954. 239 p.

HALÉVY, Daniel. *La fin des notables.* Paris: Grasset, 1930. 294 p.

HALÉVY, Daniel. *La république des ducs.* Paris: Grasset, 1937. 411 p.

HORNE, Alistair. *The fall of Paris; the siege and the Commune: 1870-71.* New York: St. Martin's, 1965. 458 p.

JELLINEK, Frank. *The Paris Commune of 1871.* London: Gollancz, 1937. 451 p. (Universal Library)

JOHNSON, Douglas. *France and the Dreyfus Affair.* New York: Walker, 1966. 242 p.

JOUGHIN, Jean T. *The Paris Commune in French politics, 1871-80; the history of the amnesty of 1880.* 2 v. Baltimore: Johns Hopkins Press, 1955. 529 p.

LANGER, William L. *The Franco-Russian Alliance, 1890-94.* Cambridge: Harvard University Press, 1929. 455 p.

44

LISSAGARAY, Prosper Olivier. *History of the Commune of 1871.* Tr. by Eleanor Marx Aveling. New York: Monthly Review Press, 1967 (c.1886). 500 p.

MASON, Edward S. *The Paris Commune: an episode in the history of the socialist movement.* New York: Fertig, 1968 (c.1930). 386 p.

MURPHY, Agnes. *The ideology of French imperialism, 1871-81.* Washington: Catholic University of America Press, 1948. 241 p. (Fertig) (OP 15,346 $15.00)

NÉRÉ, Jacques. *Le Boulangisme et la presse.* Paris: Colin, 1964. 239 p.

POWER, Thomas F. *Jules Ferry and the renaissance of French imperialism.* New York: King's Crown Press, 1944. 222 p. (Octagon) (OP 2807 $15.00)

ROUGERIE, Jacques, ed. *Procès des Communards.* Paris: Julliard, 1964. 257 p.

SEAGER, Frederic H. *The Boulanger Affair: political crossroads of France, 1886-89.* Ithaca: Cornell University Press, 1969. 276 p.

SEDGWICK, Alexander C. *The Ralliement in French politics, 1890-98.* Cambridge: Harvard University Press, 1965. 183 p.

THIBAUDET, Albert. *La république des professeurs.* Paris: Grasset, 1927. 264 p.

THOMAS, Marcel. *L'Affaire sans Dreyfus.* Paris: Fayard, 1961. 586 p.

THE THIRD REPUBLIC, 1900-1918

ANDREW, Christopher. *Théophile Delcassé and the making of the Entente Cordiale; a reappraisal of French foreign policy, 1898-1905.* New York: St. Martin's, 1968. 330 p.

CAPÉRAN, Louis. *L'invasion laique, de l'avènément de Combes au vote de la séparation.* Paris: Desclée de Brouwer, 1935. 474 p.

CHASTENET, Jacques. *Raymond Poincaré.* Paris: Julliard, 1948. 313 p.

KING, Jere Clemens. *Generals and politicians; conflict between France's high command, parliament and government, 1914-18.* Berkeley: University of California Press, 1951. 294 p.

MIQUEL, Pierre. *Poincaré.* Paris: Fayard, 1961. 636 p.

PALÉOLOQUE, Georges Maurice. *Au Quai d'Orsay à la veille de la tourmente; journal, 1913-14 (i.e. 28 juin 1914).* Paris: Plon, 1947. 328 p. (OP 60,345 $20.00)

PARTIN, Malcolm O. *Waldeck-Rousseau, Combes, and the Church: the politics of anti-clericalism, 1899-1905.* Durham: Duke University Press, 1969. 299 p.

PERREUX, Gabriel. *La vie quotidienne des civils en France pendant la Grande Guerre.* Paris: Hachette, 1966. 351 p.

POIDEVIN, Raymond. *Les relations économiques et financières entre la France et l'Allemagne de 1898 à 1914.* Paris: Colin, 1969. 917 p.

RENOUVIN, Pierre. *The forms of war government in France.* New Haven: Yale University Press, 1927. 166 p.

SORLIN, Pierre. *Waldeck-Rousseau.* Paris: Colin, 1966. 585 p.

WEBER, Eugen J. *The nationalist revival in France, 1905-14.* Berkeley: University of California Press, 1959. 237 p.

WILLIAMSON, Samuel R. *The politics of grand strategy; Britain and France prepare for war, 1904-14.* Cambridge: Harvard University Press, 1969. 409 p.

WRIGHT, Gordon. *Raymond Poincaré and the French presidency.* New York: Octagon, 1967 (c.1942). 271 p.

THE THIRD REPUBLIC, 1918-1940

BANKWITZ, Philip Charles Farwell. *Maxime Weygand and civil-military relations in modern France.* Cambridge: Harvard University Press, 1967. 445 p.

BAUMONT, Maurice. *La faillité de la paix, 1918-39.* 5. éd. 2 v. Paris: Presses universitaires de France, 1967.

BEAUFRE, André. *1940: the fall of France.* Tr. by Desmond Flower. New

York: Knopf, 1968. 227 p.

BLOCH, Marc. *Strange defeat: a statement of the evidence written in 1940.* Tr. by Gerard Hopkins. New York: Octagon, 1967 (c.1949). 178 p. (Norton)

CHAPMAN, Guy. *Why France fell: the defeat of the French army in 1940.* New York: Holt, Rinehart & Winston, 1969. 403 p.

CHAUTEMPS, Camille. *Cahiers secrets de l'armistice, 1939-40.* Paris: Plon, 1963. 330 p.

COLTON, Joel. *Leon Blum, humanist in politics.* New York: Knopf, 1966. 512 p.

DUPEUX, Georges. *Le Front populaire et les élections de 1936.* Paris: Colin, 1959. 183 p.

FOHLEN, Claude. *La France de l'entre-deux-guerres, 1917-39.* Tournai: Casterman, 1966. 226 p.

FRANÇOIS-PONCET, André. *De Versailles à Potsdam; la France et le problème allemand contemporain, 1919-43 (i.e. 1945).* Paris: Flammarion, 1949. 305 p.

FURNIA, Arthur Homer. *The diplomacy of appeasement: Anglo-French relations and the prelude to World War II, 1931-38.* Preface by James F. Brewer. Washington, D.C.: Catholic University Press, 1960. 454 p.

GÉRAUD, André (pseud. Pertinax). *The gravediggers of France: Gamelin, Daladier, Reynaud, Petain and Laval; military defeat, armistice, counter-revolution.* New York: Doubleday, 1944. 612 p.

HUGHES, Judith M. *To the Maginot Line: the politics of French military preparation in the 1920's.* Cambridge: Harvard University Press, 1971. 296 p.

JOLL, James, ed. *The decline of the Third Republic.* New York: Praeger, 1959. 127 p.

KING, Jere C. *Foch versus Clemenceau; France and German dismemberment, 1918-19.* Cambridge: Harvard University Press, 1960. 137 p.

LARMOUR, Peter J. *The French Radical Party in the 1930's.* Stanford: Stanford University Press, 1964. 327 p.

LEFRANC, Georges. *Histoire de Front populaire, 1934-38.* Paris: Payot, 1965. 501 p.

MICAUD, Charles A. *The French Right and Nazi Germany, 1933-39, a study of public opinion.* Durham: Duke University Press, 1943. 255 p.

MILZA, Pierre. *L'Italie fasciste devant l'opinion française, 1920-40.* Paris: Colin, 1967. 263 p.

MIQUEL, Pierre. *Paix de Versailles et l'opinion publique française.* Paris: Flammarion, 1972. 610 p.

PLUMYÈNE, Jean and Lasierra, Raymond. *Les fascismes française, 1923-63.* Paris: Éditions de Seuil, 1963. 318 p.

ROSSI-LANDI, Guy. *La drôle de guerre: la vie politique en France, 2 septembre 1939-10 mai 1940.* Paris: Colin, 1971. 247 p.

SHERWOOD, John M. *Georges Mandel and the Third Republic.* Stanford: Stanford University Press, 1970. 393 p.

SOUCY, Robert. *Fascism in France.* Berkeley: University of California Press, 1972.

SOULIÉ, Michel. *La vie politique d'Edouard Herriot.* Paris: Colin, 1962. 626 p.

WERTH, Alexander. *The twilight of France, 1933-40.* 2d ed. New York: Harper, 1942. 368 p.

WOLFERS, Arnold. *Britain and France between two wars; conflicting strategies of peace from Versailles to World War II.* New York: Norton, 1966 (c.1940). 467 p.

GOVERNMENT, ADMINISTRATION, EDUCATION, MILITARY

CHALLENER, Richard D. *The French theory of the nation in arms, 1866-1939.* New York: Columbia University Press, 1955. 305 p.

CHAPMAN, Brian. *Prefects and provincial France.* London: Allen & Unwin, 1955. 246 p.

GARÇON, Maurice. *Histoire de la justice sous la Troisième République.* 3 v. Paris: Fayard, 1957.

ISAMBERT-JAMATI, Viviane. *Crises de la société, crises de l'enseignement.* Paris: Presses universitaires de France, 1970. 400 p.

LA GORCE, Paul Marie, ed. *The French army: a military-political history.* Tr. by Kenneth Douglas. New York: Braziller, 1963. 568 p.

PEDRONCINI, Guy. *Les mutineries de 1917.* Paris: Presses universitaires de France, 1967. 332 p.

RALSTON, David B. *The Army of the Republic: the place of the military in the political evolution of France, 1871-1914.* Cambridge: M.I.T. Press, 1967. 395 p.

SIWEK-POUYDESSEAU, Jeanne. *Le Corps préfectoral sous la Troisième et la Quatrième Republiques.* Paris: Colin, 1969. 181 p.

TALBOTT, John E. *The politics of educational reform in France, 1918-40.* Princeton: Princeton University Press, 1969. 283 p.

SOCIAL AND ECONOMIC

AUGÉ-LARIBÉ, Michel. *La politique agricole de la France de 1880-1940.* Paris: Presses universitaires de France, 1950. 483 p.

BETTELHEIM, Charles. *Bilan de l'économie française, 1919-46.* Paris: Presses universitaires de France, 1947. 291 p.

EHRMANN, Henry W. *Organized business in France.* Princeton: Princeton University Press, 1957. 514 p.

FONTAINE, Arthur. *French industry during the war.* New Haven: Yale University Press, 1926. 477 p.

GOGUEL, François. *Modernisation économique et comportement politique.* Paris: Colin, 1969. 88 p.

IBARROLA, Jésus. *Les incidences des'deux conflits mondiaux sur l'évolution démographique française.* Paris: Librairie Dalloz, 1969. 284 p.

KEMP, Tom. *The French economy, 1913-1939.* New York: St. Martin's Press, 1972. 183 p.

KINDLEBERGER, Charles Poor. *Economic growth in France and Britain, 1851-1950.* Cambridge: Harvard University Press, 1964. 378 p.

LEVASSEUR, Émile. *Questions ouvrières et industrielles en France sous la Troisième République.* Paris: Rousseau, 1907. 968 p.

OGBURN, William F. and Jaffe, William. *The economic development of post-war France; a survey of production.* New York: Columbia University Press, 1929. 613 p.

PONTEIL, Felix. *Les Bourgeois et la démocratie sociale, 1914-68.* Paris: Michel, 1971. 571 p.

SAUVY, Alfred. *Histoire économique de la France entre deux guerres.* 2 v. Paris: Fayard, 1965-67.

SIMIAND, François. *Le salaire, l'évolution sociale et la monnaie; essai de théorie expérimentale du salaire.* 3 v. Paris: Alcan, 1932.

WARNER, Charles K. *The winegrowers and the government of France since 1875.* New York: Columbia University Press, 1960. 303 p.

WRIGHT, Gordon. *Rural revolution in France: the peasantry in the twentieth century.* Stanford: Stanford University Press, 1964. 271 p.

SOCIALISM AND THE LABOR MOVEMENT

BERNSTEIN, Samuel. *The beginnings of Marxian socialism in France.* Rev. ed. New York: Russell & Russell, 1965. 229 p.

BROWER, Daniel R. *The new Jacobins: the French Communist Party and the Popular Front.* Ithaca: Cornell University Press, 1968. 265 p.

BRUHAT, Jean, and Piolot, Marc. *Esquisse d'une histoire de la C. G. T., 1895-1965.*

47

Paris: Confédération générale du Travail, 1967. 383 p.

EHRMANN, Henry Walter. *French labor from Popular Front to liberation.* New York: Oxford University Press, 1947. 329 p.

FAUVET, Jacques. *Histoire du Parti communiste français.* 2 v. Paris: Fayard, 1964-65.

GEORGES, Bernard, and Tintant, Denise. *Léon Jouhaux; cinquante ans de synicalisme: des origines à 1921.* Paris: Presses universitaires de France, 1962. 540 p.

GOETZ-GIREY, Robert. *Le mouvement des grèves en France, 1919-62.* Paris: Sirey, 1965. 220 p.

GREENE, Nathanael. *Crisis and decline: the French Socialist Party in the Popular Front era.* Ithaca: Cornell University Press, 1969. 361 p.

KRIEGEL, Annie. *La croissance de la C.G.T., 1918-21; essai statistique.* Paris: Mouton, 1966. 254 p.

KRIEGEL, Annie. *Aux origines du communisme français, 1914-20.* 2 v. Paris: Mouton, 1964.

KRIEGEL, Annie, and Becker, Jean-Jacques. *1914: la guerre et le mouvement ouvrier française.* Paris: Colin, 1964. 243 p.

KRIEGEL, Annie, and Perrot, Michel. *Le spcialisme française et le pouvoir.* Paris: Études et Documents internationale, 1966. 221 p.

LEFRANC, Georges. *Histoire du mouvement syndical français.* Paris: Librairie syndicale, 1937. 471 p.

LEFRANC, Georges. *Jaurès et le socialisme des intellectuels, histoire du travail et de la vie économique.* Paris: Aubièr-Montaigne, 1968. 231 p.

LEFRANC, Georges. *Le mouvement socialiste sous la Troisième République, 1875-1940.* Paris: Payot, 1963. 444 p.

LICHTHEIM, George. *Marxism in modern France.* New York: Columbia University Press, 1966. 212 p.

LIGOU, Daniel. *Histoire du socialisme en France, 1871-1961.* Paris: Presses universitaires de France, 1962. 672 p.

LORWIN, Val R. *The French labor movement.* Cambridge: Harvard University Press, 1954. 346 p.

MAITRON, Jean. *Histoire du mouvement anarchiste en France, 1880-1941.* Paris: Société universitaire d'Editions et de Librarie, 1951. 744 p.

MARCUS, John T. *French socialism in the crisis years, 1933-36: Fascism and the French Left.* New York: Praeger, 1958. 216 p. (OP 41,269 $15.00)

NOLAND, Aron. *The founding of the French Socialist Party, 1893-1905.* Cambridge: Harvard University Press, 1956. 233 p.

PROST, Antoine. *La C.G.T. à l'époque du Front Populaire (1934-39); essai de description numérique.* Paris: Colin, 1964. 242 p.

RIDLEY, F. F. *Revolutionary Syndicalism in France: the direct action of its time.* New York: Cambridge University Press, 1970. 279 p.

STEARNS, Peter N. *Revolutionary Syndicalism and French labor: a cause without rebels.* New Brunswick: Rutgers University Press, 1971. 175 p.

WALTER, Gérard. *Histoire du Parti communiste française.* Paris: Somogy, 1948. 390 p.

WILLARD, Claude. *Les Guesdistes; le mouvement socialiste en France (1893-1905).* Paris: Éditions Sociales, 1965. 770 p.

WOHL, Robert. *French Communism in the making, 1914-24.* Stanford: Stanford University Press, 1966. 530 p.

REGIONAL STUDIES

BARRAL, Pierre. *Le département de l'Isère sous la Troisième République: histoire sociale et politique.* Paris: Colin, 1962. 597 p.

BERGER, Suzanne. *Peasants against politics;*

rural organization in Brittany, 1911-67. Cambridge: Harvard University Press, 1972. 298 p.

LONG, Raymond. Les élections législatives en Côte-d'Or depuis 1870; essai d'interpretation sociologique. Paris: Colin, 1958. 294 p.

MARIE, Christiane. L'évolution du comportement politique dans une ville en expansion: Grenoble 1871-1965. Paris: Colin, 1966. 227 p.

SIEGFRIED, André. Géographie électorale de l'Ardèche sous la Troisième République. Paris: Colin, 1949. 138 p.

SIEGFRIED, André. Tableau politique de la France de l'Ouest sous la Troisième République. Paris: Colin, 1913. 535 p.

INTELLECTUAL AND CULTURAL

ANDLER, Charles P. T. Vie de Lucien Herr (1864-1926). Paris: Rieder, 1932. 336p.

BENRUBI, Isaak. Les sources et les courantes de la philosophie contemporaine en France. 2 v. Paris: Alcan, 1933.

BYRNES, Robert F. Antisemitism in modern France. New York: Fertig, 1969 (c.1950). I. The prologue to the Dreyfus Affair.

CAUTE, David. Communism and the French intellectuals, 1914-60. New York: Macmillan, 1964. 412 p.

CURTIS, Michael. Three against the Third Republic: Sorel, Barrès and Maurras. Princeton: Princeton University Press, 1959. 313 p. (OP 2,000,698 $20.00)

DIGEON, Claude. La crise allemande de la pensée française, 1870-1914. Paris: Presses universitaires de France, 1959. 568 p.

HALÉVY, Daniel. Péguy and Les Cahiers de la Quinzaine. Tr. by Ruth Bethell. London: Dobson, 1946. 232 p.

HUGHES, H. Stuart. The obstructed path: French social thought in the years of desperation, 1930-60. New York: Harper & Row, 1968. 304 p.

HUMPHREY, Richard D. Georges Sorel, prophet without honor: a study in anti-intellectualism. New York: Octagon Books, 1971 (c.1951). 246 p.

JEFFERSON, Alfred Carter. Anatole France: the politics of skepticism. New Brunswick: Rutgers University Press, 1965. 294 p.

LEGRAND, Louis. L'influence du positivisme dans l'oeuvre scolaire de Jules Ferry; les origines de la laïcité. Paris: Rivière, 1961. 254 p.

MARTINO, Pierre. Le naturalisme français, 1870-95. 7. éd. rev. Paris: Colin, 1965 (1st pub., 1923). 224 p.

MEISEL, James H. The genesis of Georges Sorel, and account of his formative period followed by a study of his influence. Ann Arbor: Wahr, 1951. 320 p. (OP 23,067 $20.00)

NIESS, Robert J. Julien Benda. Ann Arbor: University of Michigan Press, 1956. 361 p. (OP 49,024 $20.00)

PASQUIER, Albert. Les doctrines sociales en France: vingt ans d'évolution, 1930-50. Paris: Pichon et Durand-Auzias, 1950. 527 p.

PIROU, Gaetan. Les doctrines économiques en France depuis 1870. Paris: Colin, 1925. 204 p.

SCHMITT, Hans A. Charles Peguy: the decline of an idealist. Baton Rouge: Louisiana State University Press, 1967. 211 p.

SCOTT, John Anthony. Republican ideas and the liberal tradition in France, 1870-1914. New York: Octagon, 1966 (c.1951). 209 p.

SHATTUCK, Roger. The banquet years: the origins of the avant-garde in France, 1885 to World War I. Rev. ed. New York: Vintage Books, 1968. 397 p.

SILVERA, Alain. Daniel Halévy and his times: a gentleman-commoner in the Third Republic. Ithaca: Cornell University Press, 1966. 251 p.

VIÉ, Louis. Renan, la guerre de 70 et la

réforme de la France. Paris: Bloud & Gay, 1949. 770 p.

RELIGION

CARON, Jeanne. *Le sillon et la démocratie chrétienne, 1894-1910.* Paris: Plon, 1966. 798 p.

DEBIDOUR, Antonin. *L'église catholique et l'état sous la Troisième République, 1870-1906.* 2 v. Paris: Alcan, 1906-09.

HOOG, Georges. *Histoire du catholicisme social en France; de l'encyclique "Rerum Novarum" à l'encyclique "Quadragesimo Anno".* Paris: Domat-Montchrestien, 1942.

LECANUET, Édouard. *L'Église en France sous la Troisième République.* Vols. 1 and 2 Nouv. ed. 4 v. Paris: Alcan, 1930-31.
I. Les dernières années du Pontificat de Pie IX, 1870-78.
II. Les premières années du Pontificat de Léon XIII, 1878-94.
III. Les signes avant-coureurs de la séparation; les dernières années de Léon XIII et l'avènement de Pie X (1894-1910).
IV. La vie de l'Église sous Léon XIII.

McMANNERS, John. *Church and state in France, 1870-1914.* London: S.P.C.K., 1972. 191 p.

ROLLET, Henri. *L'action sociale des catholiques en France (1870-1914).* 2 v. Paris: Boivin, 1947-58.

MEMOIRS AND CONTEMPORARY WRITINGS

ABETZ, Otto Friedrich. *Histoire d'une politique franco-allemande, 1930-50: mémoires d'un ambassadeur.* Paris: Stock, 1953. 356 p.

ANDRÉ, Général Louis Joseph. *Cinq ans de ministère.* Paris: Michaud, 1907. 403 p.

BARDOUX, Jacques. *Journal d'un témoin de la Troisième: Paris, Bordeaux, Vichy, Septembre 1, 1939 - 15 Juillet 1940.* Paris: Fayard, 1957. 427 p.

BLUM, Léon. *L'Oeuvre de Léon Blum.* 7 v. Paris: Michel, 1954-63.

BONNET, Georges Étienne. *Défense de la paix.* 2 v. Genève: Éditions de Cheval aile, 1946; Paris: Plon, 1967.
I. De Washington au Quai d'Orsay.
II. De Munich à la guerre. Nouv. éd. revue et augmentée.

CAILLAUX, Joseph. *Mes mémoires.* 3 v. Paris: Plon, 1942-47.

CAMBON, Paul. *Paul Cambon, ambassadeur de France, 1843-1924, par un diplomate.* Paris: Plon, 1937. 325 p.

CAMBON, Paul. *Correspondence, 1870-1924, avec un commentaire et des notes par Henri Cambon.* 3 v. Paris: Grasset, 1940-46.

CLEMENCEAU, Georges. *Grandeur and misery of victory.* Tr. by F. M. Atkinson. New York: Harcourt Brace, 1930. 432 p.

COMBES, Émile. *Mon ministère; mémoires, 1902-05.* Intro. et notes par Maurice Sorre. Paris: Plon, 1956. 293 p.

DALADIER, Édouard. *In defense of France.* New York: Doubleday, 1939. 239 p.

DREYFUS, Alfred. *The Dreyfus case, by the man—Alfred Dreyfus, and his son—Pierre Dreyfus.* Tr. and ed. by Donald C. McKay. New Haven: Yale University Press, 1937. 303 p.

DUCLOS, Jacques. *Mémoires.* 4 v. Paris: Fayard, 1968-71.

FOCH, Marshal Ferdinand. *The memoirs of Marshal Foch.* Tr. by Col. T. Bentley Mott. New York: Doubleday, 1931. 517 p.

GAMBETTA, Léon Michel. *Lettres de Gambetta, 1868-82.* Paris: Grasset, 1938. 671 p.

GAMELIN, General Maurice Gustave. *Servir.* 3 v. Paris: Plon, 1946-47.
I. Les armées françaises de 1940.
II. Le prologue du drama (1930 – Août 1939).
III. La guerre (Septembre 1939 – 19 Mai 1940).

GAULLE, Charles de. *The army of the future.* London: Hutchinson, 1940. 158 p.

GAULLE, Charles de. *The edge of the sword.*
New York: Criterion Books, 1960. 128 p.

GAULLE, Charles de. *France and her army.*
Tr. by F. L. Dash. London: Hutchinson,
1945. 104 p.

HERRIOT, Edouard. *Jadis.* 2 v. Paris:
Flammarion, 1948-52.

JAURÈS, Jean Léon. *Oeuvres de Jean Jaurès;
textes rassemblés, présentés et annotés par
Max Bonnefous.* 9 v. Paris: Rieder, 1931-
39.

JOFFRE, Maréchal Joseph Jacques Césaire.
Mémoires du maréchal Joffre, 1910-17.
2 v. Paris: Plon, 1932.

LAROCHE, Jules Alfred. *Au Quai d'Orsay
avec Briand et Poincaré, 1913-26.* Paris:
Hachette, 1957. 230 p.

LAVAL, Pierre. *The diary of Pierre Laval.*
New York: Scribner, 1948. 240 p.

MASSIS, Henri. *Maurras et notre temps:
entretiens et souvenirs.* Rev. éd. Paris:
Plon, 1961. 452 p.

MAURRAS, Charles. *Enquête sur la
monarchie; suivie de une campagne
royaliste au Figaro, et si le coup de force
est possible.* Édition definitive. Paris:
Nouvelle Librairie nationale, 1924. 615 p.

PAUL-BONCOUR, Joseph. *Entre deux
guerres: souvenirs sur la Troisième
République.* 3 v. Paris: Plon, 1945-47.
(V. 1 tr. by George Marion Jr. as *Recollec-
tions of the Third Republic.* New York:
Speller, 1957). (OP 51,399 $65.00.

v. 1—$20.00; v. 2—$25.00; v. 3—$20.00)

POINCARÉ, Raymond. *The memoirs of
Raymond Poincaré.* Tr. by Sir George
Archer. 4 v. New York: Doubleday,
1926-31.

REYNAUD, Paul. *In the thick of the fight,
1930-45.* Tr. by James D. Lambert. New
York: Simon & Schuster, 1955. 684 p.

REYNAUD, Paul. *Mémoires.* 2 v. Paris:
Flammarion, 1960-63.

SIMON, Jules. *Souvenirs du quatre septembre: le gouvernement de la défense
nationale.* Paris: Lévy, 1874. 392 p.

SOREL, Georges. *Reflections on violence.*
Tr. by T. E. Hulme and J. Roth. New
York: Collier, 1961. 286 p.

SPEARS, Sir Edward Lewis, bart. *Assign-
ment to catastrophe.* 2 v. New York:
Wyn, 1954-55.
I. Prelude to Dunkirk, July 1939-May
1940.
II. The fall of France, June 1940.

TARDIEU, André P. G. A. *La paix; préface
de Georges Clemenceau.* Paris: Payot,
1921. 520 p.

THIERS, Adolphe. *Memoirs of M. Thiers,
1870-73.* Tr. by F. M. Atkinson. London:
Allen & Unwin, 1915. 384 p.

WEYGAND, General Maxime. *Mémoires.*
3 v. Paris: Flammarion, 1950-57. (V. 3
tr. by E. W. Dickes as *Recalled to service:
the memoirs of Maxime Weygand.*
London: Heinemann, 1952).

FRANCE SINCE 1940

GENERAL AND MISCELLANEOUS

*L'ANNÉE politique, économique, sociale et
diplomatique en France.* Paris: Presses
universitaires de France, 1944/45 ff.

ARON, Raymond. *France steadfast and
changing: the Fourth and the Fifth*

Republics. Cambridge: Harvard University
Press, 1960. 201 p.

BEHR, Edward. *The Algerian problem.*
New York: Norton, 1962. 256 p.

BRINTON, Crane. *The Americans and the
French.* Cambridge: Harvard University

Press, 1968. 305 p.

CARMOY, Guy de. *The foreign policies of France, 1944-68.* Tr. by Elaine P. Halperin. Chicago: University of Chicago Press, 1970. 510 p.

CHAPSAL, Jacques. *La vie politique en France depuis 1940.* 2. éd. Paris: Presses universitaires de France, 1969. 618 p.

CLUB Jean Moulin. *L'état et le citoyen.* Paris: Éditions du Seuil, 1961. 409 p.

COGNIOT, Georges, and Joannes, Victor. *Maurice Thorez: l'homme, le militant.* Paris: Éditions Sociales, 1970. 186 p.

COTTERET, Iean-Marie; Émeri, Claude; and Lalumière, Pierre. *Lois électorales et inégalités de représentation en France (1936-60).* Paris: Colin, 1960. 409 p.

DUPEUX, Georges. *La France de 1945 à 1965.* Paris: Colin, 1969. 384 p.

DUVERGER, Maurice. *Political parties; their organization and activity in the modern state.* Tr. by Barbara and Robert North. New York: Wiley, 1963. 439 p.

FALL, Bernard B. *Street without joy: insurgency in Indochina, 1946-63.* 4th ed. Harrisburg, Pa.: Stackpole, 1964. 408 p.

FAUVET, Jacques. *Les forces politiques en France, de Thorez à de Gaulle: étude et géographie des divers partis.* 2. éd. Paris: Le Monde, 1951. 298 p.

GORDON, David C. *The passing of French Algeria.* New York: Oxford University Press, 1966. 265 p.

HAMMER, Ellen Joy. *The struggle for Indochina, 1940-55.* Stanford: Stanford University Press, 1966 (c.1955). 373 p.

HARTLEY, Anthony. *Gaullism: the rise and fall of a political movement.* New York: Dutton, 1971. 373 p.

HOFFMAN, Stanley, et al. *In search of France; the economy, society, and political system in the twentieth century.* New York: Harper & Row, 1965. 441 p.

LACOUTURE, Jean. *De Gaulle.* Rev. and enl. ed. Tr. by Francis K. Price and John Skeffington. London: Hutchinson, 1970. 253 p.

LA GORCE, Paul Marie de. *De Gaulle entre deux mondes; une vie et une époque.* Paris: Fayard, 1964. 766 p.

LEITES, Nathan C. *On the game of politics in France.* Stanford: Stanford University Press, 1959. 190 p. (OP 25,585 $15.00)

LUETHY, Herbert. *France against herself: a perceptive study of France's past, her politics and her unending crises.* Tr. by Eric Mosbacher. New York: Meridian Books, 1957. 476 p.

MENDL, Wolf. *Deterrence and persuasion: French nuclear armament in the context of national policy, 1945-69.* New York: Praeger, 1970. 256 p.

MEYNAUD, Jean. *Nouvelles études sur les groupes de pression en France.* Paris: Colin, 1962. 448 p.

MOSSUZ, Janine. *André Malraux et le gaullisme.* Paris: Colin, 1970. 312 p.

PAILLAT, Claude. *Vingt ans qui déchirèrent la France.* 2 v. Paris: Laffont, 1969-72. I. Le guêpier. II. La liquidation, 1954-62.

PICKLES, Dorothy M. *The uneasy entente: French foreign policy and Franco-British misunderstandings.* New York: Oxford University Press, 1966. 180 p.

SERFATY, Simon. *France, de Gaulle and Europe: the policy of the Fourth and Fifth Republics toward the Continent.* Baltimore: Johns Hopkins Press, 1968. 176 p.

THOMSON, David. *Two Frenchmen: Pierre Laval and Charles de Gaulle.* London: Cresset Press, 1951. 255 p.

WERTH, Alexander. *De Gaulle: a political biography.* New York: Simon & Schuster, 1966. 416 p.

WERTH, Alexander. *France, 1940-55.* New York: Holt, Rinehart & Winston, 1956. 764 p.

WILLIAMS, Philip M., with Goldey, David and Harrison, Martin. *French politicians and elections, 1951-69.* London: Cambridge University Press, 1970. 312 p.

WILLIS, Frank Roy. *France, Germany and the new Europe, 1945-67.* Rev. ed.

Stanford: Stanford University Press, 1968. 431 p.

THE OCCUPATION AND THE LIBERATION, 1940-1945

AMOUROUX, Henri. *La vie des français sous l'occupation.* Paris: Fayard, 1961. 577 p.

ARON, Robert. *France reborn: the history of the liberation, June 1944 – May 1945.* Tr. by Humphrey Hare. New York: Scribner, 1964. 490 p.

ARON, Robert. *Histoire de l'épuration.* 2 v. Paris: Fayard, 1967-69.
I. De l'indulgence aux massacres, novembre 1942-septembre 1944.
II. Des prisons clandestines aux tribunaux d'exception, septembre 1944-juin 1949.

ARON, Robert, and Elgey, Georgette. *The Vichy regime, 1940-44.* Tr. by Humphrey Hare. New York: Macmillan, 1958. 536 p.

COLE, Hubert. *Laval: a biography.* London: Heinemann, 1963. 314 p.

COTTA, Michèle. *La collaboration, 1940-44.* Paris: Colin, 1964. 333 p.

DANSETTE, Adrien. *Histoire de la libération de Paris.* Paris: Fayard, 1958. 413 p.

DE PORTE, Anton W. *De Gaulle's foreign policy, 1944-46.* Cambridge: Harvard University Press, 1968. 327 p.

FARMER, Paul. *Vichy: political dilemma.* New York: Columbia University Press, 1955. 376 p.

FUNK, Arthur L. *Charles de Gaulle: the crucial years, 1943-44.* Norman: University of Oklahoma Press, 1959. 336 p.

HYTIER, Adrienne Doris. *Two years of French foreign policy: Vichy, 1940-42.* Geneva: Droz, 1958. 402 p. (OP 62,508 $25.00)

JACKEL, Eberhard. *La France dans l'Europe de Hitler.* Tr. de l'allemand par Denise Menier. Paris: Fayard, 1966. 554 p.

MAIER, Charles S., and White, Dan S., eds. *The thirteenth of May: the advent of de Gaulle's republic.* New York: Oxford University Press, 1968. 402 p.

MALLET, Alfred. *Pierre Laval.* 2 v. Paris: Amiot-Dumont, 1954-55.
I. Des années obscures à la disgrace du 13 décembre 1940.
II. De la reconquête du pouvoir à l'exécution.

MICHEL, Henri. *Les courantes de pensée de la résistance.* Paris: Presses universitaires de France, 1962. 842 p.

MICHEL, Henri. *Vichy, année 40.* Paris: Laffont, 1966. 451 p.

NOGUÈRES, Henri. *Histoire de la résistance en France.* 2 v. Paris: Laffont, 1967-69.
I. La première année, juin 1940-juin 1941.
II. L'armée de l'ombre, juillet 1941-octobre 1942.

NOGUÈRES, Louis. *Le véritable procès du maréchal Pétain.* Paris: Fayard, 1955. 659 p.

NOVICK, Peter. *The resistance versus Vichy: the purge of the collaborators in liberated France.* New York: Columbia University Press, 1968. 245 p.

PAXTON, Robert O. *Vichy France: old guard and new order, 1940-44.* New York: Knopf, 1972. 399 p.

PICKLES, Dorothy M. *France between the Republics (1940-45).* London: Love and Malcomson, 1946. 247 p. (OP 4820 $15.00)

SOUSTELLE, Jacques. *Envers et contre tout; souvenirs et documents sur la France libre.* 2 v. Paris: Laffont, 1947-50.
I. De Londres à Alger, 1940-42.
II. D'Alger à Paris (1942-44).

WARNER, Geoffrey. *Pierre Laval and the eclipse of France.* London: Eyre & Spottiswood, 1968. 461 p.

THE FOURTH REPUBLIC

BERNARD, Stephane. *The Franco-Moroccan conflict, 1943-56.* New Haven: Yale University Press, 1968. 680 p.

DUVERGER, Maurice. *The French political system.* Tr. by Barbara and Robert North. Chicago: University of Chicago Press, 1958. 227 p.

ELGEY, Georgette. *Histoire de la IVe République.* 2 v. Paris: Fayard, 1965-68. I. La République des illusions, 1945-51: ou la vie secrète de la IVe République. II. La République des contradictions, 1951-54.

FALL, Bernard B. *Hell in a very small place: the siege of Dien Bien Phu.* Philadelphia: Lippincott, 1967. 515 p.

FAUVET, Jacques, and Planchais, Jean. *La fronde des généraux.* Paris: Arthaud, 1961. 273 p.

FREYMOND, Jacques. *The Saar conflict, 1945-55.* New York: Praeger, 1960. 395 p.

GOGUEL-NYEGAARD, François. *France under the Fourth Republic.* Tr. by Roy Pierce. Ithaca: Cornell University Press, 1952. 198 p.

GROSSER, Alfred. *La IVe République et sa politique extérieure.* Paris: Colin, 1961. 438 p.

HOFFMAN, Stanley. *Le mouvement Poujade.* Paris: Colin, 1956. 417 p.

MACRAE, Duncan. *Parliament, parties and society in France, 1946-58.* New York: St. Martin's, 1967. 375 p.

MEISEL, James Hans. *The fall of the Republic; military revolt in France.* Ann Arbor: University of Michigan Press, 1962. 309 p.

SCHEINMAN, Lawrence. *Atomic energy policy in France under the Fourth Republic.* Princeton: Princeton University Press, 1965. 259 p.

SIEGFRIED, André. *De la IVe à la Ve République au jour le jour.* Paris: Grasset, 1958. 321 p.

TOURNOUX, Jean-Raymond. *Le mois de mai du général, livre blanc des événements.* Paris: Plon, 1969. 527 p.

WALLACE-HADRILL, John M., and McManners, John, eds. *France: government and society.* London: Methuen, 1957. 275 p.

WILLIAMS, Philip M. *Crisis and compromise: politics in the Fourth Republic.*
3d ed. Hamden, Conn.: Archon Books, 1964. 546 p.

WILLIAMS, Philip M. *Wars, plots and scandals in postwar France.* Cambridge: University Press, 1970. 232 p.

WILLIS, Frank Roy. *The French in Germany, 1945-49.* Stanford: Stanford University Press, 1962. 308 p.

WRIGHT, Gordon. *The reshaping of French democracy.* New York: Reynal & Hitchcock, 1948. 277 p. (Beacon)

THE FIFTH REPUBLIC

ARON, Raymond. *The elusive revolution: anatomy of a student revolt.* Tr. by Gordon Clough. New York: Praeger, 1969. 200 p.

ARON, Robert. *An explanation of de Gaulle.* Tr. by Marianne Sinclair. New York: Harper & Row, 1966. 210 p.

AVRIL, Pierre. *Le régime politique de la Ve République.* 2. éd. Paris: Librairie générale de Droit et de Jurisprudence, 1966. 439 p.

BURNIER, Michel Antoine, et al. *La chute du Général.* Paris: Editions et Publications premières, 1969. 275 p.

COUVE DE MURVILLE, Maurice. *Une politique étrangère, 1958-69.* Paris: Plon, 1971. 503 p.

DOGAN, M., éd. *L'établissement de la Ve République; le référendum de septembre et les élections de novembre 1958.* Paris: Colin, 1960. 390 p.

DUVERGER, Maurice. *La Ve République.* 4. éd. Paris: Presses universitaires de France, 1968. 291 p.

DUVERGER, Maurjce. *La démocratie sans le peuple.* Paris: Éditions du Seuil, 1967. 249 p.

FURNISS, Edgar S. *De Gaulle and the French army; a crisis in civil-military relations.* New York: Twentieth Century Fund, 1964. 331 p.

GOGUEL, François, et al. *Les élections législatives de Mars 1967.* Paris: Colin, 1971. 415 p.

GROSSER, Alfred. *French foreign policy under de Gaulle*. Tr. by Louis A. Pattison. Boston: Little, Brown, 1967. 175 p.

KULSKI, Wladislaw W. *De Gaulle and the world: the foreign policy of the Fifth Republic*. Syracuse: Syracuse University Press, 1966. 428 p.

LAPONCE, J. A. *The government of the Fifth Republic: French political parties and the Constitution*. Berkeley: University of California Press, 1961. 415 p.

MACRIDIS, Roy C., ed. *De Gaulle: implacable ally*. New York: Harper & Row, 1966. 248 p.

MACRIDIS, Roy C., and Brown, Bernard E. *The de Gaulle republic: quest for unity*. Homewood, Ill.: Dorsey Press, 1960. 400 p. (Supplement, 1963. 141 p.)

MENARD, Orville D. *The army and the Fifth Republic*. Lincoln: University of Nebraska Press, 1967. 265 p.

PICKLES, Dorothy. *The Fifth French Republic*. 3d ed. New York: Praeger, 1966. 261 p.

PIERCE, Roy. *French politics and political institutions*. New York: Harper & Row, 1968. 275 p.

SEALE, Patrick, and McConville, Maureen. *Red flag, black flag: French Revolution of 1968*. New York: Ballantine Books, 1968. 240 p.

TANNENBAUM, Edward R. *The new France*. Chicago: University of Chicago Press, 1961. 251 p.

TOURAINE, Alain. *The May movement: revolt and reform. May 1968—the student rebellion and workers strikes—the birth of a social movement*. Tr. by Leonard Mayhew. New York: Random House, 1971. 373 p.

WILLIAMS, Philip M., and Harrison, Martin. *De Gaulle's Republic*. 2d ed. London: Longmans, 1962. 279 p.

WILLIAMS, Philip M. *The French Parliament: politics in the Fifth Republic*. New York: Praeger, 1968. 136 p.

WILLIAMS, Philip M., and Harrison, Martin.

Politics and society in de Gaulle's republic. London: Longmans, 1971. 404 p.

WILSON, Frank L. *The French democratic Left, 1963-69: toward a modern party system*. Stanford: Stanford University Press, 1971. 258 p.

GOVERNMENT, ADMINISTRATION, EDUCATION, MILITARY

AMBLER, John Steward. *The French army in politics, 1945-62*. Columbus: Ohio State University Press, 1966. 427 p. (Anchor title: *Soldiers against the state*.)

AVRIL, Pierre. *Le gouvernement de la France*. Paris: Éditions universitaires, 1969. 228 p.

BELORGEY, Gerard. *Le gouvernement et l'administration de la France*. Paris: Colin, 1967. 447 p.

COGNIOT, Georges. *Laïcité et reforme démocratique de l'enseignement*. Paris: Éditions sociales, 1963. 288 p.

CROZIER, Michel. *La société bloquée*. Paris: Editions du Seuil, 1970. 251 p.

GIRARDET, Raoul, éd. *La crise militaire française, 1945-62: aspects sociologiques et idéologiques*. Paris: Colin, 1964. 235 p.

KELLY, George Armstrong. *Lost soldiers; the French army and empire in crisis, 1947-62*. Cambridge: M.I.T. Press, 1965. 404 p.

PAXTON, Robert O. *Parades and politics at Vichy: the French officer corps under Marshal Petain*. Princeton: Princeton University Press, 1966. 472 p.

SOCIAL AND ECONOMIC

ARDAGH, John. *The new French revolution: a social and economic study of France, 1945-67*. New York: Harper & Row, 1968. 501 p.

BAUCHET, Pierre. *La planification française du premier au sixième plan*. 5. éd. Paris: Editions du Seuil, 1966. 383 p.

BAUM, Warren C. *The French economy and the state*. Princeton: Princeton University

Press, 1958. 391 p.

FAURE, Marcel. *Les paysans dans la société française*. Paris: Colin, 1966. 343 p.

FAUVET, Jacques, and Mendras, Henri, éds. *Les paysans et la politique dans la France contemporaine*. Paris: Colin, 1958. 531 p.

HACKETT, John, and Hackett, Ann-Marie. *Economic planning in France*. Cambridge: Harvard University Press, 1963. 418 p.

JEANNENEY, Jean Marcel. *Forces et faiblesses de l'économie française, 1945-59*. 2. éd. Paris: Colin, 1959. 362 p.

MALLET, Serge. *Les paysans contre le passé*. Paris: Éditions de Seuil, 1962. 237 p.

MENDRAS, Henri. *The vanishing peasant: innovation and change in French agriculture*. Tr. by Jean Lerner. Cambridge: M.I.T. Press, 1970. 289 p.

MEYNAUD, Jean. *La révolte paysanne*. Paris: Payot, 1963. 312 p.

MILWARD, Alan S. *The new order and the French economy*. New York: Oxford University Press, 1970. 320 p.

SERVAN-SCHREIBER, J.-J. *The American challenge*. New York: Atheneum, 1968. 291 p.

SHEAHAN, John. *Promotion and control of industry in postwar France*. Cambridge: Harvard University Press, 1963. 301 p.

SOCIALISM AND THE LABOR MOVEMENT

ADAM, Gérard; Bon, Frédéric; Capdeville, Jacques; and Mouriaux, René. *L'Ouvrier français en 1970; enquête nationale auprès de 1116 ouvriers d'industrie*. Paris: Colin, 1970. 276 p.

BELLEVILLE, Pierre. *Une nouvelle classe ouvrière*. Paris: Julliard, 1963. 316 p.

FEJTÖ, François. *The French communist party and the crisis of international communism*. Cambridge: M.I.T. Press, 1967. 225 p.

GRAHAM, Bruce Desmond. *The French*

socialists and tripartism, 1944-47. Toronto: University of Toronto Press, 1965. 299 p.

HAMILTON, Richard F. *Affluence and the French worker in the Fourth Republic*. Princeton: Princeton University Press, 1967. 323 p.

KAËS, René. *Images de la culture chez les ouvriers français*. Paris: Éditions Cujas, 1968. 347 p.

KRIEGEL, Annie. *The French Communists: profile of a people*. Tr. by Elaine P. Halperin. Chicago: University of Chicago Press, 1972. 408 p.

MALLET, Serge. *La nouvelle classe ouvrière*. Paris: Éditions de Seuil, 1963. 265 p.

SIMMONS, Harvey G. *French socialists in search of a role, 1957-67*. Ithaca: Cornell University Press, 1970. 313 p.

TOURAINE, Alain. *L'évolution du travail ouvrier aux usines Renault*. Paris: Centre nationale de la Recherche scientifique, 1955. 202 p. (OP 64,413 $15.00)

REGIONAL STUDIES

BETTELHEIM, Charles, and Frère, Suzanne. *Une ville français moyenne: Auxerre en 1950*. Paris: Colin, 1951. 270 p.

MORIN, Edgar. *The red and the white: report from a French village*. Tr. by A. M. Sheridan-Smith. New York: Pantheon, 1970. 263 p.

RAMBAUD, Placide. *Économie et sociologie de la montagne: Albiez-le-Vieux en Maurienne*. Paris: Colin, 1962. 292 p.

WYLIE, Laurence William, ed. *Chanzeaux, a village in Anjou*. Cambridge: Harvard University Press, 1966. 383 p.

WYLIE, Laurence William. *Village in the Vaucluse*. 2d ed. Cambridge: Harvard University Press, 1964. 377 p.

INTELLECTUAL AND CULTURAL

ARON, Raymond. *The opium of the intellectuals*. Tr. by Terence Kilmartin. New York: Doubleday, 1957. 324 p. (Norton)

BURNIER, Michel Antoine. *Choice of action: the French existentialists on the political front line.* Tr. by Bernard Murchland. New York: Random House, 1968. 206 p.

BURNIER, Michel Antoine, and Bon, Frédéric. *Les nouveaux intellectuels.* Paris: Editions Cujas, 1966. 383 p.

CHATELAIN, Abel. *"Le Monde" et ses lecteurs sous la Quatrième République.* Paris: Colin, 1962. 279 p.

GILPIN, Robert. *France in the age of the scientific state.* Princeton: Princeton University Press, 1968. 474 p.

PARK, Julian, ed. *The culture of France in our time.* Ithaca: Cornell University Press, 1954. 345 p.

PIERCE, Roy. *Contemporary French political thought.* New York: Oxford University Press, 1966. 276 p.

RELIGION

BOSWORTH, William. *Catholicism and crisis in modern France.* Princeton: Princeton University Press, 1962. 407 p.

DOMENACH, Jean-Marie, and Montvalon, Robert de. *The Catholic avant-garde: French Catholicism since World War II.* New York: Holt, Rinehart & Winston, 1967. 245 p.

POULAT, Émile. *Naissance des prêtres ouvriers.* Paris: Casterman, 1965. 538 p.

RÉMOND, René, éd. *Forces religieuses et attitudes politiques dans la France contemporaine.* Paris: Colin, 1965. 397 p.

MEMOIRS AND CONTEMPORARY WRITINGS

BIDAULT, Georges. *Resistance: the political autobiography of Georges Bidault.* Tr.

by Marianne Sinclair. New York: Praeger, 1967. 348 p.

ELY, Paul. *Mémoires.* Paris: Plon, 1964. I. l'Indochine dans la tourmente.

FRANCE during the German occupation: a collection of 292 statements on the government of Marechal Pétain and Pierre Laval. Tr. by Philip W. Whitcomb. 3 v. Stanford: Stanford University Press, 1958-59.

GAULLE, Charles de. *The complete war memoirs.* Tr. by J. Griffin & R. Howard. 3 v. in 1. New York: Simon & Schuster, 1964. 1048 p.

GAULLE, Charles de. *Memoirs of hope: renewal and endeavor.* Tr. by T. Kilmartin. New York: Simon & Schuster, 1971. 392 p.

JUIN, Alphonse Pierre. *Mémoires.* 2 v. Paris: Fayard, 1959-60.

LEBRUN, Albert François. *Témoignage.* Paris: Plon, 1945. 260 p.

MALRAUX, André. *Felled Oaks: conversation with de Gaulle.* Tr. by Irene Clephane. New York: Holt, Rinehart & Winston, 1972. 128 p.

MENDÈS-FRANCE, Pierre. *A modern French republic.* Tr. by Anne Carter. New York: Hill & Wang, 1963. 205 p.

MICHEL, Henri. *Les idées politiques et sociales de la résistance (documents clandestins, 1940-44).* Paris: Presses universitaires de France, 1954. 410 p.

PÉTAIN, Maréchal Henri Philippe. *Quatre années au pouvoir.* 3. éd. Paris: Couronne littéraire, 1949. 178 p.

SCHNAPP, Alain, and Vidal-Naquet, Pierre. *Journal de la commune étudiante; textes et documents, novembre 1967 – juin 1968.* Paris: Éditions de Seuil, 1969. 876 p.

PART II: DISSERTATIONS

HISTORIES AND SPECIAL STUDIES COVERING
MORE THAN ONE CENTURY

CAMP, Wesley Douglass. *Marriage and the family in France since the revolution: an essay in the history of population.* Columbia University, 1957. DAI 18/04, p. 1405. Order No. 58-1334.

COWAN, Laing G. *France and the Saar, 1680-1948.* Columbia University, 1950.

COX, Henry Bartholomew. *"To the victor": a history of the French spoliation claims controversy, 1793-1955.* George Washington University, 1967.

DOSHER, Harry Randall. *The concept of the ideal prince in French political thought, 800-1760.* University of North Carolina at Chapel Hill, 1969. DAI 30/09-A, p. 3879. Order No. 70-3226.

GOLDSMITH, James Lowth. *The rural nobles of Auvergne under the Old Regime: the Seigneurs of Salers and Mazerolles and their domains.* Harvard University, 1971.

GOREUX, Louis-Marie. *Agricultural productivity and economic development in France.* University of Chicago, 1955.

GREENE, Christopher Morrill. *Historical consciousness and historical monuments in France after 1789.* Harvard University, 1964.

HANNAWAY, John Joseph. *The Canal of Burgundy 1720-1853: a study of a mixed enterprise.* Johns Hopkins University, 1971. DAI 32/05-A, p. 2602. Order No. 71-29,148.

HIGONNET, Patrick Louis-René. *Social background of political life in two villages of central France, 1700-1962.* Harvard University, 1964.

JACKSON, Richard Arlen. *The royal coronation ceremony in France from Charles III to Charles X.* University of Minnesota, 1967. DAI 28/06-A, p. 2175. Order No. 67-14,620.

LOUGHREY, Mary E. *France and Rhode Island, 1686-1800.* Columbia University, 1945.

MACHEN, Mary Gresham. *Images of Joan of Arc: their political uses in modern France.* Johns Hopkins University, 1959.

RIESENFELD, Stephan A. *The French system of administrative justice.* Harvard University, 1950.

SARGENT, Frederic O. *Land tenure in the agriculture of France.* University of Wisconsin, 1952.

SCHRAM, Stuart R. *Protestantism and politics in France.* Columbia University, 1954.

TIHANY, Leslie Charles. *French Utopian thought, 1676-1790.* University of Chicago, 1943.

WEINBERG, Michael Albert. *The liberal image of America in France and England, 1789-1890.* Harvard University, 1960.

THE SEVENTEENTH CENTURY, 1600-1715

GENERAL AND MISCELLANEOUS

CARMACK, David English. *Law in French diplomacy from the Treaty of Westphalia to the French Revolution, 1648-1789.* University of Virginia, 1963. DAI 24/07, p. 2971. Order No. 64-699.

FOLMER, Henri. *Franco-Spanish rivalry in North America, 1524-1763.* University of Chicago, 1949.

IDLE, Dunning. *The post of the St. Joseph River during the French regime 1679-1761.* University of Illinois, 1946.

REED, Gervais Eyer. *Claude Barbin (c. 1628-1698): Paris bookseller during the reign of Louis XIV.* Brown University, 1964. DAI 25/08, p. 4707. Order No. 65-2241.

SOLOMON, Howard Mitchell. *The innocent inventions of Theophraste Renaudot: public welfare, science, and propaganda in seventeenth century France.* Northwestern University, 1969. DAI 30/07-A, p. 2952. Order No. 70-163.

HENRY IV AND THE REGENCY, 1589-1624

DICKERMAN, Edmund Howard. *The kings' men: the minsters of Henry III and Henry IV, 1574-1610.* Brown University, 1965. DAI 26/08, p. 4602. Order No. 65-13,644.

HAYDEN, J. Michael. *The Estates General of 1614.* Loyola University of Chicago, 1963.

LINDSAY, Robert Orval. *Antoine Lefèvre de la Boderie's mission to England: a study of French-English relations, 1606-1611.* University of Oregon, 1966. DAI 27/03-A, p. 652. Order No. 66-8069.

MITCHELL, John H. *The tribunal of the Connétablie et Maréchaussée de France under Henri IV.* Yale University, 1941.

ROTHROCK, George A. *The French crown and the Estates General of 1614.* University of Minnesota, 1958. DAI 19/06, p. 1358. Order No. 58-7020.

SOMAN, Alfred. *Book censorship in France (1599-1607) with emphasis upon diplomatic relations between Paris and Rome.* Harvard University, 1968.

THOROUGHMAN, Thomas Vernon. *Some political aspects of Anglo-French relations, 1610-1619.* The University of North Carolina at Chapel Hill, 1968. DAI 30/01-A, p. 261. Order No. 69-10,209.

RICHELIEU AND LOUIS XIII, 1624-1642

BECKER, Michael Kelleher. *The Santarelli affair: a case study of ecclesiastical policy in the early years of the Richelieu ministry.* University of California, Berkeley, 1970. DAI 32/02-A, p. 870. Order No. 71-20,772.

COBB, William Henry. *French diplomatic relations with Spain: 1632-1635.* Tulane University, 1970. DAI 31/06-A, p. 2837. Order No. 70-24,513.

McKENNAN, William Whipple. *Gaston d'Orléans and the grands: the opposition to absolutism under Louis XIII.* Brown University, 1972.

MAZARIN, 1642-1661

DOOLIN, Paul R. *The Fronde.* Harvard University, 1934.

DYKEMA, Frank Edward. *Commercial rivalry between the French and the Dutch from 1646 to 1667.* University of Michigan, 1940.

FREUDMANN, Felix Raymond. *Memoirs of the Fronde. A literary study.* Columbia University, 1957. DAI 17/06, p. 1337. Order No. 21,114.

KORR, Charles Paul. *Cromwell and France, 1653-1658.* University of California, Los Angeles, 1969. DAI 30/11-A, p. 4915. Order No. 70-8169.

METZGER, Fraser Kirk. *The political role of the Prince of Conde during the Fronde.* Rutgers University, 1966. DAI 27/11-A, p. 3817. Order No. 67-5270.

MOOTE, Alanson Lloyd. *The Parlement of Paris, the French crown, and royal absolutism during the Fronde, 1643-1652.* University of Minnesota, 1958. DAI 19/10, p. 2591. Order No. 58-7016.

RUSSO, Severino A. *Unpublished letters of Jules Cardinal Mazarin written during the Fronde, 1649-1650.* University of Pennsylvania, 1967. DAI 28/10-A, p. 4074. Order No. 68-4612.

WESTRICH, Sal Alexander. *The Ormée of Bordeaux: a revolution within the Fronde.* Columbia University, 1970. DAI 33/10-A, p. 5666. Order No. 73-8993.

LOUIS XIV, 1661-1715

BINGHAM, Richard Boyd. *Louis XIV and the war for peace: the genesis of a peace offensive, 1686-1690.* University of Illinois at Chicago Circle, 1972. DAI 33/10-A, p. 5648. Order No. 73-8228.

BOGLE, Emory Crockett. *A stand for tradition: the rejection of the Anglo-French commercial Treaty of Utrecht.* University of Maryland, 1972. DAI 33/10-A, p. 5650. Order No. 73-9677.

EKBERG, Carl J. *From Dutch war to European war: a study in French high politics during 1673.* Rutgers University, 1970. DAI 31/11-A, p. 5981. Order No. 71-12,242.

FREGAULT, Guy. *La carriere de Pierre Le Moyne, Sieur D'Iberville.* Loyola University of Chicago, 1942.

GAEDDERT, Dale Albert. *The Franco-Bavarian alliance during the war of the Spanish succession.* Ohio State University, 1969. DAI 30/10-A, p. 4371. Order No. 70-6777.

GISSELQUIST, Orloue Neander. *The French ambassador, Jean Antoine de Mesmes, Comte d'Avaux, and French diplomacy at the Hague, 1678-1684.* University of Minnesota, 1968. DAI 29/08-A, p. 2639. Order No. 69-1502.

HANDEN, Ralph Donnelly, Jr. *The Savoy negotiations of the Comte de Tessé, 1693-1696.* Ohio State University, 1970. DAI 31/07-A, p. 3469. Order No. 70-26,296.

KLAITS, Joseph Aaron. *Diplomacy and public opinion. Louis XIV, Colbert de Torcy and French war propaganda, 1700-1713.* University of Minnesota, 1970. DAI 31/05-A, p. 2311. Order No. 70-20,203.

MARTIN, Ronald Dale. *The Marquis de Chamlay, friend and confidential advisor to Louis XIV: the early years, 1650-1691.* University of California, Santa Barbara, 1972. DAI 33/10-A, p. 5657. Order No. 73-8102.

O'CONNOR, John Thomas. *William Egon von Fürstenberg and French diplomacy in the Rhineland prior to the outbreak of the war of the League of Augsburg in 1688.* University of Minnesota, 1965. DAI 26/01, p. 340. Order No. 65-7900.

PLACE, Frank Richard. *French policy and the Turkish war, 1679-1688.* University of Minnesota, 1965. DAI 26/12, p. 7285. Order No. 65-1029.

RILEY, Philip F. *Moral rigorism in the character of Louis XIV: a study of the Sun King's interest in the moral behavior of Frenchmen between 1683 and 1715.* University of Notre Dame, 1971. DAI 32/05-A, p. 2617. Order No. 71-27,769.

ROOSEN, William James. *The ambassador's craft: a study of the functioning of French ambassadors under Louis XIV.* University of Southern California, 1967. DAI 28/07-A, p. 2632. Order No. 67-17,697.

ROTHKRUG, Lionel Nathan. *Government and reform in France, 1660-1700.* University of California, Berkeley, 1963. DAI 24/05, p. 2003. Order No. 63-5548.

ROWEN, Herbert Harvey. *Pomponne and De Witt (1669-1671): a study of the French policy on the eve of the Dutch war.* Columbia University, 1951. DAI 12/01, p. 50. Order No. 3381.

SAMRAS, Kharaiti R. *Colbert and the founding of the French East India Company.* University of California, Berkeley, 1934.

SHAPIRO, Sheldon. *The relations between Louis XIV and Leopold of Austria from the Treaty of Nymegen to the Truce of Ratisbon.* University of California, Los

Angeles, 1966. DAI 27/06-A, p. 1771. Order No. 66-11,920.

SONNINO, Paul Mark. *Louis XIV's correspondence, memoires, and his view of the papacy (1661-1667).* University of California, Los Angeles, 1964. DAI 24/12, p. 5368. Order No. 64-6386.

STURGILL, Claude C. *Marshall Villars in the war of the Spanish succession.* University of Kentucky, 1963. DAI 30/07-A, p. 2928. Order No. 70-314.

SYMCOX, Geoffrey Walter. *Louis XIV and the war in Ireland, 1689-91: a study of his strategic thinking and decision-making.* University of California, Los Angeles, 1967. DAI 28/06-A, p. 2191. Order No. 67-16,019.

VALONE, James Samuel. *The Huguenots and the war of the Spanish marriages.* University of Michigan, 1965. DAI 26/06, p. 3265. Order No. 65-11,053.

WILSON, Lester Newton. *François de Callières (1645-1717): diplomat and man of letters.* University of Illinois, 1963. DAI 24/05, p. 2006. Order No. 63-5161.

GOVERNMENT, ADMINISTRATION, EDUCATION, MILITARY

ASHER, Eugene Leon. *The resistance against the inscription maritime, principally in Languedoc and Provence, 1668-1690.* University of California, Los Angeles, 1958.

BAXTER, Douglas Clark. *French intendants of the army, 1630-1670.* University of Minnesota, 1971. DAI 32/10-A, p. 5700. Order No. 71-22,269.

BERNARD, Louis L. *Nicolas-Joseph Foucault: the case study of an intendant in the age of Louis XIV.* University of North Carolina at Chapel Hill, 1951.

FERGUSON, Ronald Thomas. *Blood and fire: contribution policy of the French armies in Germany (1668-1715).* University of Minnesota, 1970. DAI 32/01-A, p. 354. Order No. 71-18,722.

KIERSTEAD, Raymond Foster, Jr. *Pomponne de Bellièvre: a study of the*

elite of high administrators in the age of Henry IV. Northwestern University, 1964. DAI 25/06, p. 3539. Order No. 64-12,298.

RANUM, Orest Allen. *The creatures of Richelieu, a study of the secretaries of state and superintendents of finance in the ministry of Richelieu, 1635-1642.* University of Minnesota, 1960. DAI 21/10, p. 3081. Order No. 61-587.

ZACCANO, Joseph Peter, Jr. *French colonial administration in Canada to 1760.* University of Pittsburgh, 1961. DAI 23/03, p. 1007. Order No. 62-3410.

SOCIAL AND ECONOMIC

BAMFORD, Paul Walden. *French naval timber: a study of the relation of forests to French sea power, 1660-1789.* Columbia University, 1951. DAI 12/01, p. 41. Order No. 3318.

BITTON, Ronald Davis. *The French nobility as seen by contemporaries, 1560-1630.* Princeton University, 1961. DAI 23/05, p. 1669. Order No. 62-1881.

LOUGEE, Carolyn Edna Chappell. *Feminism and social stratification in seventeenth-century France.* University of Michigan, 1972. DAI 33/09-A, p. 5097. Order No. 73-6868.

ONION, Charles Clary. *The social status of musicians in seventeenth century France.* University of Minnesota, 1959. DAI 20/06, p. 2238. Order No. 59-5084.

SIPPEL, Cornelius, III. *The Noblesse de la Robe in early seventeenth-century France: a study in social mobility.* University of Michigan, 1963. DAI 24/04, p. 1598. Order No. 63-6953.

WEBSTER, Jonathan Howes. *The merchants of Bordeaux in trade to the French West Indies, 1664-1717.* University of Minnesota, 1972. DAI 33/11-A, p. 6293. Order No. 73-10,651.

REGIONAL STUDIES

BEIK, William Humphrey. *Governing Languedoc: the practical functioning of absolutism in a French province, 1633-1685.* Harvard University, 1969.

FESSENDEN, Nicholas Buck. *Epernon and Guyenne: provincial politics under Louis XIII.* Columbia University, 1972. DAI 33/10-A, p. 5637. Order No. 73-9013.

HURT, John Jeter. *The Parlement of Brittany in the reign of Louis XIV.* University of North Carolina at Chapel Hill, 1970. DAI 31/05-A, p. 2309. Order No. 70-21,200.

KETTERING, Sharon Kathleen. *Red robes and barricades: the Parlement of Aix-en-Provence in a period of popular revolt, 1629-1649.* Stanford University, 1969. DAI 30/12A, p. 5385. Order No. 70-10,472.

LOWENSTEIN, Steven Mark. *Resistance to absolutism: Huguenot organization in Languedoc, 1621-1622.* Princeton University, 1972. DAI 33/05-A, p. 2294. Order No. 72-29,801.

PEARL, Johathan Lewis. *Guise and Provence: political conflict in the epoch of Richelieu.* Northwestern University, 1968. DAI 29/11A, p. 3961. Order No. 69-6975.

TROUT, Andrew Patrick. *The jurisdiction and role of the municipality of Paris during the Colbert ministry: a study based on registres des délibérations du bureau de la ville.* University of Notre Dame, 1968. DAI 29/09-A, p. 3061. Order No. 69-4083.

INTELLECTUAL AND CULTURAL

BOWERS, Alice Tremain. *Allusions to the private life of Louis XIV in the dramatic literature of the seventeenth century.* University of Missouri, 1968. DAI 29/08-A, p. 2701. Order No. 69-3215.

BURKETT, John Howard. *Descartes: a sympathetic reading.* University of Texas at Austin, 1971. DAI 32/10-A, p. 5835. Order No. 72-11,324.

BUTTURFF, Diane Livingston. *The ambigu de vers et de prose: the art of polite satire in seventeenth century France.* The University of Illinois at Urbana-Champaign,

1970. DAI 31/09-A, p. 4756. Order No. 71-5063.

CAMPBELL, Lytle Blair. *The ideology of egocentrism in seventeenth and eighteenth century France: some proponents and antagonists.* Princeton University, 1966. DAI 27/07-A, p. 2180. Order No. 66-13,297.

DERBY, Roger Dan. *Some medieval religious and philosophical survivals in seventeenth century France.* University of Minnesota, 1953. DAI 13/05, p. 769. Order No. 5527.

EMONT, Milton David. *Seventeenth-century French society in the novels of Charles Sorel.* The University of Wisconsin, 1958. DAI 18/06, p. 2139. Order No. 58-1896.

GREEN, Robert William. *The political theories of Bishop Bossuet and Louis XIV.* State University of Iowa, 1953. DAI 13/03, p. 378. Order No. 4968.

HIRSCHFIELD, John M. *The Académie Royale des Sciences (1666-83): inauguration and initial problems of method.* University of Chicago, 1958.

ISHERWOOD, Robert M. *Music in the service of the royal absolutism: France in the seventeenth century.* University of Chicago, 1965.

ISRAELS, Elisabeth Miriam. *The historical argument in French religious controversy, 1671-1691.* University of California, Los Angeles, 1967. DAI 28/01-A, p. 1765. Order No. 67-14,267.

KING, James E. *Science and nationalism in the government of Louis XIV, 1661-1683.* Johns Hopkins University, 1948.

LANDER, John Albert. *The new life and its educational correlates in France from Rabelais to Rousseau.* University of Pennsylvania, 1962. DAI 23/04, p. 1265. Order No. 62-4319.

LEFFLER, Phyllis Koran. *L'histoire raisonnée: a study of French historiography, 1660-1720.* Ohio State University, 1971. DAI 32/07-A, p. 3895. Order No. 72-4546.

McMILLAN, Cynthia Anne. *The concept of the mathematical infinite in French thought, 1670-1760.* University of Virginia, 1970. DAI 31/09-A, p. 4683. Order No. 70-26,571.

MILLER, Leslie Coombs. *Music and poetry in seventeenth-century France.* The University of Rochester, 1969. DAI 30/09-A, p. 3950. Order No. 70-2891.

MORBY, John Edwin. *Musicians at the royal chapel of Versailles, 1683-1792.* University of California, Berkeley, 1971.

ROELKER, Annie L. *Pierre de l'Estoile's account of the Paris League.* Radcliffe College, 1953.

SOULEYMAN, Elizabeth V. *The vision of world peace in seventeenth and eighteenth-century France.* Columbia University, 1941.

STEEN, Charlie Rupert, III. *A survey of the notion of Christendom principally in France, 1580-1690.* University of California, Los Angeles, 1970. DAI 31/08-A, p. 4102. Order No. 71-4882.

THORMANN, Wolfgang Ernst. *Attitudes of seventeenth century France toward Germany.* Columbia University, 1955. DAI 15/07, p. 1238. Order No. 12,073.

WYNN, Malcolm Morgan. *Agrippa d'Aubigné: Huguenot historian.* Ohio State University, 1958. DAI 19/09, p. 2332. Order No. 59-434.

RELIGION

CALLAHAN, Maria Theresa. *The gallicanism of Claude Fleury.* Boston College, 1971.

CHILL, Emanuel Stanley. *The Company of the Holy Sacrament (1630-1666): social aspects of the French counter-reformation.* Columbia University, 1960. DAI 21/07, p. 1925. Order No. 60-5085.

DINSMORE, Richard B. *Pierre Bayle and the development of the idea of religious liberty in late seventeenth century France.* New York University, 1971. DAI 32/10-A, p. 5705. Order No. 72-13,347.

DOSH, Terence Leonard. *The growth of the congregation of Saint Maur, 1618-1672.* University of Minnesota, 1971. DAI 32/05-A, p. 2596. Order No. 71-28,230.

KLEINMAN, Ruth. *Saint François de Sales and the Protestants.* Columbia University, 1959. DAI 20/02, p. 652. Order No. 59-2854)

KLEVGARD, Paul Albert. *Society and politics in counter-reformation France: a study of Bérulle, Vincent de Paul, Olier, and Bossuet.* Northwestern University, 1971. DAI 32/06-A, p. 3211. Order No. 71-30, 71-30,858.

SCHLOSSBERG, Herbert. *Pierre Bayle and the politics of the Huguenot Diaspora.* University of Minnesota, 1965. DAI 27/12-A, p. 4202. Order No. 67-8061.

WILL, Joseph Stanley. *Protestantism in France.* Columbia University, 1921.

THE EIGHTEENTH CENTURY, 1715-1789

GENERAL AND MISCELLANEOUS

ABARCA, Ramón Eugenio. *Bourbon 'revanche' against England: the balance of power, 1763-1770.* University of Notre Dame, 1965. DAI 27/04-A, p. 1010. Order No. 66-10,157.

ACOMB, Frances Dorothy. *Anti-English opinion in France, 1763-89.* University of Chicago, 1943.

CAVANAUGH, Gerald John. *Vauban, d'Argenson, Turgot: from absolutism to constitutionalism in eighteenth-century*

France. Columbia University, 1967. DAI 28/04-A, p. 1368. Order No. 67-12,240.

CORWIN, Edward Samuel. *French policy and the American alliance of 1778.* University of Pennsylvania, 1905.

DALTON, Roy Clinton. *The history of the Jesuits' estates. 1760-1888.* University of Minnesota, 1957. DAI 18/01, p. 212. Order No. 23,929.

DONAGHAY, Marie Martenis. *The Anglo-French negotiations of 1786-1787.* University of Virginia, 1970. DAI 31/09-A, p. 4668. Order No. 71-6667.

DUDDY, Frank Edward, Jr. *The d'Argenson strategy and French diplomacy, 1748-1756.* Harvard University, 1942.

DULL, Jonathan Romer. *The French Navy and American independence: naval factors in French diplomacy and war strategy, 1774-1780.* University of California, Berkeley, 1972. DAI 33/03-A, p. 1106. Order No. 72-24,439.

FOX, Frank. *French-Russian commercial relations in the eighteenth century and the French-Russian commercial treaty of 1787.* University of Delaware, 1966. DAI 28/12-A, p. 4988. Order No. 67-11,724.

HACKMANN, William Kent. *English military expeditions to the coast of France, 1757-1761.* The University of Michigan, 1969. DAI 30/09-A, p. 3884. Order No. 70-4094.

HALL, Thadd E. *France and the eighteenth century Corsican question.* University of Minnesota, 1966. DAI 27/09-A, p. 2986. Order No. 67-1484.

HARDY, James Daniel, Jr. *The Parlement of Paris during the Regency, 1715-1723.* University of Pennsylvania, 1961. DAI 22/04, p. 1140. Order No. 61-3521.

HUDSON, David Carl. *Maupeou and the Parlements: a study in propaganda and politics.* Columbia University, 1967. DAI 28/10-A, p. 4093. Order No. 68-5601.

KENNEDY, John Hopkins. *New France and the European conscience. I. The matter of New France.* Yale University, 1942. DAI

31/01-A, p. 340. Order No. 70-10,719.

KILLION, Howard Ray. *The Suffren expedition: French operations in India during the War of American Independence.* Duke University, 1972. DAI 33/10-A, p. 5654. Order No. 73-8084.

KRAUSKOPF, Frances C. *The French in Indiana, 1700-1760: a political history.* Indiana University, 1953. DAI 13/05, p. 781. Order No. 5869.

LAMBERT, Francis X. *The foreign policy of the Duke de Choiseul, 1763-1770.* Harvard University, 1953.

LUNN, Jean. *Economic development in New France—1713-1760.* McGill University, 1943.

LUPO, Larry Waller. *The Abbé Ferdinando Galiani in Paris, 1759-1769.* University of Georgia, 1971. DAI 32/09-A, p. 5155. Order No. 72-10,998.

MENG, John Joseph. *The Comte de Vergennes; European phases of his American diplomacy (1774-1780).* Catholic University of America, 1932.

MIDDLETON, Robert Nelson. *French policy and Prussia after the peace of Aix-La-Chapelle, 1749-1753: a study of the pre-history of the diplomatic revolution of 1756.* Columbia University, 1968. DAI 28/12-A, p. 4972. Order No. 68-8600.

MURPHY, Orville Theodore, Jr. *French contemporary opinion of the American Revolutionary Army.* University of Minnesota, 1957. DAI 18/03, p. 1024. Order No. 24,670.

OLIVA, Lawrence Jay. *French policy in Russia: 1755-1762.* Syracuse University, 1960. DAI 22/01, p. 240. Order No. 61-1497.

OTT, Edward R. *The influence of church and trade on French colonial policy as seen in the history of Detroit, 1700-1752.* Northwestern University, 1937.

PACHECO, Josephine F. *French secret agents in America, 1763-1778.* University of Chicago, 1951.

PULLEY, Judith Poss. *Thomas Jefferson at the court of Versailles: an American philosophe and the coming of the French Revolution.* University of Virginia, 1966. DAI 27/08-A, p. 2485. Order No. 66-15,193.

RAMSEY, John F. *Anglo-French relations, 1763-1770: a study of Choiseul's foreign policy.* University of California, Berkeley, 1935.

RAVITCH, Norman. *Government and episcopate in the age of aristocracy: France and England in the 18th century.* Princeton University, 1962. DAI 23/08, p. 2896. Order No. 63-554.

SEDGWICK, Charlene Maute. *The politics of the Cour Des Aides of Paris, 1750-1771.* Harvard University, 1969.

SINGH, Roopnarine John. *French foreign policy, 1763-1778, with special reference to the Caribbean.* The University of Oklahoma, 1972. DAI 33/10-A, p. 5640. Order No. 73-9173.

SMITH, Ronald Dwight. *French interests in Louisiana: from Choiseul to Napoleon.* University of Southern California, 1964. DAI 25/06, p. 3545. Order No. 64-13,539.

STINCHCOMBE, William Charles. *The French-American alliance in American politics, 1778-1783.* The University of Michigan, 1967. DAI 28/06-A, p. 2191. Order No. 67-15,702.

THOMPSON, Virginia M. *Dupleix and his letters (1742-1745).* Columbia University, 1934.

WALSH, Mary Madeline. *The role of Dubois in French foreign affairs, 1715-1721.* Fordham University, 1965. DAI 26/04, p. 2172. Order No. 65-9519.

WINZERLING, Oscar W. *The removal of Acadians from France to Louisiana: 1763-1785.* University of California, Berkeley, 1949.

ZOLTVANY, Yves-François. *Philippe de Rigaud de Vaudreuil, governor of New France (1703-1725).* University of Alberta, 1964.

GOVERNMENT, ADMINISTRATION, EDUCATION, MILITARY

BAILEY, Charles Randall. *The college at Moulins (1761-1780): an example of the former Jesuit colleges outside Paris but within the jurisdiction of the Parlement of Paris.* University of Chicago, 1969.

BEIK, Paul H. *A judgment of the old régime, being a survey by the Parlement of Provence of French economic and fiscal policies at the close of the Seven Years War.* Columbia University, 1944.

BOULLE, Pierre Henri. *The French colonies and the reform of their administration during and following the Seven Years' War.* University of California, Berkeley, 1968. DAI 29/12-A, p. 4412. Order No. 69-10,257.

GRUDER, Vivian Rebecca. *The Royal Provincial Intendants: a governing elite in eighteenth-century France.* Harvard University, 1966.

GUERLAC, Henry Edward. *Science and war in the old regime.* Harvard University, 1941.

KENNETT, Lee Boone. *The French armies in the Seven Years' War: a study in military organization and administration.* University of Virginia, 1962. DAI 23/11, p. 4333. Order No. 62-5930.

MATTHEWS, George Tennyson. *The royal general farms in eighteenth-century France with special reference to the period 1726 to 1786.* Columbia University, 1954. DAI 14/09, p. 1380. Order No. 8730.

QUIMBY, Robert Sherman. *The antecedents of Napoleonic warfare: a study of military theory in eighteenth century France.* Columbia University, 1952. DAI 12/05, p. 740. Order No. 4232.

WRONG, Charles John. *The French infantry officer at the close of the Ancien Régime.* Brown University, 1968. DAI 30/01-A, p. 264. Order No. 69-10,037.

SOCIAL AND ECONOMIC

ADAMS, Thomas McStay. *An approach to the problem of beggary in eighteenth-*

century France: the dépôts de mendicité.
The University of Wisconsin, 1972. DAI
33/07-A, p. 3520. Order No. 72-27,307.

ALLEN, Turner Wharton. *The highway and
canal system in eighteenth-century France.*
University of Kentucky, 1953. DAI
20/09, p. 3703. Order No. 60-628.

BARBER, Elinor G. *The position of the
bourgeoisie in the class structure of 18th
century France.* Radcliffe College, 1951.

BRANDENBURG, David John. *French
agriculture: technology and enlightened
reform, 1750-1789.* Columbia University,
1954. DAI 14/08, p. 1206. Order No.
8616.

CARSON, John Woodruff. *The social position of a French lawyer (1718-1763): an
appraisal of the advocate Barbier.* The University of Nebraska, 1957. DAI 17/09,
p. 1990. Order No. 22,126.

CLINCH, Vernie Clinel Francesco. *The
problem of unemployment relief in France
during the revolutionary eighteenth century.* University of Kansas, 1949. DAI
11/03, p. 653. Order No. 2502.

DUNHAM, Douglas. *The French element in
the American fur trade, 1760-1816.* The
University of Michigan, 1950. DAI 10/04,
p. 193. Order No. 1961.

FORD, Franklin L. *The high noblesse de
robe and the regrouping of the French
aristocracy, 1715-1748.* Harvard University, 1950.

FOSTER, Charles A. *Honoring commerce
and industry in eighteenth-century France:
a case study of changes in traditional social
functions.* Harvard University, 1950.

FRIEDMAN, Leonard M. *The nature and
role of women as conceived by representa-
tive authors of eighteenth century France.*
New York University, 1970. DAI 31/10-A,
p. 5400. Order No. 71-5611.

GREENLAW, Ralph Weller, Jr. *The French
nobility on the eve of the revolution: a
study of its aims and attitudes, 1787-89.*
Princeton University, 1952. DAI 15/04,
p. 569. Order No. 11,218.

HAFTER, Daryl Maslow. *Critics of mercantilism in France, 1751-1789: the industrial*

reformers. Yale University, 1964. DAI
26/09, p. 5397. Order No. 66-1135.

HEDMAN, Edwin Randolph. *Early French
feminism: from the eighteenth century to
1848.* New York University, 1954. DAI
17/10, p. 2253. Order No. 22,950.

HERTZBERG, Arthur. *The Jews in France
before the revolution: prelude to emancipation.* Columbia University, 1966. DAI
30/04-A, p. 1499. Order No. 69-15,558.

KLIN, George. *Woman in eighteenth century
French fiction.* Wayne State University,
1963. DAI 28/11-A, p. 4633. Order No.
68-6656.

MASON, Paul Taylor, Jr. *Industrial technology in the Encyclopédie.* St. Louis University, 1964. DAI 25/08, p. 4673. Order
No. 64-13,446.

ROBERTS, Warren Errol. *Mortality and the
social classes in eighteenth century French
literature and painting.* University of
California, Berkeley, 1966. DAI 28/05-A,
p. 1745. Order No. 67-5149.

ROGERS, John West, Jr. *The opposition to
the physiocrats: a study of economic
thought and policy in the Ancien Regime,
1750-1780.* The Johns Hopkins University,
1971. DAI 32/05-A, p. 2618. Order No.
71-29,179.

SMITH, Cecil Oliver, Jr. *The Parisian
bourgeoisie under Louis XVI and Louis
Philippe: education and marriage.* Harvard
University, 1959.

THOMPSON, Dorothy Gillian. *The confiscation and administration of Jesuit property under the jurisdiction of the Parlement
of Paris, 1762-1798.* University of British
Columbia, 1972.

WILLIAMS, Preston B. *The French
bourgeoisie on the eve of the revolution.*
University of Texas at Austin, 1950.

REGIONAL STUDIES

DATER, Henry M. *Municipal administration
of Lyon, 1764-1790.* Yale University, 1936.

SHEPPARD, Thomas Frederick. *A provincial village in eighteenth century France:
Lourmarin, 1680-1800.* The Johns Hopkins

University, 1969. DAI 33/02-A, p. 710. Order No. 72-16,871.

VILES, Perry. *The shipping interest of Bordeaux, 1774-1793.* Harvard University, 1965.

INTELLECTUAL AND CULTURAL*

BARNETT, Gary Lew. *A comparison of the moral and political ideas of Jean-Jacques Rousseau and Jean-Jacques Burlamaqui.* University of Arizona, 1970. DAI 31/05-A, p. 2373. Order No. 70-20,702.

BARZUN, Jacques. *The French race: theories of its origins and their social and political implications prior to the revolution.* Columbia University, 1932.

BILLINGSLEY, Susan Vaughan. *L'Académie Royale des Sciences, Paris, 1785-1793: an interpretation.* University of California, Berkeley, 1958.

BURKHARDT, Richard Wellington, Jr. *The evolutionary thought of Jean-Baptiste Lamarck.* Harvard University, 1972.

CHAPIN, Seymour Leon. *Astronomy and the Paris Academy of Sciences during the eighteenth century.* University of California, Los Angeles, 1964. DAI 25/06, p. 3531. Order No. 64-12,181.

CLARK, Beatrice Stith. *The development of the nature-man motif in the rustic novel from Rousseau to Giono.* The George Washington University, 1969. DAI 30/08-A, p. 3426. Order No. 70-2347.

COLEMAN, William Robert. *Georges Cuvier and the fixity of species.* Harvard University, 1962.

CONNELLY, James Leo, Jr. *The movement to create a national gallery of art in eighteenth-century France.* University of Kansas, 1962. DAI 24/02, p. 713. Order No. 63-5634.

CRAWFORD, Frederic Mull, Jr. *The* Mercure Historique et Politique *1715-1781: a critical analysis.* University of Kentucky, 1969. DAI 31/01-A, p. 335. Order No. 70-12,344.

---

* See next section for the French Enlightenment.

DE RYCKE, Robert Marie Emile. *The preoccupations of Pierre Bayle in the* Dictionnaire Historique et Critique. University of Illinois, 1966. DAI 27/07-A, p. 2149. Order No. 66-12,313.

ERICKSON, Robert Finn. *The French Academy of Sciences expedition to Spanish America 1735-1744.* University of Illinois, 1955. DAI 16/03, p. 523. Order No. 15,202.

EVERDELL, William R. *Christian apologetics in France from 1750 to the Concordat of 1801.* New York University, 1972. DAI 33/11-A, p. 6270. Order No. 73-11,691.

GALLANAR, Joseph Milton. *Studies in the idea of anxiety and dissolution in French thought from Jean-Jacques Rousseau to Pierre Simon Ballanche.* The Johns Hopkins University, 1959.

GARRETT, Clarke William. *French nationalism on the eve of the French revolution.* The University of Wisconsin, 1961. DAI 22/06, p. 1960. Order No. 61-5926.

GILLMOR, Charles Stewart. *Charles Augustin Coulomb: physics and engineering in eighteenth century France.* Princeton University, 1968. DAI 29/08-A, p. 2622. Order No. 69-2741.

GREENE, John C. *The discovery of the history of nature, natural history and world view in the eighteenth century.* Harvard University, 1952.

GRIFFIN, Janet. *Anticlericalism among the Englist deists.* St. Louis University, 1969. DAI 31/05-A, p. 2307. Order No. 70-20,392.

HEALY, George Robert. *Mechanistic science and the French Jesuits: a study of the responses of the* Journal de Trevoux *(1701-1762) to Descartes and Newton.* University of Minnesota, 1956. DAI 17/05, p. 1065. Order No. 20,515.

HUBBARD, Genevieve G. *French travelers in America, 1775-1840: a study of their observations.* American University, 1936.

JENNISON, Earl Wilson, Jr. *Intrigue and philosophy: Prussia in Mirabeau's career and thought.* Columbia University, 1969.

67

DAI 33/01-A, p. 238. Order No. 72-19,067.

KESSLER, Eugene Edmond. *The role of Abraham Chaumeix'* Préjugés *in the official condemnation of the* Encyclopédie. University of California, Irvine, 1970. DAI 31/08-A, p. 4123. Order No. 71-4279.

KNAPP, Richard Gilbert. *The fortunes of Pope's* Essay on Man *in eighteenth-century France: Du Resnel, Silhouette, Voltaire and Fontanes.* Columbia University, 1969. DAI 32/11-A, p. 6380. Order No. 72-15,580.

KOHLER, Maurice Emile. *L'image de Louis XIV en France avant 1750.* The University of Connecticut, 1969. DAI 30/02-A, p. 728. Order No. 69-12,744.

KOSTOROSKI, Emilie Pauline. *Corneille and Racine in the literary criticism of eighteenth-century France.* Case Western Reserve University, 1970. DAI 31/07-A, p. 3553. Order No. 70-25,880.

LEITH, James Andrews. *The idea of art as propaganda in France 1750-1799: a study in the history of ideas.* University of Toronto, 1961.

LEVY, Darline Gay Shapiro. *Social realism and the politics of revolt in eighteenth century France: an intellectual portrait of Simon Nicolas Henri Linguet (1736-1794).* Harvard University, 1968.

MACCANNELL, Juliet Flower. *The autobiography of the fictional self: reflections on the problem of fiction in* Rousseau Juge de Jean-Jacques. Cornell University, 1971. DAI 32/09-A, p. 5235. Order No. 72-8963.

McNEIL, Gordon H. *The cult of Rousseau and the revolutionary spirit in France, 1750-1800.* University of Chicago, 1941.

MARSAK, Leonard Mendes. *Bernard de Fontenelle: the idea of science in eighteenth century France.* Cornell University, 1957. DAI 17/11, p. 2583. Order No. 23,138.

NEWCOMB, Donald Richard. *The evolution of ethical thought in the eighteenth-century French novel.* University of Missouri,

1967. DAI 28/08-A, p. 3194. Order No. 68-320.

O'CONNOR, Thomas A., Sister. *An evaluation of Voltaire's method of writing history.* Saint Louis University, 1949.

PALMER, Robert R. *The French idea of American independence on the eve of the French revolution.* Cornell University, 1934.

PASKVAN, Raymond Frank. *The Jardin du Roi: the growth of its plant collection (1715-1750).* University of Minnesota, 1971. DAI 32/07-A, p. 3930. Order No. 71-28,304.

PERMENTER, Wayne Edward. *The academy of science at Toulouse in the eighteenth century.* The University of Texas at Austin, 1964. DAI 25/09, p. 5244. Order No. 65-4341.

RAPPAPORT, Rhoda. *Guettard, Lavoisier, and Monnet: geologists in the service of the French monarchy.* Cornell University, 1964. DAI 25/06, p. 3544. Order No. 64-13,136.

RICHTMAN, Jack. *Adrienne Lecouvreur: actress and woman under the Ancien Régime.* Columbia University, 1969. DAI 30/05-A, p. 1993. Order No. 69-17,612.

SEGAL, Lester Abraham. *Nicholas Lenglet du Fresnoy (1674-1755): a study of historical criticism and methodology in early eighteenth-century France.* Columbia University, 1968. DAI 30/02-A, p. 641. Order No. 69-13,000.

SINGLETON, Ira Custer. *The rationality of eighteenth century musical classicism: a study of the relationships between the rationalistic philosophies of Descartes, Spinoza and Leibniz and the classicism of Haydn, Mozart and Beethoven.* New York University, 1954. DAI 14/05, p. 842. Order No. 8012.

STOUFFER, Phyllis Carol. *Voltaire as Horatian lyric poet.* The Pennsylvania State University, 1969. DAI 31/04-A, p. 1816. Order No. 70-19,479.

STRICKLEN, Charles Gilmer, Jr. *The emergence of modern liberal constitutionalism in France, 1770-1789.* Yale University,

1966. DAI 27/08-A, p. 2488. Order No. 66-15,019.

THIELEMANN, Leland James. *The tradition of Hobbes in eighteenth-century France.* Columbia University, 1950. DAI 11/02, p. 388. Order No. 2489.

VAHLKAMP, Charles Gustav. *Voltaire's literary career: 1770-1778.* Vanderbilt University, 1970. DAI 31/06-A, p. 2943. Order No. 70-24,896.

VARTANIAN, Aram. *Diderot and Descartes: the role of Cartesian ideas in the growth of scientific naturalism in eighteenth-century France.* Columbia University, 1951. DAI 11/04, p. 1078. Order No. 2866.

VYVERBERG, Henry S. *Decadence and historical flux: French anti-progressionist thought in the eighteenth century (1715-1789).* Harvard University, 1950.

WARDEN, Annie Chirac. *La notion d'espace dans un choix de romans français de la deuxième moitié du XVIIIᵉ siècle.* University of Southern California, 1971. DAI 32/05-A, p. 265. Order No. 71-27,966.

WITSCHI, Astrid Nilsdotter Bernz. *The evolution of theoretical historical methodology in France and Germany: 1690-1770.* Harvard University, 1971.

WORMUTH, Diana Wells. *Epistemology and scepticism in the* Encyclopédie: *the Pyrrhonian tradition and the emergence of modern scientific methodology.* Yale University, 1972. DAI 33/07-A, p. 3608. Order No. 73-805.

INTELLECTUAL AND CULTURAL — THE FRENCH ENLIGHTENMENT

ADE, Walter Frank Charles. *Voltaire on education.* Indiana University, 1960. DAI 21/03, p. 537. Order No. 60-2988.

ANDERSON, Jane Jaspersen. *Political necessity in the literature of the French Enlightenment: Diderot and the* Encyclopédie. Brown University, 1962. DAI 23/06, p. 2104. Order No. 63-1002.

BOSS, Ronald Ian. *Rousseau's answer to Bayle's paradox—the civil religion and the meaning of belief.* Columbia University,

1970. DAI 33/07-A, p. 3524. Order No. 72-33,410.

BRIGGS, Josiah M., Jr. *D'Alembert: mechanics, matter, and morals.* Columbia University, 1962. DAI 24/04, p. 1584. Order No. 63-6103.

CALLAHAN, Anne Marie. *The role of the legislator in the political philosophy of the eighteenth century French philosophes.* Case Western Reserve University, 1970. DAI 31/06-A, p. 2907. Order No. 70-25,853.

CARSON, George B., Jr. *The Chevalier de Chastellux, soldier and philosophe.* University of Chicago, 1942.

CHAPMAN, John William. *Rousseau and liberalism.* Columbia University, 1954. DAI 14/12, p. 2384. Order No. 8627.

COOK, Terrence Edward. *Rousseau: education and politics.* Princeton University, 1971. DAI 32/03-A, p. 1578. Order No. 71-23,352.

DEDECK-HÉRY, Ernestine. *Jean-Jacques Rousseau et le projet de constitution pour la Corse; histoire des pourparlers de J.-J. Rousseau avec ses correspondants corses et des répercussions de ces pourparlers dans le monde des lettres.* University of Pennsylvania, 1932.

GOLIN, Stephen Jeffrey. *Madame de Stael and the rejection of happiness: a study in the end of the enlightenment.* Brandeis University, 1968. DAI 29/08-A, p. 2641. Order No. 69-2051.

GONZALEZ, Carlos Ignacio. *J. J. Rousseau, metaphysician of human nature.* St. Louis University, 1970. DAI 32/02-A, p. 1015. Order No. 71-21,390.

HAMILTON, James Francis. *Rousseau's socio-political concept of literature.* The Ohio State University, 1970. DAI 31/04-A, p. 1800. Order No. 70-19,315.

JARRETT, Horace Marshall. *D'Alembert and the* Encyclopédie. Duke University, 1962. DAI 24/05, p. 1999. Order No. 63-7507.

KAPLAN, Jane Payne. *On the margin of philosophy: the abbé Coyer in the French*

Enlightenment. The Louisiana State University and Agricultural and Mechanical College, 1970. DAI 31/04-A, p. 1802. Order No. 70-18,538.

KNIGHT, Isabel Frances. *Condillac: a study in the geometric spirit of the French Enlightenment.* Yale University, 1964.

KORS, Alan Charles. *The Coterie Holbachique: an enlightenment in Paris.* Harvard University, 1969.

KRA, Pauline. *Religion in Montesquieu's Lettres Persanes.* Columbia University, 1968. DAI 31/10-A, p. 5365. Order No. 71-6206.

LANGDON, David Jeffrey. *Diderot's moral and social thought.* The University of British Columbia, 1970. DAI 31/12-A, p. 6616.

LIBBY, Margaret S. *The attitude of Voltaire to magic and the sciences.* Columbia University, 1935.

MALKIN, Edward Ezekiel. *Aspects of stoicism in Diderot and Rousseau.* The University of Arizona, 1972. DAI 33/06-A, p. 2862. Order No. 72-31,849.

MARSHALL, Terence Edward. *Freedom and nature in Rousseau's political philosophy.* University of Pennsylvania, 1972. DAI 33/07-A, p. 3730. Order No. 73-1419.

MEYER, Henry Pierre. *Voltaire: philosophe pacifiste?* University of Maryland, 1970. DAI 31/08-A, p. 4129. Order No. 71-4075.

O'KEEFE, Cyril Blaise. *Contemporary reactions to the Enlightenment, 1728-1762. A study of three critical journals: the Jesuit* Journal de Trévoux, *the Jansenist* Nouvecles ecclésiastiques, *and the secular* Journal des Savants. University of Toronto, 1959.

PETERSON, Ronald Maurice. *The moral philosophy of Montesquieu.* Claremont Graduate School, 1972. DAI 33/09-A, p. 5255. Order No. 73-7234.

POOR, Matile Rothschild. *A study of the political ideas of Denis Diderot.* Columbia University, 1969. DAI 30/10-A, p. 4382. Order No. 70-7047.

RIZK, Samir Habib. *Le réalisme chez Diderot: image de la société contemporaine.* University of Illinois at Urbana-Champaign, 1970. DAI 31/05-A, p. 2399. Order No. 70-21,051.

ROCKWOOD, Raymond O. *The cult of Voltaire (1778-91).* University of Chicago, 1935.

ROGERS, Adrienne. *References to Voltaire and Rousseau in the manuscript journal (1750-1769) of Joseph D'Hémery.* State University of New York at Albany, 1970. DAI 31/06-A, p. 2888. Order No. 70-25,476.

SANDOMIRSKY, Lilian Natalie. *Diderot et la morale.* Yale University, 1956. DAI 31/05-A, p. 2354. Order No. 70-20,363.

SCHLERETH, Thomas John. *The cosmopolitan ideal in Enlightenment thought: its form and function in the ideas of Franklin, Hume, and Voltaire, 1694-1790.* State University of Iowa, 1969. DAI 30/07-A, p. 2951. Order No. 69-21,725.

SHERMAN, Sandra Elaine. *A portrait of woman through the eyes of Denis Diderot.* Columbia University, 1968. DAI 32/01-A, p. 400. Order No. 71-17,618.

STREIFF, Eric Jewell. *The politics of Enlightenment historiography. Studies in the development of historical thought in France, Scotland, and Germany during the later eighteenth century.* Yale University, 1969. DAI 30/08-A, p. 3415. Order No. 70-2810.

VANCE, Christie McDonald. La Nouvelle Héloïse: *a study of the pastoral vision in Rousseau.* Yale University, 1969. DAI 30/08-A, p. 3438. Order No. 70-2824.

WEBER, Marie-Louise. *Présence de Montaigne dans les* Rêveries de Rousseau. Rice University, 1970. DAI 31/06-A, p. 2945. Order No. 70-23,592.

WESTBROOK, Rachel Horwitz. *John Turberville Needham and his impact on the French Enlightenment.* Columbia University, 1972. DAI 33/07-A, p. 3606. Order No. 72-28,111.

WILBERGER, Carolyn Hope. *Voltaire, Russia, and the party of civilization.* Cornell University, 1972. DAI 33/04-A, p. 1748. Order No. 72-27,991.

WITTES, Sarah-Sue. *La Nouvelle Héloïse: Rousseau and authority.* Columbia University, 1970. DAI 31/09-A, p. 4741. Order No. 71-6277.

YOUNG, David Bruce. *Montesquieu's standards and his relativism in the* Lettres Persanes: *their origins, significance, and development.* Columbia University, 1971. DAI 32/06-A, p. 3236. Order No. 72-1409.

RELIGION

ADAMS, Francis G. W. *The struggle of the French Protestants for civil rights (1750-1787).* University of Chicago, 1955.

ARMAND, Laura Maslow. *Protestantism in La Rochelle, 1755-1830: the consequences of bourgeois rule.* Harvard University, 1969.

BELLEROSE, Leo M. *The ecclesiastical theory of the Parlement of Paris in the eighteenth century.* Georgetown University, 1947.

BIEN, David Duckworth. *Calas and the Catholics—the end of religious persecution in the Old Regime, 1750-1789.* Harvard University, 1958.

BREATHETT, George Amitheat. *The religious missions in colonial French Saint-Domingue.* State University of Iowa, 1954. DAI 14/12, p. 2323. Order No. 9570.

DELANGLEZ, Jean. *The French Jesuits in lower Louisiana (1700-1763).* Catholic University of America, 1935.

GREENBAUM, Louis S. *The ecclesiastical career of Charles-Maurice de Talleyrand-Périgord, 1780-1788.* Harvard University, 1955.

KREISER, Bernard Robert. *Miracles and convulsions in Paris, 1727-1737: an episode in the politics of religion during the ancien régime.* University of Chicago, 1971.

MAXWELL, Margaret. *The French Protestants in the eighteenth century: the struggle for civil rights and the advent of tolerance.* New York University, 1952.

RICHTER, Jean Beatrice. *Currents of spirituality in eighteenth century France: nuns, sisters, and philosophes.* University of Wisconsin, 1972. DAI 33/04-A, p. 1658. Order No. 72-22,112.

VAN KLEY, Dale Kenneth. *The Jansenists and the expulsion of the Jesuits from France, 1757-1765.* Yale University, 1970. DAI 32/01-A, p. 373. Order No. 71-17,157.

WILLIAMS, William Hayes. *The priest in history: a study in divided loyalties in the French lower clergy from 1776 to 1789.* Duke University, 1965. DAI 27/02-A, p. 449. Order No. 66-7930.

THE REVOLUTION AND THE NAPOLEONIC EMPIRE, 1789-1815

GENERAL AND MISCELLANEOUS

BONAR, Hugh S., Jr. *Joachim Murat, soldier of the Republic.* University of Wisconsin, 1952.

BOWMAN, Albert Hall. *The struggle for neutrality: a history of the diplomatic relations between the United States and France, 1790-1801.* Columbia University, 1954. DAI 14/08, p. 1205. Order No. 8612.

CHILDS, Frances S. *French refugee life in the United States, 1790-1800; an American chapter of the French Revolution.* Columbia University, 1940.

DOMKE, George W. *The life and writings of Jacques-Nicolas Billaud-Varennes (1756-1819).* New York University, 1953.

ELLERY, Eloise. *Brissot de Warville; a study in the history of the French Revolution.* Cornell University, 1902.

IGNATIEFF, Leonide. *French émigrés in Russia, 1789-1825: the interaction of cultures in time of stress.* The University of Michigan, 1963. DAI 24/12, p. 5360. Order No. 64-6697.

NALL, Charles Thomas. *The role of the Swiss in France in the Revolution, 1789-1799.* University of Kentucky, 1966. DAI 30/06-A, p. 2443. Order No. 69-20,418.

QUINNEY, Valerie Yow. *The Committee on Colonies of the French Constituent Assembly, 1789-91.* The University of Wisconsin, 1967. DAI 28/03-A, p. 1033. Order No. 67-3409.

REIFF, Paul Friedrich. *Friedrich Gentz, an opponent of the French Revolution and Napoleon.* University of Illinois, 1912.

ROBISON, Georgia. *Revellière-Lepeaux, citizen director, 1753-1824.* Columbia University, 1939.

WEITMAN, Sasha Reinhard. *Bureaucracy, democracy and the French Revolution.* Washington University, 1968. DAI 30/04-A, p. 1514. Order No. 69-15,226.

THE REVOLUTION, 1789-1794

APPLEWHITE, Harriet Verdier Branson. *Political culture in the French Revolution, 1788-1791.* Stanford University, 1972. DAI 32/12-A, p. 7050. Order No. 72-16,683.

CALHOUN, Dougald Thomas. *The deputies and revolution: new views on French revolutionary problems, 1789-1791.* The University of North Carolina at Chapel Hill, 1953. DAI 30/08-A, p. 3388. Order No. 70-3209.

CREIGHTON, John Kellogg. *Georges-Jacques Danton: a re-evaluation of aspects of his political career from August 10, 1792 to April 5, 1794.* University of Colorado, 1965. DAI 26/11, p. 6670. Order No. 66-2771.

CUBBERLY, Ray Ellsworth. *The Committee of General Security during the Reign of Terror.* University of Wisconsin, 1967. DAI 28/08-A, p. 3104. Order No. 67-12,114.

CULVER, Kenneth L. *The Brissotin Robespierrist struggle during the Legislative Assembly with reference to the fear of a dictator.* University of California, Berkeley, 1936.

CURL, Peter V. *Talleyrand and the révolution nobiliaire, an interpretation of his role in the French Revolution.* Cornell University, 1951.

DOZIER, Robert Raymond. *Ministerial efforts to combat revolutionary propaganda, 1789-1793.* University of California, Berkeley, 1969. DAI 30/10-A, p. 4368. Order No. 70-6092.

DUNKEL, G. Rainer. *Policies of Necker during his second administration, 1788-1790.* University of California, Berkeley, 1934.

DURHAM, Mary Jay. *The sans-jupons' crusade for liberation during the French Revolution.* Washington University, 1972. DAI 33/08-A, p. 4298. Order No. 73-5033.

EAGAN, James M. *Maximilien Robespierre: nationalist dictator.* Columbia University, 1939.

EPSTEIN, David Manford. *The role of Mirabeau in the French Revolution.* The University of Nebraska, 1967. DAI 28/02-A, p. 588. Order No. 67-10,661.

GERSHOY, Leo. *Barère, the mediator of the revolution.* Cornell University, 1925.

GOUTOR, Jacques Roger. *Robespierre and the French historians.* University of Illinois, 1960. DAI 21/11, p. 3437. Order No. 61-128.

HARRINGTON, Donald Bruce. *French historians and the terror: the origins, development, and present-day fate of the thèse du complot and the thèse des circonstances.* The University of Connecticut, 1970. DAI 31/12-A, p. 6517. Order No. 71-15,989.

HAYWORTH, Ronald Lee. *The trial of Louis XVI.* Emory University, 1968. DAI 29/09-A, p. 3073. Order No. 69-5232.

HOMAN, Gerlof Douwe. *The revolutionary career of Jean-François Reubell.* University of Kansas, 1959.

HYSLOP, Beatrice F. *French nationalism in 1789 according to the general cahiers.* Columbia University, 1935.

JACKSON, Melvin Hoffman. *The French privateers in American waters, 1793-1798: the failure of a mission.* Harvard University, 1957.

KIDNER, Frank L., Jr. *The Girondists and the "Propaganda War" of 1792: a reevaluation of French revolutionary foreign policy from 1791 to 1793.* Princeton University, 1971. DAI 32/04-A, p. 2033. Order No. 71-25,947.

KOLODY, Philip. *The Right in the French National Assembly, 1789-1791.* Princeton University, 1967. DAI 29/01-A, p. 213. Order No. 68-8938.

LANDIN, Harold William. *Thomas Jefferson and the French Revolution.* Cornell University, 1928.

LeGUIN, Charles A. *The first Girondin ministry, March-June 1792: a revolutionary experiment.* Emory University, 1956. DAI 19/11, p. 2927. Order No. 58-5158.

LITCHFIELD, Robert Burr. *The expansion of the French Revolution in Tuscany, 1790-1801.* Princeton University, 1965. DAI 28/02-A, p. 599. Order No. 66-5000.

LONG, Richard Melville. *The relations of the Grand Duchy of Tuscany with revolutionary France, 1790-1799.* The Florida State University, 1972. DAI 33/11-A, p. 6280. Order No. 73-11,319.

McGRATH, Paul C. *Secretary Jefferson and revolutionary France, 1790-1793.* Boston University, 1950.

MARKOFF, John. *Who wants bureaucracy? A study of French public opinion in 1789.* The Johns Hopkins University, 1972. DAI 33/04-A, p. 1853. Order No. 72-25,019.

PFEIFFER, Laura Belle. *The uprising of June 20, 1792.* The University of Nebraska-Lincoln, 1912.

ROBERTSON, George M. *The Society of the Cordeliers and the French Revolution, 1790-1794.* The University of Wisconsin, 1972. DAI 33/07-A, p. 3557. Order No. 72-27,346.

ROGERS, Cornwell B. *The spirit of revolution in 1789, a study of public opinion as revealed in political songs and other popular literature at the beginning of the French Revolution.* Columbia University, 1949.

SALA, Fred Russell. *The influence of physiocracy on the programme of reform instituted by the National Assembly of France, 1789-1791.* University of California, Berkeley, 1943.

SCHADT, Richard Schuyler. *The French Revolution in contemporary American thought.* Syracuse University, 1960. DAI 21/09, p. 2695. Order No. 61-522.

SHANKWILER, William N. *The idea of the nobility and the third estate of a constitution of France.* Cornell University, 1935.

SIRICH, John B., Jr. *The revolutionary committees in the departments of France during the Reign of Terror (1793-1794).* Harvard University, 1937.

SLAVIN, Morris. *Left of the mountain: the Enragés and the French Revolution.* Western Reserve University, 1961.

THE REVOLUTION, 1794-1799

KENNEDY, William Benjamin. *French projects for the invasion of Ireland, 1796-1798.* University of Georgia, 1966. DAI 27/10-A, p. 3399. Order No. 67-3563.

MORSE, Darrell Pierce. *Soldiers in politics during the first French Republic, 1795-1799.* University of California, Berkeley, 1962.

MURDOCH, Richard K. *French intrigue along the Georgia-Florida frontier, 1793-1796.* University of California, Los Angeles, 1948.

WOLOCH, Isser. *The democratic movement of the year VI: the evolution and revival of Jacobinism in France, 1797-98.* Princeton University, 1965. DAI 26/06, p. 3290. Order No. 65-12,334.

THE CONSULATE AND THE EMPIRE, 1799-1815

BAIRD, Thomas Reynolds. *The Napoleonic counts and barons 1808-1814, a political and social study.* New York University, 1968. DAI 30/11-A, p. 4903. Order No. 70-7385.

BEATTY, John Louis. *Napoleon and the governance of non-French subject peoples.* University of Washington, 1953. DAI 13/05, p. 773. Order No. 5891.

BECK, Thomas Davis. *The characteristics of French elected legislators, 1800-1834.* University of California, Berkeley, 1972.

BJELOVUCIC, Harriet Towers. *The Ragusan Republic: victim of Napoleon and its own conservatism.* Columbia University, 1964. DAI 25/05, p. 2938. Order No. 64-11,283.

BUTTRICK, Don Francis. *The administrative and political career of the Duke de Richelieu, 1803-1815: an episode in French-Russian relations.* University of California, Berkeley, 1959.

CAREY, Raymond G. *The liberals of France and their relation to the development of Bonaparte's dictatorship, 1799-1804.* University of Chicago, 1945.

CONNELLY, Owen Sergeson, Jr. *Joseph Bonaparte, King of Spain, 1808-1813.* The University of North Carolina at Chapel Hill, 1960. DAI 21/06, p. 1539. Order No. 60-4833.

CORTADA, Rafael Leon. *The government of Spain under Joseph Bonaparte, 1808-1814.* Fordham University, 1968. DAI 29/08-A, p. 2636. Order No. 69-2587.

CURRAN, Carleton Edgar. *The Corps Législatif during the supremacy of Napoleon the First, 1799-1813.* The University of Wisconsin, 1956. DAI 17/03, p. 611. Order No. 19,078.

DUNBAR, Robert G. *The Napoleonic regime in Piedmont and Liguria, 1801-1814.* University of Wisconsin, 1936.

EGAN, Clifford Lewis. *Franco-American relations, 1803-1814.* University of Colorado, 1969. DAI 30/02-A, p. 652. Order No. 69-13,405.

FRIEDRICH, Ruth I. *Napoleon's failing diplomatic battle, 1813-1814.* University of Iowa, 1938.

GRIFFITHS, Gordon. *Napoleon's Adriatic policy.* University of California, Berkeley, 1942.

HORWARD, Donald David. *The French invasion of Portugal, 1810-1811.* University of Minnesota, 1962. DAI 26/05, p. 2711. Order No. 65-7844.

KLANG, Daniel Michael. *Bavaria and the Age of Napoleon.* Princeton University, 1963. DAI 25/01, p. 435. Order No. 64-6273.

KNAPTON, Ernest J. *A reconsideration of the diplomatic policy of Prince Talleyrand, 1814-1815.* Harvard University, 1934.

KOENIG, Duane Walter. *The Napoleonic regime in Tuscany, 1807-1814.* University of Wisconsin, 1943.

ONSGARD, Henry A. *The influence of the French Revolution on Baden during the Napoleonic period.* The University of Wisconsin, 1935.

RAGSDALE, Hugh Appleton, Jr. *Russian diplomacy in the Age of Napoleon: Franco-Russian rapprochement of 1800-1801.* University of Virginia, 1964. DAI 25/05, p. 3544. Order No. 64-12,408.

RATH, Reuben J. *The fall of the Napoleonic kingdom of Italy (1814).* Columbia University, 1942.

SHULIM, Joseph I. *The Old Dominion and Napoleon Bonaparte; a study in American opinion.* Columbia University, 1952.

WEBSTER, Thomas Stewart. *Napoleon and Canada.* University of Chicago, 1962.

GOVERNMENT, ADMINISTRATION, EDUCATION, MILITARY

ARNOLD, Eric A., Jr. *Administrative leadership in a dictatorship, the position of Joseph Fouché in the Napoleonic police, 1800-1810.* Columbia University, 1969. DAI 33/01-A, p. 243. Order No. 72-19,044.

74

CROAL, Ralph F. *The idea of the école spéciale militaire and the founding of Saint-Cyr.* University of Arizona, 1970. DAI 31/05-A, p. 2299. Order No. 70-22,228.

GODFREY, James L. *The organization, procedure, and personnel of the French revolutionary tribunal.* University of Chicago, 1942.

HOLTMAN, Robert Barney. *The use of propaganda by Napoleon.* University of Wisconsin, 1941.

MONROE, Charles Rexford. *The origins of the French prefectural system.* The University of Wisconsin, 1941.

MOODY, Walton Smith. *The introduction of military conscription in Napoleonic Europe, 1798-1812.* Duke University, 1971. DAI 32/10-A, p. 5717. Order No. 72-11,111.

OJALA, Jeanne Adell Melin. *The military career of Auguste Colbert, 1793-1809.* The Florida State University, 1969. DAI 33/03-A, p. 1122. Order No. 72-21,325.

PUGH, Wilma Jennings. *Methods of communication and propaganda of the revolutionary government of France, 1789 to 1793.* Cornell University, 1931.

READ, Ira Bulger. *The origin and development of the idea of the levée en masse in the French Revolution.* Emory University, 1965. DAI 26/10, p. 6006. Order No. 66-2880.

RINGGOLD, Gordon B. *The French National Guard; its origin, organization and role in the first phase of the French Revolution.* Georgetown University, 1951.

SCHUSTER, Alice. *The struggle between clericals and anti-clericals for control of French schools (1789-1879).* Columbia University, 1967. DAI 28/02-A, p. 605. Order No. 67-10,606.

SCOTT, Samuel Francis. *The French Revolution and the line army, 1787-1793.* The University of Wisconsin, 1968. DAI 29/03-A, p. 858. Order No. 68-9127.

VESS, David Marshall. *French military medicine during the Revolution, 1792-*

1795. University of Alabama, 1965. DAI 26/10, p. 6012. Order No. 66-2948.

VIGNERY, John Robert. *Jacobin educational theories and policies in the French National Convention, 1792-1794.* The University of Wisconsin, 1960. DAI 21/06, p. 1547. Order No. 60-5802.

WATSON, Robert James. *The legislative basis of army organization and administration in France under the National Convention, 1792-1794.* University of Virginia, 1953. DAI 14/07, p. 1069. Order No. 7991.

SOCIAL AND ECONOMIC

CHAIKIN, William. *Youth groups in the French Revolution, 1788-1795.* University of California, Berkeley, 1939.

CLARK, Priscilla Parkhurst. *The bourgeois in the French novel, 1789-1848.* Columbia University, 1967. DAI 28/05-A, p. 1814. Order No. 67-12,243.

DAELEY, Albert J. *The Continental system in France as illustrated by American trade.* University of Wisconsin, 1949.

GEIGER, Reed Glenn. *The Anzin Company: the history of a French coal mining firm, 1800-1833.* University of Minnesota, 1965. DAI 26/10, p. 5994. Order No. 66-1661.

HARDY, Charles Oscar. *The Negro question in the French Revolution.* University of Chicago, 1916.

HUGHES, Henry Stuart. *The crisis of the French imperial economy, 1810-1812.* Harvard University, 1940.

MELVIN, Frank Edgar. *Napoleon's navigation system; a study of trade control during the continental blockade.* University of Pennsylvania, 1913.

MILLER, Genevieve. *The adoption of inoculation for smallpox in England and France.* Cornell University, 1955. DAI 16/01, p. 109. Order No. 15,418.

NUSSBAUM, Frederick Louis. *Commercial policy in the French Revolution; a study of the career of G.J.A. Ducher.* University of Pennsylvania, 1923.

RODIS, Themistocles C. *Morals: marriage, divorce, and illegitimacy during the French Revolution, 1789-1795.* Case Western Reserve University, 1968. DAI 30/03-A, p. 1119. Order No. 69-9369.

SARICKS, Ambrose, Jr. *Pierre Samuel Du Pont de Nemours and the French Revolution.* The University of Wisconsin, 1950.

SHEPARD, William F. *Decontrol during the French Revolution: the destruction of an economic dictatorship after the fall of Robespierre.* University of California, Berkeley, 1952.

SMITH, Herbert B. *The social implications of the rise and fall of the Paris Commune, 1789-1794.* University of California, Berkeley, 1952.

TAYLOR, George V. *Business enterprise and the French Revolution.* University of Wisconsin, 1951.

TERR, Sidney D. *Grain trade legislation in France during the French Revolution (1789-1792).* Ohio State University, 1938.

TRAER, James Frederick. *Marriage and the family in French law and social criticism from the end of the ancien régime to the civil code.* The University of Michigan, 1970. DAI 31/05-A, p. 2327. Order No. 70-21,806.

REGIONAL STUDIES

BEELER, Azel Dale. *The revolution at Bordeaux, France, 1789-1795: an experiment in democracy.* Indiana University, 1940.

BRACE, Richard M. *La Gironde in arms: a study of the revolution in southwestern France with special emphasis upon the National Guard (1789-1793).* University of California, Berkeley, 1941.

CAMERON, John Burton, Jr. *The revolution of the sections of Marseilles: federalism in the Department of the Bouches-du-Rhône in 1793.* University of North Carolina at Chapel Hill, 1971. DAI 32/05-A, p. 2591. Order No. 71-30,544.

HOOD, James Norton. *The riots in Nîmes in 1790 and the origins of a popular counter-revolutionary movement.* Princeton University, 1969. DAI 30/05-A, p. 1958. Order No. 69-18,166.

KENNEDY, Michael Lee. *The Club of the Rue Thubaneau: a study of the Popular Society of Marseilles, 1790-1794.* Tulane University, 1970. DAI 31/09-A, p. 4680. Order No. 71-8062.

MAGE, Lily Diana. *Public spirit and public opinion in Auvergne before and during the French Revolution to 1791.* Columbia University, 1963. DAI 24/09, p. 3713. Order No. 64-2775.

INTELLECTUAL AND CULTURAL

APT, Leon Jerome. *Louis-Philippe de Ségur: an intellectual in a revolutionary age.* University of Chicago, 1966.

BEECHER, Jonathan French. *Charles Fourier and his early writings: 1800-1820.* Harvard University, 1968.

BRUNET, Joseph, Jr. *Science and the early École Polytechnique, 1794-1806: the impact of the early polytechniciens on the science of the eighteenth century and on the Revolution in the nineteenth century.* University of Kentucky, 1969. DAI 30/08-A, p. 3377. Order No. 70-2565.

DIELMANN, Reta Hazel. *Dramatic representation as a means of popular instruction in the French Revolution.* Cornell University, 1924.

DUNN, Seymour Ballard. *The national festival in the French Revolution, 1794-1797: a study in revolutionary propaganda.* Cornell University, 1940.

EDELSTEIN, Melvin Allen. *La Feuille Villageoise: communication and rural modernization in the French Revolution.* Princeton University, 1965. DAI 26/12, p. 7277. Order No. 66-4992.

ELBOW, Matthew H. *French corporative theory, 1789-1948; a chapter in the history of ideas.* Harvard University, 1953.

FRIGUGLIETTI, James. *The social and religious consequences of the French revolutionary calendar.* Harvard University, 1966.

FULTON, Roger L. *The political significance of the Parisian theater, 1789-1793.*
University of California, Berkeley, 1953.

GORDON, David Crockett. *A philosophe
views the French Revolution: the Abbé
Morellet (1727-1819).* Princeton University, 1957. DAI 19/09, p. 2327. Order
No. 58-7844.

GREGORY, Allene. *The French Revolution
and the English novel.* Radcliffe College,
1913.

HAHN, Roger. *The fall of the Paris Academy
of Sciences during the French Revolution.*
Cornell University, 1962. DAI 23/06,
p. 2101. Order No. 62-5977.

HARRIS, Robert Dalton. *Equality as interpreted by the French revolutionaries.*
University of California, Berkeley, 1960.

IDZERDA, Stanley J. *Art and the State
during the French Revolution, 1789-1795.*
Western Reserve University, 1952.

KAFKER, Frank Arthur. *The Encyclopedists
and the French Revolution.* Columbia University, 1961. DAI 22/04, p. 1141. Order
No. 61-3440.

LEACOCK, Ruth Marie. *Jacques Mallet-
DuPan: publicist for conservatism during
the French Revolution.* University of
California, Berkeley, 1959.

MAIORINO, Giancarlo. *An interpretation
of the Napoleonic myth in literature and
art.* The University of Wisconsin, 1971.
DAI 32/06-A, p. 3313. Order No.
71-25,734.

MALAKIS, Emile. *French travellers in
Greece (1770-1820) an early phase of
French Philhellenism.* University of
Pennsylvania, 1925.

MARAS, Raymond J. *Napoleon: patron of
the arts and sciences.* University of California, Berkeley, 1955.

MERSHART, Ronald Valere. *S.-N.-H.
Linguet: the regretful prophet.* University
of Chicago, 1970.

POE, William Allen. *The suppression of the
academies during the French Revolution.*
University of Alabama, 1968. DAI
29/05-A, p. 1501. Order No. 68-15,504.

ROBINOVE, Phyllis Susan. *The reputation
of the philosophes in France, 1789-1799,
as reflected in the periodical press.* Columbia University, 1955. DAI 16/03, p. 539.
Order No. 15,748.

SMITH, Agnes Monroe. *The first historians
of the French Revolution.* Western Reserve
University, 1966.

STANSELL, Harold L. *The Puritan spirit in
the French Revolution.* St. Louis University, 1948.

STEIN, Jay Wobith. *The Ideologues, their
theories and politics: intellectuals under
the governments of the French Revolution
and Napoleonic Regime.* Columbia University, 1952. DAI 13/03, p. 425. Order No.
5208.

STEVENS, John Christopher. *Anacharsis
Cloots and French cosmopolitanism: the
death of an idea.* University of Arkansas,
1954. DAI 14/08, p. 1210. Order No.
8375.

SULLIVAN, Harriet Varrell. *Defenders of
privilege: a study of the political ideas
which lay behind the defense of privilege
at the French Constituent Assembly of
1789.* Radcliffe College, 1956.

VAN DUZER, Charles H. *Contributions of
the Ideologues to French revolutionary
thought.* Johns Hopkins University, 1934.

WALDINGER, Renee. *Voltaire and reform
in the light of the French Revolution.* Columbia University, 1953. DAI 14/01,
p. 1130. Order No. 6732.

RELIGION

CARVEN, John Winslow. *Napoleon and the
Lazarists, 1804-1809.* State University of
New York at Buffalo, 1972. DAI 33/08-A,
p. 4294. Order No. 73-5087.

GLIOZZO, Charles Anthony. *The anti-
Christian movement in Paris during the
French Revolution, 1789-1794.* State Uni-
versity of New York at Buffalo, 1966.
DAI 27/06-A, p. 1754. Order No.
66-12,113.

GRAHAM, Ruth. *The English press on the
ecclesiastical changes in the French Revolution.* City University of New York, 1971.

DAI 32/06-A, p. 3204. Order No. 72-992.

GREYTAK, William Joseph. *Henri Grégoire, a study in French church-state relations from 1790 to 1802.* University of Colorado, 1967. DAI 29/01-A, p. 212. Order No. 68-10,622.

HOFFMAN, Frances Malino. *Abraham Furtado and the Sephardi Jews of France: a study of emancipation during the French Revolution and Napoleonic Era.* Brandeis University, 1971. DAI 32/12-A, p. 6867. Order No. 71-20,333.

JOHNSON, Dale Arthur. *The political and religious thought of Henri Grégoire: a contribution to the study of the church-state issues in France, 1789-1830.* Union Theological Seminary in the City of New York, 1967. DAI 28/02-A, p. 768. Order No. 67-8817.

LEVACK, Arthur Paul. *The principal immediate non-parliamentary origins of the civil constitution of the clergy.* Harvard University, 1941.

NECHELES, Ruth F. *The Abbé Grégoire and the constitutional church: 1794-1802.*

University of Chicago, 1964.

O'LOUGHLIN, John E. *The influence of the French Revolution on the relations between Great Britain and the Vatican.* Boston College, 1938.

POLAND, Burdette Crawford. *French Protestantism and the French Revolution: a study in church and state , thought and religion, 1685-1815.* Princeton University, 1954. DAI 14/10, p. 1699. Order No. 9441.

RUSKOWSKI, Leo Francis. *French emigré priests in the United States (1791-1815.)* The Catholic University of America, 1940.

STEWART, John Hall. *The life and works of Jean Paul Rabaut de Saint-Étienne, the Huguenot patriot.* Cornell University, 1930.

TAYLOR, Wallace Willard. *The confiscation of church property in France in 1789.* University of Iowa, 1941.

TRUE, Wallace M. *The de-christianizing movement during the Terror, 1793-94.* Harvard University, 1939.

THE NINETEENTH CENTURY, 1815-1870

GENERAL AND MISCELLANEOUS

BARNWELL, Stephen B. *The Duc de Persigny, 1808-1872.* University of California, Berkeley, 1955.

BISING, James Albert. *The admirals' government: a history of the naval colony that was French Cochinchina, 1862-1879.* New York University, 1972. DAI 33/11-A, p. 6265. Order No. 73-11,674.

BRANCH, Anthony Douglas. *Dr. Thomas W. Evans, American dentist in Paris, 1847-1897.* University of California, Santa Barbara, 1971. DAI 32/08-A, p. 4519. Order No. 72-7450.

CAMPBELL, John Coert. *French influence and the rise of Roumanian nationalism,*

1830-1857. Harvard University, 1940.

DUNN, Gustus Albert, Jr. *The French intervention in Syria, 1860-1861.* University of Texas, 1940.

EISENSTEIN, Elizabeth L. *The evolution of the Jacobin tradition in France—the survival and revival of the ethos of 1793 under the Bourbon and Orleanist regimes.* Radcliffe College, 1953.

GRAY, Walter Dennis. *The opposition of the notables to Napoleon III: 1839-1864.* University of Notre Dame, 1959. DAI 20/07, p. 2772. Order No. 59-6600.

GRIFFETH, Robert Ross. *Varieties of African resistance to the French conquest of the western Sudan, 1850-1900.* Northwestern University, 1968. DAI 29/10-A, p. 3556. Order No. 69-6930.

KELLY, George H. *The political development of the French overseas empire.* Stanford University, 1955. DAI 16/01, p. 149. Order No. 15,374.

KENNEDY, Melvin D. *The suppression of the African slave trade to the French colonies and its aftermath, 1814-48.* University of Chicago, 1947.

KIESWETTER, James Kay. *The political career of Etienne-Denis Pasquier.* University of Colorado, 1969. DAI 29/10-A, p. 3548. Order No. 69-4302.

KLEIN, Martin Allen. *Sine-Saloum, 1847-1914: the traditional states and the French conquest.* University of Chicago, 1965.

METCALF, Helen. *The problem of Tunisia in Franco-Italian relations, 1835-1838.* University of Maryland, 1942.

PERINBAM, Barbara Marie. *Trade and politics on the Senegal and Upper Niger 1854-1900: African reaction to French penetration.* Georgetown University, 1969. DAI 30/10-A, p. 4382. Order No. 70-5927.

PUTNEY, Martha Settle. *The slave trade in French diplomacy, 1814-1865.* University of Pennsylvania, 1955. DAI 16/01, p. 110. Order No. 13,422.

RUEDY, John Douglas. *The origins of the rural public domain in French Algeria, 1830-1851.* University of California, Los Angeles, 1965. DAI 26/01, p. 342. Order No. 65-7321.

SCOTT, Robert C. L. *American travelers in France, 1830-1860.* Yale University, 1940.

SONGY, Benedict Gaston. *Alexis de Tocqueville and slavery: judgments and predictions.* St. Louis University, 1969. DAI 30/08-A, p. 3413. Order No. 70-1872.

STEELE, Hollins McKim, Jr. *European settlement vs. Muslim property: the foundation of colonial Algeria, 1830-1880.* Columbia University, 1965. DAI 28/12-A, p. 4973. Order No. 68-8555.

WITHERELL, Julian Wood. *The response of the peoples of Cayor to French pene-*

tration, 1850-1900. The University of Wisconsin, 1964. DAI 25/03, p. 1886. Order No. 64-9703.

THE RESTORATION, 1815-1830

BEACH, Vincent Woodrow. *Charles X of France.* University of Illinois, 1950. DAI 10/04, p. 187. Order No. 2058.

BROWN, Nicolette Friederich. *Ultra-royalist deputies in the Chambre Introuvable, 1815-1816.* Duke University, 1969. DAI 30/08-A, p. 3387. Order No. 70-2144.

CAPPADOCIA, Ezio. *The history of the Liberal party in France, 1814-1826.* University of Chicago, 1958.

DEAN, Edgar P. *Royalism and constitutionalism in France, 1814-1816.* Harvard University, 1939.

FAIR, Eugene R. *Anglo-French relations concerning Spain and Portugal and their American colonies, 1822-1827.* University of Iowa, 1938.

HARTMAN, Mary Susan. *The liberalism of Benjamin Constant during the Bourbon Restoration in France.* Columbia University, 1970. DAI 31/09-A, p. 4675. Order No. 71-6184.

HATTON, Roy Odell. *Prince Camille de Polignac: the life of a soldier.* The Louisiana State University and Agricultural and Mechanical College, 1970. DAI 31/09-A, p. 4675. Order No. 71-6576.

HEARN, Jana Srba. *The schoolmaster of liberty or the political views of Benjamin Constant de Rebecque.* Indiana University, 1970. DAI 31/07-A, p. 3470. Order No. 70-26,928.

KELLY, Daniel Kemp. *Ultra-royalism: ideology and politics under the Bourbon Restoration.* The University of Wisconsin, 1964. DAI 25/06, p. 3538. Order No. 64-12,730.

McBRIDE, John Dewitt, Jr. *America in the French mind during the Bourbon Restoration.* Syracuse University, 1954. DAI 15/03, p. 417. Order No. 10,414.

McNEALLY, Douglass Hall. *Constitutional monarchy in France, 1814-1848.* Northwestern University, 1963. DAI 24/09, p. 3715. Order No. 64-2503.

MELLON, Stanley. *The politics of history: a study of the historical writing of the French Restoration.* Princeton University, 1954. DAI 14/10, p. 1697. Order No. 9435.

MITCHELL, Marilyn L. *Chateaubriand and Hyde de Neuville: the loyal opposition.* University of Kansas, 1972. DAI 33/06-A, p. 2865. Order No. 72-32,909.

NEWMAN, Edgar Leon. *Republicanism during the Bourbon Restoration in France, 1814-1830.* University of Chicago, 1970.

RADER, Daniel L. *The political role of French journalism in the last years of the Bourbon Restoration, 1828-1830.* University of California, Berkeley, 1953.

RESNICK, Daniel Philip. *The white terror and the political reaction of 1815-1816 in France.* Harvard University, 1962.

THE JULY MONARCHY, 1830-1848

BRUSH, Elizabeth Parnham. *Guizot in the early years of the Orleanist monarchy.* University of Illinois, 1927.

FASEL, George William. *The French moderate republicans, 1837-48.* Stanford University, 1965. DAI 26/07, p. 3900. Order No. 65-12,772.

GORDON, Evelyn B. *The significance of political caricature during the reign of Louis-Philippe 1830-1835.* University of Pennsylvania, 1970. DAI 31/06-A, p. 2843. Order No. 70-25,653.

HAYNIE, Kenneth Eugene. *The constitutional left under the July monarchy: Orleanist party of opposition.* University of Michigan, 1970. DAI 31/05-A, p. 2308. Order No. 70-21,679.

JACOBS, Vincil Dale. *Toward a consensus: the political crisis in the French Chamber of Deputies, 1839-40.* University of Washington, 1972. DAI 33/08-A, p. 4306. Order No. 73-3730.

JONES, Russell Mosley. *The French image of America: 1830-1848.* University of

Missouri, 1957. DAI 17/12, p. 2992. Order No. 22,757.

KOEPKE, Robert Louis. *François Guizot and the formation of a conservative party in France, 1840-48.* Stanford University, 1967. DAI 28/11-A, p. 4576. Order No. 68-6446.

LAWLOR, Mary. *Alexis de Tocqueville in the Chamber of Deputies; his views on foreign and colonial policy.* Catholic University of America, 1959.

LYNN, Ralph L. *The picture of Louis-Philippe in French historiography.* University of Wisconsin, 1952.

RIDLEY, Jack Blaine. *Marshal Bugeaud, the July monarchy and the question of Algeria, 1841-1847: a study in civil-military relations.* The University of Oklahoma, 1970. DAI 31/06-A, p. 2855. Order No. 70-23,002

RODKEY, Frederick Stanley. *The Turco-Egyptian question in the relations of England, France, and Russia, 1832-1841.* University of Illinois at Urbana-Champaign, 1921.

SWEET, James S. *France during the last two years of the July monarchy: the climate of opinion, 1846-1848.* University of California, Los Angeles, 1955.

THE REVOLUTION OF 1848 AND THE SECOND REPUBLIC, 1848-1852

AMANN, Peter. *A French revolutionary club in 1848: the Société Démocratique Centrale.* University of Chicago, 1959.

BAUGHMAN, John Joseph. *The political banquet campaign in France, 1847-1848.* The University of Michigan, 1953. DAI 13/05, p. 773. Order No. 5637.

BERNSTEIN, Paul. *The Rhine problem during the Second Republic and Second Empire.* University of Pennsylvania, 1955. DAI 15/05, p. 805. Order No. 11,394.

BRESCIA, Anthony Mark. *Richard Rush and the French Revolution of 1848.* St. John's University, 1968. DAI 29/10-A, p. 3553. Order No. 69-4148.

80

CALMAN, Alvin Rosenblatt. *Ledru-Rollin and the Second French Republic.* Columbia University, 1922.

CHASTAIN, James Garvin. *French Kleindeutsch policy in 1848.* The University of Oklahoma, 1967. DAI 28/07-A, p. 2620. Order No. 68-724.

COX, Marvin Rountree. *The legitimists under the Second French Republic.* Yale University, 1966. DAI 27/09-A, p. 2980. Order No. 66-5416.

DE LUNA, Frederick Adolph. *The republic of Cavaignac.* State University of Iowa, 1963. DAI 23/08, p. 2888. Order No. 63-914.

GARGAN, Edward. *The education of Alexis de Tocqueville, the critical years, 1848-1851.* Catholic University of America, 1955.

GUSTAFSON, Richard Elmer. *Louis Blanc and the Revolution of 1848.* University of Wisconsin, 1945.

HAHN, Robert John. *The attitude of the French revolutionary government toward German unification in 1848.* The Ohio State University, 1955. DAI 16/04, p. 741. Order No. 16,076.

JENNINGS, Lawrence Charles. *The conduct of French foreign affairs in 1848: the diplomacy of a republic divided within itself.* Wayne State University, 1967. DAI 28/08-A, p. 3112. Order No. 68-2093.

Mc NIFF, Franklin Joseph. *Auguste de Morny and the coup d'état of December, 1851, in France.* St. John's University, 1972. DAI 33/02-A, p. 701. Order No. 72-21,728.

MARTIN, Kenneth Robert. *British and French diplomacy and the Sardinian War, 1848-1849.* University of Pennsylvania, 1965. 26/09, p. 5401. Order No. 66-283.

PINCETL, Stanley J., Jr. *Republics in conflict: episodes in Franco-American relations, 1848-1851.* University of California, Berkeley, 1955.

SCOTT, Lawrence Sherwood. *Paris and the June days of 1848: a case study of revolutionary leadership.* Boston University

Graduate School, 1972. DAI 33/04-A, p. 1660. Order No. 72-25,324.

WATKINS, Sharon Brown. *The working class deputies in the French Constituent Assembly May 4, 1848-May 26, 1849.* University of North Carolina at Chapel Hill, 1971. DAI 32/02-A, p. 900. Order No. 71-21,008.

THE SECOND EMPIRE, 1852-1870

ADAMS, Henry M. *The immediate origins of the Franco-Prussian war, 1870-1871.* Stanford University, 1937.

BARKER, Nancy N. *The influence of the Empress Eugénie on foreign affairs of the Second Empire.* University of Pennsylvania 1955.

BLOOMFIELD, James Robert. *Count Walewski's foreign ministry 1855-1860.* University of Pennsylvania, 1972. DAI 32/08-A, p. 4510. Order No. 72-6137.

BUSH, John William. *Napoleon III and the redeeming of Venetia, 1864-1866.* Fordham University, 1961. DAI 22/11, p. 3992. Order No. 62-1016.

CASE, Lynn Marshall. *Franco-Italian relations, 1860-1865; the Roman question and the Convention of September.* University of Pennsylvania, 1931.

CUMMINGS, Raymond Leo. *France and the fall of the kingdom of the two Sicilies, 1860.* University of Pennsylvania, 1964. DAI 25/04, p. 2469. Order No. 64-10,362.

ECHARD, William Earl. *Napoleon III and the Concert of Europe: conference diplomacy and the congress idea to 1863.* University of Pennsylvania, 1960. DAI 21/11, p. 3435. Order No. 60-6155.

EVANS, Elliot Arthur Powell. *Napoleon III and the American Civil War.* Stanford University, 1941.

FLETCHER, Willard Allen. *Vincent Benedetti, French ambassador to Berlin, 1864-1870.* University of Pennsylvania, 1956. DAI 16/05, p. 951. Order No. 16,326.

GANNON, Francis X. *The Washburne Mission to France, 1869-1871.* Georgetown University, 1950.

GAVRONSKY, Serge. *The French liberal opposition and the American Civil War.* Columbia University, 1965. DAI 26/12, p. 7278. Order No. 65-9160.

GERRITY, Francis X. *American editorial opinion of the French intervention in Mexico, 1861-1867.* Georgetown University, 1952.

GOOCH, Brison D. *French leadership in the Crimean War.* University of Wisconsin, 1955.

HAGG, Harold T. *The Congress of Paris of 1856.* University of Iowa, 1937.

HARNEY, Robert Forest. *The last crusade: France and the papal army of 1860.* University of California, Berkeley, 1966. DAI 27/03-A, p. 728. Order No. 66-8321.

HOUSTON, Douglas William. *The negotiations for a triple alliance between France, Austria, and Italy, 1869-70.* University of Pennsylvania, 1959. DAI 20/05, p. 1756. Order No. 59-4632.

HOWARD, Mary Katherine. *The French Parliament and the Italian-Roman questions, 1859-1865.* University of Pennsylvania, 1963. DAI 24/05, p. 1998. Order No. 63-7052.

HUNTER, Stephen Carl. *Franco-Spanish relations in the era of Napoleon III and Isabel II.* Stanford University, 1967. DAI 28/11-A, p. 4574. Order No. 68-6436.

HUSLEY, Fabian Val. *Napoleon III and the confederacy: a reappraisal.* Mississippi State University, 1970. DAI 31/07-A, p. 3472. Order No. 71-1199.

JORDAN, James Edward. *Prince Napoleon Bonaparte and the unification of Italy.* University of California, Berkeley, 1965. DAI 26/07, p. 3904. Order No. 65-13,515.

LALLY, Frank Edward. *French opposition to the Mexican policy of the Second Empire.* Johns Hopkins University, 1930.

LANCASTER, John Ezekiel. *France and the United States, 1870-71: diplomatic relations during the Franco-Prussian War and the insurrection of the Commune.* University of Georgia, 1972. DAI 33/09-A, p. 5095. Order No. 73-5726.

LORANTAS, Raymond Martin. *Lord Cowley's mission to Paris, 1852-1856.* University of Pennsylvania, 1963. DAI 25/01, p. 436. Order No. 64-7386.

McDONALD, Michael Joseph. *Napoleon III and his ideas of Italian confederation: 1856-1860.* University of Pennsylvania, 1969. DAI 30/03-A, p. 1112. Order No. 69-15,089.

McFARLANE, Larry Allen. *Anglo-French relations and the London Conference of 1864.* University of Georgia, 1972. DAI 33/09-A, p. 5098. Order No. 73-5738.

McLARTY, Vivian Kirkpatrick. *The relations of Napoleon III with England.* University of Illinois, 1930.

MALLOY, George W. *The United States and the French intervention in Mexico, 1861-1867.* University of California, Berkeley, 1938.

MANGE, Alyce Edythe. *The principal phases of the Near Eastern policy of the Emperor Napoleon III.* University of Illinois, 1930.

MEIDZINI, Meron. *French policy in Japan during the closing years of the Tokugawa Regime.* Harvard University, 1964.

MOSS, Herbert J. *Napoleon III and Belgium, 1866-1870: a study in Belgian neutrality.* Harvard University, 1938.

POTTINGER, Evelyn Ann. *Napoleon III and the German crisis, 1865-66.* Radcliffe College, 1962.

RICHARDSON, Charles O. *The ideas of Napoleon III on the principle of self-determination of nationalities and their influence on his foreign policies.* Georgetown University, 1963.

ROSE, Klaras Blevins. *Napoleon III and the Austro-Sardinian War of 1859.* The University of Texas, 1963. DAI 26/04, p. 2169. Order No. 65-8019.

SCHWERTMAN, Elmer Chester. *Napoleon III and the Bonapartist clique: a study in political power.* Columbia University, 1953. DAI 14/01, p. 102. Order No. 6701.

SCOTT, Ivan Carl. *The powers and the French occupation of Rome, 1859-1865.* University of Pennsylvania, 1964. DAI 25/12, p. 7232. Order No. 65-5804.

STEVENS, John Knox. *Franco-Russian relations, 1856-1863.* University of Illinois, 1962. DAI 23/07, p. 2509. Order No. 62-6235.

WEST, Warren Reed. *Contemporary French opinion on the American Civil War.* Johns Hopkins University, 1922.

WHEELER, Lawrence Jefferson. *The conflict between the government of Napoleon III and the Society of Saint Vincent de Paul, 1860-1862,* University of Georgia, 1972. DAI 33/07-A, p. 3565. Order No. 72-34,163.

WILLIAMS, Roger Lawrence. *The Duc de Morny and Franco-Russian relations, 1856-63.* The University of Michigan, 1951. DAI 11/02, p. 327. Order No. 2475.

WOLFE, Robert David. *The origins of the Paris Commune: the popular organizations of 1868-71.* Harvard University, 1966.

ZARUR, Claire A. *Prince Napoleon (Jerome) during the Second Empire.* Georgetown University, 1965. DAI 26/06, p. 3291. Order No. 65-6991.

GOVERNMENT, ADMINISTRATION, EDUCATION, MILITARY

ADRIANCE, Thomas James. *The mobilization and concentration of the French army in 1870.* Columbia University, 1968. DAI 29/09-A, p. 3057. Order No. 69-3047.

DAY, Charles Rodney. *Freedom of conscience and Protestant education in France, 1815-1885.* Harvard University, 1964.

EISENSTEIN, Hester. *Victor Cousin and the war on the University of France.* Yale University, 1968. DAI 29/02-A, p. 539. Order No. 68-11,178.

GAISSER, Charles Thomas. *The bourgeois regime and the French University, 1830-*
1848. Yale University, 1956.

GARNER, Reuben. *Watchdogs of empire: the French colonial inspection service in action: 1815-1913.* The University of Rochester, 1970. DAI 31/07-A, p. 3468. Order No. 71-1391.

HARRIGAN, Patrick Joseph. *Catholic secondary education in France, 1851-1882.* University of Michigan, 1971. DAI 32/03-A, p. 1440. Order No. 71-23,770.

HORVATH, Sandra Ann. *Victor Duruy and French education, 1863-1869.* The Catholic University of America, 1971. DAI 32/04-A, p. 2030. Order No. 71-25,242.

McCLEARY, John W. *Anglo-French naval rivalry, 1815-1848.* Johns Hopkins University, 1947.

MEYERS, Peter Vroom. *The French instituteur 1830-1914: a study of professional formation.* Rutgers University The State University of New Jersey, 1972. DAI 33/08-A, p. 4314. Order No. 73-4765.

OLIVER, James Montgomery, III. *The Corps des Ponts et Chaussées, 1830-1848.* University of Missouri-Columbia, 1967. DAI 28/07-A, p. 2628. Order No. 67-13,888.

OLIVER, Lew D. *Reorganization of the French army, 1866-1870.* University of California, Berkeley, 1941.

PADBERG, John William. *The Jesuit colleges in France between the Falloux Law and the Ferry Decrees—1850-1880.* Harvard University, 1965.

PAYNE, Howard C. *French regionalism, 1851-1914: a study of the principal alternatives to administrative centralization.* University of California, Berkeley, 1948.

RANDOLPH, Paul Gene. *The role of Protestantism in the founding of public primary instruction in France, 1814-1833.* The University of Michigan, 1972. DAI 33/05-A, p. 2304. Order No. 72-29,177.

WALLIN, Franklin W. *The French navy during the Second Empire: a study of the effects of technological development on French governmental policy.* University of California, Berkeley, 1954.

SOCIAL AND ECONOMIC

ADAMS, Paul Vauthier. *Economic and demographic change in Mediterranean France, 1850-1914.* State University of New York at Buffalo, 1972. DAI 33/05-A, p. 2274. Order No. 72-27,231.

BARKER, Richard John. *Casimir Périer (1777-1832) and William Ternaux (1763-1833): two French capitalists.* Duke University, 1958. DAI 19/06, p. 1352. Order No. 58-3388.

CAMERON, Rondo. *French foreign investment, 1850-1880.* University of Chicago, 1953.

CARLISLE, Robert Bruce. *The Saint-Simonians and the foundation of the Paris-Lyon railroad, 1832-52.* Cornell University, 1957. DAI 17/07, p. 1538. Order No. 21,076.

DOUKAS, Kimon A. *The French railroads and the State.* Columbia University, 1946.

GRANTHAM, George William, Jr. *Technical and organizational change in French agriculture between 1840 and 1880: an economic interpretation.* Yale University, 1972. DAI 33/05-A, p. 1957. Order No. 72-29,544.

HILL, Michael J. *Industrialization and cultural change: the French experience, 1815-1830.* University of Kansas, 1972. DAI 33/11-A, p. 6273. Order No. 73-11,897.

KRANZBERG, Melvin. *The siege of Paris, 1870-71: a social history.* Harvard University, 1942.

KULSTEIN, David I. *Louis Napoleon and the social and economic policy of the Second Empire: a new approach to the social problem.* Harvard University, 1955.

LANDES, David S. *Bankers and pashas: international finance and imperialism in the Egypt of the 1860's.* Harvard University, 1953.

MORROW, Dwight Whitney, Jr. *The impact of American agricultural machinery on France, 1851-1914, with some consideration of the general agricultural impact until 1880.* Harvard University, 1957.

NEWELL, William Henry. *Population change and agricultural development in nineteenth century France.* University of Pennsylvania, 1971. DAI 32/12-A, p. 6661. Order No. 72-17,404.

SHERMAN, Dennis Marvin. *Governmental attitudes toward economic modernization in France during the July monarchy, 1830-1848.* University of Michigan, 1970. DAI 31/08-A, p. 4100. Order No. 71-4728.

SUSSMAN, George David. *From yellow fever to cholera: a study of French government policy, medical professionalism and popular movements in the epidemic crises of the restoration and the July Monarchy.* Yale University, 1971. DAI 32/06-A, p. 3231. Order No. 71-31,018.

WEBER, William. *Music and the midlde class: the social structure of the middle-class concert public in London, Paris, and Vienna between 1830 and 1848.* University of Chicago, 1971.

SOCIALISM AND THE LABOR MOVEMENT

BUSH, Robert Donald. *Individualism and the role of the individual in British and French socialism: the early years, 1800-1848.* University of Kansas, 1969. DAI 30/07-A, p. 2935. Order No. 69-21,499.

HOFFMAN, Robert Louis. *The social and political theory of P. J. Proudhon.* Brandeis University, 1968. DAI 29/03-A, p. 851. Order No. 68-12,435.

JOHNSON, Christopher Howard. *Étienne Cabet and the Icarian Communist movement in France 1839-1848.* The University of Wisconsin, 1968. DAI 28/12-A, p. 4993. Order No. 68-5320.

LOUBERE, Leo A. *Louis Blanc in exile.* Northwestern University, 1953. DAI 13/06, p. 1175. Order No. 6218.

MOSS, Bernard Haym. *Origins of the French labor movement: the socialism of skilled workers.* Columbia University, 1972. DAI 33/05-A, p. 2299. Order No. 72-28,068.

PHILIPS, R. Craig. *The life and political thought of Simonde de Sismondi.* University of Chicago, 1969.

SPEAR, Lois C. *Pierre Joseph Proudhon and the revolution of 1848.* Loyola University of Chicago, 1971. DAI 32/05-A, p. 2622. Order No. 71-28,138.

SPITZER, Alan Barrie. *The revolutionary theories of Louis-Auguste Blanqui.* Columbia University, 1955. DAI 15/06, p. 1055. Order No. 12,071.

STEARNS, Peter Nathaniel. *Employer and worker in France, 1820-1848: a study of attitudes.* Harvard University, 1963.

VEXLER, Robert Irwin. *The intellectual origins of the French labor movement, 1852-1870.* University of Minnesota, 1965. DAI 27/03-A, p. 838. Order No. 66-9057.

REGIONAL STUDIES

ARCHER, Julian Pratt Waterman. *The First International and the Lyon Revolutionary Movement, 1864-1871.* University of Wisconsin, 1970. DAI 31/11-A, p. 5974. Order No. 70-24,730.

BEZUCHA, Robert Joseph. *Association and insurrection: the Republican party and the worker movement in Lyon, 1831-1835.* University of Michigan, 1968. DAI 30/01-A, p. 237. Order No. 69-12,040.

HAMMOND, William Eugene. *A political and economic history of the Marne-Rhine Canal, 1820-1860.* University of Missouri, 1962. DAI 23/07, p. 2505. Order No. 63-1553.

LEONARD, Charlene Marie. *The transformation of Lyon: public works of the second empire, 1853-1864.* University of California, Berkeley, 1958.

MARGADANT, Ted Winston. *The insurrection of 1851 in southern France: two case studies.* Harvard University, 1972.

MERRIMAN, John Mustard. *Radicalization and repression: the experience of the Limousin, 1848-1851.* University of Michigan, 1972. DAI 33/05-A, p. 2297. Order No. 72-29,149.

PINKNEY, David Henry. *Paris in the nineteenth century: a study in urban growth.* Harvard University, 1941.

SCOTT, Joan Wallach. *Les verriers de Carmaux, 1850-1914.* The University of Wisconsin, 1969. DAI 31/03-A, p. 1210. Order No. 70-3700.

SEWELL, William Hamilton. *The structure of the working class of Marseille in the middle of the nineteenth century.* University of California, Berkeley, 1971.

SMITH, J. Harvey. *Village revolution: agricultural workers of Cruzy (Herault), 1850-1910.* University of Wisconsin, 1972.

INTELLECTUAL AND CULTURAL

BALL, Rex Harrison. *America in the French liberal mind, 1815-1871.* Harvard University, 1970.

BEIRER, Dora. *Ernest Renan: his role in the culture of modern France.* Columbia University, 1951. DAI 11/04, p. 995. Order No. 2797.

CAMPBELL, Stuart Lorin. *Historical objectives and objective history: perspectives on the historiography of the Second Empire.* University of Rochester, 1969. DAI 30/09-A, p. 3880. Order No. 70-2851.

CLARK, Linda Loeb. *Social Darwinism and French intellectuals, 1860-1915.* The University of North Carolina at Chapel Hill, 1968. DAI 18/24-A, p. 4417. Order No. 69-10,141.

COOLEY, Martha Helms. *Nineteenth century French historical research on Russia— Louis Leger, Alfred Rambaud, Anatole Leroy-Beaulieu.* Indiana University, 1971. DAI 32/05-A, p. 2595. Order No. 71-29,564.

CORDOVA, Abraham Albert. *Intellectuals in culture and politics: a study of French men of ideas in the first half of the nineteenth century.* Brandeis University, 1971. DAI 32/02-A, p. 1083. Order No. 71-20,326.

COUSE, G. S. *The historical consciousness of the doctrinaires as represented by Pierre Paul Royer-Collard, François Guizot, and Victor Cousin.* University of Chicago, 1965.

DERBY, Donald. *Edgar Quinet: a French historian and his work.* Harvard University, 1940.

DREHER, Robert Edward. *Arthur de Gobineau: an intellectual portrait.* The University of Wisconsin, 1970. DAI 31/9-A, p. 4668. Order No. 70-22,047.

DUNN, Richard Maxwell. *The portrait in France, 1830-1850: the study of a literary genre.* Yale University, 1969. DAI 31/03-A, p. 1269. Order No. 70-16,259.

FRANKEL, Eugene. *Jean-Baptiste Biot: the career of a physicist in nineteenth century France.* Princeton University, 1972.

FURMAN, Nelly. *La* Revue des Deux Mondes *et le romantisme français (1831-1848).* Columbia University, 1972. DAI 33/05-A, p. 2371. Order No. 72-28,036.

GALE, John Edward. *The literary image of Napoleon III in the works of Victor Hugo.* University of Colorado, 1967. DAI 29/02-A, p. 597. Order No. 68-10,595.

GORJANC, Adele Alexandra. *Voltaire's conception of the four great ages of civilization: its fortune among nineteenth century French critics and historians.* University of Missouri, 1967. DAI 28/07-A, p. 2683. Order No. 68-296.

HOLMES, Frederic Lawrence. *Claude Bernard and the concept of the internal environment.* Harvard University, 1962.

HUPPERT, Ellen Taylor. *The image of the city: the Paris of the novelists from Stendhal to Zola.* University of California, Berkeley, 1970. DAI 31/10-A, p. 5320. Order No. 71-9835.

KELLNER, Hans Dodds. *Frédéric Le Play and the development of modern sociology.* University of Rochester, 1972. DAI 33/06-A, p. 2861. Order No. 72-28,762.

KENISTON, Muriel Cleverly. *Romanticism and conservatism in France (1815-1848).* University of Illinois, 1949. DAI 9/03, p. 124. Order No. 1397.

MAZLISH, Bruce. *Burke Bonald and de Maistre: a study in conservatism.* Columbia University, 1955. DAI 15/07, p. 1228. Order No. 12,314.

NIMMONS, Phyllis Ann Boden. *The novels of Alphonse Daudet: the influence of money in the French society of his time.* Rice University, 1970. DAI 31/06-A, p. 2930. Order No. 70-23,560.

NISBET, Robert O. *The social group in French thought.* University of California, Berkeley, 1940.

O'CONNOR, M. Consolata. *The historical thought of François Guizot.* Catholic University of America, 1955.

PEARSON, Charles S. *The politico-social ideas of Hugues Félicité Robert de Lamennais, 1830-1854.* New York University, 1936.

PETRI, Barbara Patricia. *The historical thought of P.-J.-B. Buchez.* Catholic University of America, 1959.

POWERS, Richard Howard. *Edgar Quinet: a study in anti-clerical and nationalistic aspects of French liberalism.* The Ohio State University, 1953. DAI 18/03, p. 1025. Order No. 58-712.

QUINLAN, M. Hall, Mother. *The historical thought of the Vicomte de Bonald.* Catholic University of America, 1953.

REARICK, Charles Walter. *Historians and folklore in nineteenth-century France.* Harvard University, 1968.

SMITH, Mary Agnes Monroe. *The first historians of the French Revolution.* Western Reserve University, 1966. DAI 27/12-A, p. 4204. Order No. 67-4655.

STEBBINS, Robert Ernest. *French reactions to Darwin, 1859-1882.* University of Minnesota, 1965. DAI 26/08, p. 4615. Order No. 65-15,223.

TURBOW, Gerald Dale. *Wagnerism in France, 1839-1870: a measure of a social and political trend.* University of California, Los Angeles, 1965. DAI 26/07, p. 3919. Order No. 65-12,688.

86

WEINBERG, Arthur Myron. *The artist and the social philosopher: the debate between art and morality in mid-nineteenth century France.* Columbia University, 1951. DAI 12/01, p. 84. Order No. 3398.

WHITEHILL, David P. *The Philhellenic movement in France, 1821-1830.* Harvard University, 1939.

RELIGION

ALLISON, John Maudgridge Snowden. *Church and state in the reign of Louis Philippe, 1830-1848.* Princeton University, 1914.

AUGUSTINE, Flavia. *Le Correspondant: French liberal Catholic journal, 1843-1855.* Catholic University of America, 1959.

COLLINS, Ross William. *Catholicism and the second French republic, 1848-1852.* Columbia University, 1923.

GHEZZI, Bertil William. *L'Univers and the definition of papal infallibility.* University of Notre Dame, 1969. DAI 30/11-A, p. 4911. Order No. 70-7889.

GOLDSTEIN, Doris Silk. *Church and society: a study of the religious outlook of Alexis de Tocqueville.* Bryn Mawr, 1956. DAI 16/08, p. 1434. Order No. 16,950.

HASSETT, Mary Barat. *Dupanloup on the "Roman Question".* St. Louis University, 1967. DAI 28/08-A, p. 3110. Order No. 68-1269.

HUCKABY, John Keith. *Liberal Catholicism in France, 1843-1870.* The Ohio State University, 1957. DAI 18/03, p. 1023. Order No. 58-539.

McCARTHY, Joan M. *French native policy and the Church in Algeria.* University of California, Berkeley, 1938.

MAY, Anita Marie Rasi. *The challenge of the French Catholic press to episcopal authority, 1842 to 1860: a crisis of modernization.* University of Pittsburgh, 1970. DAI 31/05-A, p. 2315. Order No. 70-20,330.

OSEN, James Lynn. *The revival of the French Reformed Church, 1830-1852.* The University of Wisconsin, 1966. DAI 28/02-A, p. 601. Order No. 66-1302.

THE THIRD REPUBLIC, 1870-1940

GENERAL AND MISCELLANEOUS

ALLEN, Mary Kibbe. *The relations between France and Italy, 1885-1915.* Clark University, 1927

ALROY, Gil Carl. *Radicalism and modernization: the French problem.* Princeton University, 1962. DAI 24/02, p. 809. Order No. 63-494.

ATKINSON, John L. B. *Camille Barrère, ambassador to Rome: the first eight years of a mission.* University of Pennsylvania, 1951.

BAIN, Chester Arthur. *The history of Vietnam from the French penetration to 1939. (Parts I-III).* The American University, 1956. DAI 17/03, p. 610. Order No. 17,524.

BETTS, Raymond Frederick. *The Problem of French colonial doctrine, 1890-1914: assimilation and association.* Columbia University, 1958. DAI 21/04, p. 860. Order No. 60-3044.

BOWIE, Leland Louis. *The protégé system in Morocco, 1880-1904.* The University of Michigan, 1970. DAI 31/08-A, p. 4076. Order No. 71-4571.

BROWN, Edmund Alden. *French parties and the electoral law, 1871-1956.* Columbia University, 1957. DAI 18/03, p. 1019. Order No. 25,141.

BROWN, Leon Carl. *The modernization of Tunisia: a study of ideological changes under the impact of the French protectorate.* Harvard University, 1962.

BUNCHE, Ralph J. *French administration in Togoland and Dahomey.* Harvard University, 1934.

BURKE, Edmund, III. *Moroccan political responses to French penetration, 1900-1912.* Princeton University, 1970. DAI 31/06-A, p. 2834. Order No. 70-23,603.

CALKINS, Mary Ann. *The political career of Maurice Barrès, 1888-1923: the trial of a nationalist ideology.* Bryn Mawr College, 1969.

CARDON, Louis Bellamy. *The economic bases of Franco-German rivalry in Morocco, 1906-1909.* University of California, Berkeley, 1966. DAI 27/05-A, p. 1314. Order No. 66-8284.

CARRIER, Fred J. *Jacques Doriot, a political biography.* University of Wisconsin, 1968. DAI 29/12-A, p. 4415. Order No. 69-885.

COHEN, William Benjamin. *Rulers of empire: the French colonial service in Africa, 1880-1960.* Stanford University, 1968. DAI 29/12-A, p. 4418. Order No. 69-8165.

CONFER, Carl V. *Lyautey and the Moroccan problem, 1903 to 1907.* University of Pennsylvania, 1939.

COOKE, James Jerome. *Eugène Étienne and new French imperialism 1880-1910.* University of Georgia, 1969. DAI 30/12-A, p. 5371. Order No. 70-10,173.

DeTARR, Francis. *Men, ideas, and politics: the French Radical party from Herriot to Mendès-France.* Yale University, 1958.

DILLA, Geraldine P. *France and England: a bibliographical study of mutual analyses 1898-1914.* George Peabody College for Teachers, 1935.

DOIRON, Gerald Joseph. *The policy of association in Morocco under Marshal Lyautey, 1912-1925.* Boston University Graduate School, 1971. DAI 32/04-A, p. 2023. Order No. 71-26,398.

DOWNUM, Joel G. *The place of Madagascar in Anglo-French rivalry.* University of Texas at Austin, 1939.

DUNN, Ross Edmunds. *The colonial offensive in southeastern Morocco, 1881-1912: patterns of response.* The University of Wisconsin, 1969. DAI 30/01-A, p. 244. Order No. 69-4388.

ECHENBERG, Myron Joel. *African reaction to French conquest: upper Volta in the late nineteenth century.* University of Wisconsin, 1971. DAI 32/06-A, p. 3200. Order No. 71-25,467.

ENNIS, Thomas E. *The French administration and problems in Indochina.* University of Minnesota, 1935.

GOLDMAN, Minton Forman. *Origins and development of the colonial conflicts resolved by the Anglo-French Entente of 1904.* Fletcher School of Law and Diplomacy (Tufts University), 1965.

HAFFAR, Ahmad Rafic. *France in the establishment of greater Lebanon: a study of French expansionism on the eve of the First World War.* Princeton University, 9161. DAI 22/07, p. 2447. Order No. 61-4780.

HARTEL, William Clark. *The French Colonial party, 1895-1905.* The Ohio State University, 1962. DAI 23/09, p. 3333. Order No. 63-2499.

HEISSER, David Calvin Reynolds. *The impact of the great war on French imperialism, 1914-1924.* University of North Carolina at Chapel Hill, 1972. DAI 33/04-A, p. 1643. Order No. 72-24,796.

JESSNER, Sabine L. M. *Edouard Herriot: patriarch of the republic.* Columbia University, 1964. DAI 25/12, p. 7225. Order No. 64-9886.

KABBANI, Rashid. *Morocco: from protectorate to independence, 1912-1956.* The American University, 1957. DAI 17/09, p. 2051. Order No. 21,963.

LAFFEY, John Francis. *French imperialism and the Lyon mission to China.* Cornell University, 1967. DAI 28/01-A, p. 176. Order No. 67-1390.

LaFUZE, George L. *Great Britain, France, and the Siamese question, 1885-1904.* University of Illinois, 1936.

88

LEOPARD, Donald Dean. *The French conquest and pacification of Madagascar, 1885-1905.* The Ohio State University, 1966. DAI 27/05-A, p. 1321. Order No. 66-10,026.

LING, Dwight L. *The French occupation and administration of Tunisia, 1881-1892.* University of Illinois, 1955. DAI 15/11, p. 2181. Order No. 13,514.

McKAY, Donald V. *The French acquisition of Tunis.* Cornell University, 1939.

McNIVEN, James Daniel. *French aid policies toward the African territories: from empire to independence, 1900-1966.* The University of Michigan, 1972. DAI 33/11-A, p. 6416. Order No. 73-11,204.

MANSUR, Abed Al-Hafiz. *Anglo-French rivalry in the Levant and the question of Syrio-Lebanese independence, 1939-1943.* University of Oregon, 1964. DAI 25/10, p. 5890. Order No. 65-2473.

MITCHELL, Royal Judson. *Coalition theory and multi-party politics: application of Riker's theory to the problem of government formation in the Third and Fourth French Republics.* University of Notre Dame, 1968. DAI 29/09-A, p. 3196. Order No. 69-4072.

O'DONNELL, Joseph Dean, Jr. *Charles Cardinal Lavigerie and the establishment of the 1881 French protectorate in Tunisia.* Rutgers University The State University of New Jersey, 1970. DAI 31/11-A, p. 5994. Order No. 71-12,266.

OSGOOD, Samuel Maurice. *The life and politics of Henri, Comte de Paris.* Clark University, 1953. DAI 13/05, p. 781. Order No. 5847.

PERSELL, Stuart Michael. *The French colonial lobby, 1899-1914.* Stanford University, 1969. DAI 30/12-A, p. 5393. Order No. 70-10,505.

RHOADES, James N. *Alexandre Ribot, French parliamentarian and statesman, 1878-1923: a study of significant phases of his career.* University of California, Berkeley, 1952.

RIFE, John Merle, Jr. *The political career of Louis Barthou, 1889-1913.* The Ohio State

University, 1964. DAI 25/02, p. 1178. Order No. 64-9587.

ROLAND, Joan Gardner. *The Alliance Israelite Universelle and French policy in North Africa, 1860-1918.* Columbia University, 1969. DAI 30/10-A, p. 4384. Order No. 70-7058.

SANJIAN, Avedis Krikor. *The Sanjak of Alexandretta (Hatay): a study in Franco-Turco-Syrian relations.* The University of Michigan, 1956. DAI 17/06, p. 1322. Order No. 21,356.

SHERWOOD, John Michael. *The life of Georges Mandel: a study in French politics from Clemenceau to Pétain.* Columbia University, 1967. DAI 31/04-A, p. 1740. Order No. 70-18,853.

SHORROCK, William Irwin. *France in Syria and Lebanon 1901-1914: pre-war origins of the mandate.* The University of Wisconsin, 1968. DAI 29/06-A, p. 1853. Order No. 68-13,661.

SLAWECKI, Leon M. S. *French policy towards the Chinese in Madagascar.* Yale University, 1969. DAI 31/03-A, p. 1351. Order No. 70-17,441.

THE THIRD REPUBLIC, 1870-1900

BERTOCCI, Philip Anton. *Jules Simon, 1814-1896: a study of republican religious politics in France.* Yale University, 1970. DAI 31/12-A, p. 6508. Order No. 71-16,119.

BLAISDELL, Lowell L. *Jules Ferry and the Government of National Defense.* University of Wisconsin, 1949.

BLICK, Boris Andre. *Waldeck-Rousseau (1894-1904).* The University of Wisconsin, 1958. DAI 22/06, p. 1955. Order No. 61-5892.

BROWN, Roger Glenn. *The Dreyfus Affair and Fashoda: a study of the interaction of domestic and international politics, 1893-1898.* University of California, Berkeley, 1968. DAI 29/09-A, p. 3067. Order No. 69-3573.

BUCKLEY, John James. *The Anglo-German convention of 1898 and French foreign policy.* St. Louis University, 1972. DAI 33/03-A, p. 1103. Order No. 72-23,908.

BYRD, Edward Leavell, Jr. *Paul Déroulède, revanchist.* Texas Tech University, 1970. DAI 31/05-A, p. 2297. Order No. 70-20,685.

BYRNES, Robert F. *Anti-Semitism in France, 1870-1894.* Harvard University, 1947.

CARNES, Jess G. *The French army officers and the establishment of the Republic, 1876-1889.* Cornell University, 1950.

CLARY, Norman James. *French antisemitism during the years of Drumont and Dreyfus, 1886-1906.* The Ohio State University, 1970. DAI 31/07-A, p. 3462. Order No. 70-26,265.

DOTY, Charles Stewart. *Maurice Barrès and the fate of Boulangism: the political career of Maurice Barrès (1888-1906).* The Ohio State University, 1964. DAI 25/11, p. 6564. Order No. 65-3845.

DRIGGS, Orval T., Jr. *French reaction to the Central European alliances, 1871-1890.* University of Pennsylvania, 1950.

EASTMAN, Lloyd Eric. *Reaction of Chinese officials to foreign aggression: a study of the Sino-French controversy, 1880-1885.* Harvard University, 1963.

ELWITT, Sanford Harold. *The radicals enter French politics, 1870-1875.* Cornell University, 1963. DAI 24/09, p. 3708. Order No. 64-3676.

EMERY, Harold Wilson, Jr. *The mission of Albert Billot in Rome, 1890-1898, and the Franco-Italian rapprochement.* University of Pennsylvania, 1964. DAI 25/09, p. 5236. Order No. 64-10,370.

GILLEN, James Frederick John. *The Christian monarchy in France, 1870-1880: a study of the nature and influence of legitimism.* Harvard University, 1942.

GOODE, James Hubbard. *The Fashoda crisis: a survey of Anglo-French imperial policy on the Upper Nile question, 1882-1899.* North Texas State University, 1972. DAI 32/12-A, p. 6890. Order No. 72-17,008.

GRIFFIN, David Eugene. *Adolphe Thiers, the mayors, and the coming of the Paris Commune of 1871.* University of California, Santa Barbara, 1971. DAI 32/12-A, p. 6891. Order No. 72-18,239.

HAUSE, Steven Charles. *Théophile Delcassé's first years at the Quai D'Orsay: French diplomacy between Britain and Germany, 1898-1901.* University of Washington, 1969. DAI 30/07-A, p.2941. Order No. 69-22,532.

HINGER, George W. *The attitudes of Le Correspondent and La Revue Des Deux Mondes toward the political role of Austria-Hungary during the years 1890-1914.* Catholic University of America, 1961.

HIRSHFIELD, Claire. *The Marquis of Dufferin and Ava, ambassador to France.* University of Pennsylvania, 1965. DAI 26/09, p. 5399. Order No. 66-271.

HSIEH, Pei-Chih. *Diplomacy of the Sino-French War, 1883-1885.* University of Pennsylvania, 1968. DAI 29/07-A, p. 2181. Order No. 69-122.

IIAMS, Thomas Marion, Jr. *Gabriel Hanotaux at the Quai D'Orsay: the foreign policy of France, 1894-1898.* Columbia University, 1960. DAI 21/03, p. 607. Order No. 60-2453.

IRVINE, Dallas D. *French military policy and the Russian alliance of 1891.* University of Pennsylvania, 1934.

KANE, Nancy Ann. *The Egyptian question in French foreign policy, 1881-1904.* Stanford University, 1959. DAI 19/09, p. 2328. Order No. 59-271.

KATZ, Bruno J. *French attempts to bring about cooperation with Germany, 1871-1900.* University of California, Berkeley, 1951.

KNOX, Clinton Everett. *French interests and policy in the Ottoman Empire, 1887-1905.* Harvard University, 1940.

KYTE, George Wallace. *Louis Adolphe Thiers, liberator of French territory, 1871-1873.* University of California, Berkeley, 1944.

LEATHERS, Noel L. *France and the Balkans, 1871-1879.* The University of Oklahoma,

1963. DAI 24/04, p. 1594. Order No. 63-6607.

LOCKE, Bobby Ray. *The Legitimists: a study in social mentality. The Royalists right in the French National Assembly of 1871.* University of California, Los Angeles, 1965. DAI 26/01, p. 339. Order No. 65-6948.

MACDONALD, John Frederick. *Camille Barrère and the conduct of Delcassian diplomacy in Italy, 1898-1902.* University of California, Los Angeles, 1970. DAI 31/02-A, p. 713. Order No. 70-14,305.

MARSHALL, Philip Ray. *France and the Congress of Berlin.* University of Pennsylvania, 1969. DAI 30/06-Á, p. 2464. Order No. 69-21,401.

MUIRHEAD, George R. *French attitudes toward the problems of defeat and occupation, 1870-1873.* The University of Iowa, 1951.

MURPHY, Agnes L. *The ideology of French imperialism, 1871-1881.* The Catholic University of America, 1949.

OFFEN, Karen Marie Stedtfeld. *The political career of Paul de Cassagnac.* Stanford University, 1971. DAI 32/02-A, p. 893. Order No. 71-19,737.

PERKINS, Charles Alfred. *French Catholic opinion and imperial expansion, 1880-1886.* Harvard University, 1965.

POWER, Thomas F. *Jules Ferry and the renaissance of French imperialism.* Columbia University, 1944.

ROTHNEY, John Alexander Murray. *The resurgence and eclipse of Bonapartism, 1870-1879.* Harvard University, 1964.

RUTKOFF, Peter Maxim. *Revanche and revision: Paul Déroulède and the Ligue des Patriotes 1897-1900.* University of Pennsylvania, 1971. DAI 32/04-A, p. 2042. Order No. 71-26,079.

SCHMIDT, Martin Edward. *The diplomacy of Alexandre Ribot, 1890-1893.* University of Pennsylvania, 1966. DAI 27/12-A, p. 4202. Order No. 67-7874.

SCHOTT, Carl Gerard. *The Franco-German duel for Russian support: the Russian*

mission of General Adolphe Le Flô, 1871-79. University of Notre Dame, 1971. DAI 32/05-A, p. 2619. Order No. 71-27,770.

SCOTT, John Anthony. *Republican ideas and the liberal tradition in France 1870-1914.* Columbia University, 1950. DAI 10/03, p. 204. Order No. 1724.

SEAGER, Frederic H. *The Boulanger Affair, political crossroad of France, 1886-1889.* Columbia University, 1965. DAI 27/02-A, p. 429. Order No. 66-6956.

SEDGWICK, Alexander. *The Ralliement in French politics, 1890-98.* Harvard University, 1963.

SHIELDS, Dorothy Axford. *Solidarity: a French doctrine of state intervention.* University of Pittsburgh, 1942.

SWEITZER, Vesta C. *French political parties, 1885-99.* University of Chicago, 1934.

THOMPSON, Dorothy L. *France, the Czechs, and the question of Austria, 1867-1885.* Stanford University, 1946.

THORSON, Winston Bernard. *Charles de Freycinet as foreign minister of France: a study in the diplomacy of the early Third Republic.* University of Minnesota, 1940.

VON VORYS, Karl. *The foundations of the French Third Republic. A socio-political analysis of its first twenty-five years, 1870-1895.* Georgetown University, 1956.

WARD, James Edward. *Franco-Vatican relations, 1878-1892. The diplomatic origins of the Ralliement.* Cornell University, 1963. DAI 23/12, p. 4671. Order No. 63-3154.

WHITEHEAD, James Louis. *French reaction to American imperialism, 1895-1908.* University of Pennsylvania, 1942.

WILLIAMS, Richmond Dean. *Lord Salisbury's policy toward France, 1886-1892.* University of Pennsylvania, 1959. DAI 20/05, p. 1760. Order No. 59-4677.

WILSON, John H. *Nationalist demonstrations in France, 1880-1900.* University of Chicago, 1971.

WOODALL, John Burwell. *The Ralliement in France: origins and early history, 1876-1894.* Columbia University, 1964. DAI 28/02-A, p. 611. Order No. 67-10,394.

THE THIRD REPUBLIC, 1900-1918

ADAMS, Wallace Earl. *André Tardieu and French foreign policy 1902-1919.* Stanford University, 1959. DAI 20/04, p. 1334. Order No. 59-3676.

BENNETT, Harry L. *From entente to alliance, a history of the Entente Cordiale, 1904-1914.* Yale University, 1954.

BURNIKEL, Catherine T. *Camille Barrère and the Franco-Italian rapproachment: 1898-1902.* Loyola University of Chicago, 1972. DAI 33/04-A, p. 1630. Order No. 72-25,090.

CAIRNS, John C. *France in the international crisis, 1911-1914: foreign policy, diplomacy and their national background.* Cornell University, 1951.

CHAMBERS, Samuel T. *Franco-American relations, 1897-1914.* Georgetown University, 1951.

CHAPMAN, Geoffrey Williams. *Decision for war: the domestic political context of French diplomacy, 1911-1914.* Princeton University, 1972. DAI 33/01-A, p. 245. Order No. 72-18,766.

CLAYPOOL, James Chester. *The early political career of Aristide Briand, 1902-1914.* University of Kentucky, 1968. DAI 33/05-A, p. 1951. Order No. 69-18,197.

CLEVELAND, Robert Eugene. *French attitudes toward the 'German problem', 1914-1919.* The University of Nebraska, 1957. DAI 17/09, p. 1991. Order No. 22,128.

DAVIDSON, Kerry. *The French Socialist party and parliamentary efforts to achieve social reform, 1906-1914.* Tulane University, 1970. DAI 31/06-A, p. 2838. Order No. 70-24,515.

EUBANK, Weaver K., Jr. *The diplomatic career of Paul Cambon.* University of Pennsylvania, 1952.

FARMAKIDES, Anna. *French foreign policy under the "Bloc des Gauches."* McGill University, 1960.

FARMER, Marlin K. *The foreign policy of M. Théophile Delcassé.* Ohio State University, 1937.

FARRAR, Marjorie Milbank. *French blockade policy, 1914-1918: a study in economic warfare.* Stanford University, 1968. DAI 29/07-A, p. 2177. Order No. 69-218.

GOMPF, Eloise. *France and the Vatican: the break in relations, 1904.* Indiana University, 1958. DAI 19/03, p. 517. Order No. 58-2912.

GRAHAM, James Quentin, Jr. *The French Radical and Radical-Socialist party, 1906-1914.* The Ohio State University, 1962. DAI 23/02, p. 615. Order No. 62-3583.

HILL, Albert Seymour. *The Radical-Socialist party: promise and performance, 1900-1910.* Harvard University, 1963.

HUNTER, John Cleary. *The strength of France on the eve of World War I: a study of French self-confidence as evidenced in the parliamentary debate on the Three-Year Service Law of 1913.* Harvard University, 1959.

JONES, Francis L. *French foreign policy, 1911-1913.* Clark University, 1952.

KIEFFER, Martin John. *French "defeatism" in World War I.* Columbia University, 1961. DAI 21/11, p. 3439. Order No. 61-864.

KING, Jere C., Jr. *The conflict between the high command and the French National Assembly, 1914-1918; a study of the struggle between the military and civilian forces directing France's war policy.* University of California, Berkeley, 1946.

LAGOW, Thomas Kenneth, Jr. *Tensions in the Triple Entente, as viewed from Paris and London, 1911-1914.* University of Georgia, 1968. DAI 29/08-A, p. 2644. Order No. 69-3464.

LEAMAN, Bertha R. *French foreign and colonial policy under Radical Socialist party control, 1898-1905.* University of Chicago, 1935.

LEWIS, Tom Tandy. *Franco-American diplomatic relations, 1898-1907.* The University of Oklahoma, 1970. DAI 31/07-A, p. 3475. Order No. 71-1492.

McGEOCH, Lyle Archibald. *The role of Lord Lansdowne in the diplomatic negotiations connected with the Anglo-French agreement of 8 April 1904.* University of Pennsylvania, 1965. DAI 26/01, p. 340. Order No. 65-5785.

MARKOFF, Robert Allen. *Opposition to the war in France, 1914-1918.* University of Pennsylvania, 1962. DAI 23/12, p. 4666. Order No. 63-4164.

MATHEWS, Joseph J. *Egypt and the formation of the Anglo-French entente of 1904.* University of Pennsylvania, 1935.

MATHIEU, Donald Roland. *The role of Russia in French foreign policy, 1908-1914.* Stanford University, 1968. DAI 29/11-A, p. 3957. Order No. 69-8225.

MERRIMAN, Howard M. *The French and Woodrow Wilson, 1912-1918: a study in public opinion.* Harvard University, 1937.

NEWHALL, David Sowle. *Georges Clemenceau, 1902-1906: "An Old Beginner."* Harvard University, 1963.

PARTIN, Malcolm Overstreet. *The politics of anticlericalism: Waldeck-Rousseau, Combes, and the church, 1899-1905.* Duke University, 1967. DAI 28/09-A, p. 3614. Order No. 68-3439.

PAYNE, David Sylvester. *The foreign policy of Georges Clemenceau: 1917-1920.* Duke University, 1970. DAI 31/10-A, p. 5330. Order No. 71-10,408.

PICKETT, Ralph H. *French foreign policy during the first Poincaré ministry, January 14, 1912 to January 18, 1913.* University of Pennsylvania, 1937.

REYNOLDS, Michael Connolly. *Paul Painlevé and the parliamentary crisis in France in 1917.* Northwestern University, 1966. DAI 27/07-A, p. 2123. Order No. 66-14,052.

STELOFF, Charles Gustav. *France and Weltpolitik: the image and role of France in German public opinion, 1911-14.* Stanford University, 1971.

STEYTLER, Edmund John. *France and the Wilsonian program, a study of conflicting conceptions of victory, 1914-1918, with special emphasis on French nationalist criticism of Wilson's peace program.* University of North Carolina at Chapel Hill, 1957.

STUART, Graham Henry. *French foreign policy from Fashoda to Sarajevo (1898-1914).* University of Wisconsin, 1920.

SUMLER, David E. *Polarization in French politics, 1909-1914.* Princeton University, 1969. DAI 30/03-A, p. 1122. Order No. 69-14,439.

TANENBAUM, Jan Karl. *The radical republican general: a political and military study of General Sarrail, 1900-1917.* University of California, Berkeley, 1969. DAI 30/10-A, p. 4390. Order No. 70-6238.

TANNENBAUM, Edward R. *The Action française before the First World War.* University of Chicago, 1950.

TEWELL, Wendell H. *Two protectorate relationships in the international community: France and Tunisia, France and Morocco.* Columbia University, 1952. DAI 12/05, p. 742. Order No. 4242.

WATSON, Cicely M. *The campaign against the religious orders, 1901-1904: an analysis of the legislation passed by the Waldeck-Rousseau and Combes ministries.* Radcliffe College, 1951.

WHITE, Dorothy S. *Franco-American relations in 1917-1918: war aims and peace prospects.* University of Pennsylvania, 1954. DAI 14/05, p. 820. Order No. 7821.

WILCOX, Carol Harting. *The Franco-Russian alliance, 1908-1911.* Clark University, 1968. DAI 29/08-A, p. 2662. Order No. 69-2806.

WILEY, Evelyn Virginia. *Jean Jules Jusserand and the first Moroccan crisis, 1903-1906.* University of Pennsylvania, 1959. DAI 20/05, p. 1760. Order No. 59-4676.

WRIGHT, Gordon Justin. *Raymond Poincaré and the French presidency.* Stanford University, 1940.

THE THIRD REPUBLIC, 1918-1940

ADAMS, Derrik Brian. *The role of military considerations in Anglo-French decision-making in the Munich crisis.* University of Denver, 1971.

ALLEN, Luther. *The French Left and Soviet Russia to 1936: interaction between French party alliances and Franco-Soviet diplomacy.* University of Chicago, 1956.

BANKWITZ, Philip C. F. *Weygand: a biographical study.* Harvard University, 1952.

BERNARD, Laureat Odilon Joseph. *Democratic crisis of 1934 in France.* Boston University, 1957. DAI 17/12, p. 2988. Order No. 21,410.

BINION, Rudolph. *Defeated leaders: the political fate of Caillaux, Jouvenel, and Tardieu.* Columbia University, 1960.

BIRN, Donald S. *Britain and France at the Washington Conference, 1921-1922.* Columbia University, 1964. DAI 26/04, p. 2156. Order No. 65-7340.

BRANDSTADTER, Michael. *Paul Reynaud and the Third French Republic, 1919-1939: French political conservatism in the interwar years.* Duke University, 1971. DAI 32/10-A, p. 5702. Order No. 72-11,070.

BURNETT, Robert Adair. *Georges Clemenceau in the Paris Peace Conference 1919.* The University of North Carolina at Chapel Hill, 1968. DAI 29/07-A, p. 2171. Order No. 69-1585.

CAMERON, Elizabeth Ripley. *France turns to appeasement. A study in foreign policy, 1933-1936.* University of Pennsylvania, 1941.

CLAPHAM, Noel Pavitt. *Anglo-French influence on Hitler's Northern policy, September, 1939-April, 1940.* The University of Nebraska, 1968. DAI 29/07-A, p. 2175. Order No. 68-18,013.

COX, Frederick J. *French strategy at the Paris Peace Conference: a study of the conflict between Foch and Clemenceau over the problem of security.* University of California, Berkeley, 1947.

DeMYER, William F. *The role of Léon Blum in the French Chamber of Deputies, 1919-1933.* Georgetown University, 1954.

DREIFORT, John E. *Yvon Delbos and the formulation of French foreign policy*

during the Front Populaire, 1936-1938.* Kent State University, 1970. DAI 31/12-A, p. 6513. Order No. 71-13,429.

ENDRESS, Charles Albert. *The Republican-Radical and Radical-Socialist party in the French Popular Front, 1934-1938.* Tulane University, 1968. DAI 29/05-A, p. 1491. Order No. 68-15,243.

FRANCELLO, Joseph Anthony. *The Anglo-French-Russian negotiations of 1939.* Syracuse University, 1960. DAI 21/09, p. 2772. Order No. 61-508.

FRIEDBERG, Robert Michael. *French radical opinion and French foreign policy, 1933-1939.* University of Connecticut, 1972. DAI 33/06-A, p. 2858. Order No. 72-32,213.

FURNIA, Arthur Homer. *Anglo-French relations, 1931-1938.* Georgetown University, 1958.

GAY, Albert Carl, Jr. *The Daladier administration, 1938-1940.* University of North Carolina at Chapel Hill, 1970. DAI 31/08-A, p. 4085. Order No. 71-3556.

GOLDMAN, Aaron Leon. *Crisis in the Rhineland: Britain, France and the Rhineland crisis of 1936.* Indiana University, 1967. DAI 28/12-A, p. 4991. Order No. 68-2295.

GORDON, Richard A. *France and the Spanish civil war.* Columbia University, 1971.

GRAYSON, Jasper Glenn. *The foreign policy of Léon Blum and the Popular Front government in France.* University of North Carolina at Chapel Hill, 1962. DAI 23/12, p. 4664. Order No. 63-3492.

HAIGHT, John McVickar, Jr. *The Paris press and the neutrality policy of the United States, 1935-1939.* Northwestern University, 1953. DAI 13/06, p. 1171. Order No. 6199.

HALL, Hines Holt, III. *The Eastern question in Anglo-French relations, 1920-1922.* Vanderbilt University, 1971. DAI 32/02-A, p. 882. Order No. 71-20,287.

HARVEY, James C. *The French security thesis and French foreign policy from*

Paris to Locarno, 1919-1925. University of Texas, 1955.

HEADLEY, Anne Renouf. *National interests and supranational delegation: discontinuities and developments in Anglo-French Western European treaty systems during the 1920's.* Yale University, 1966. DAI 27/08-A, p. 2585. Order No. 67-80.

HEALEY, Gordon Daniel. *The reaction of the European powers to the Franco-Soviet Pact.* The University of Texas, 1963. DAI 24/12, p. 5358. Order No. 64-6604.

HOISINGTON, William Arch, Jr. *A businessman in politics in France, 1935-1955: the career of Jacques Lemaigre Dubreuil.* Stanford University, 1968. DAI 29/11-A, p. 3950. Order No. 69-8197.

HOLDER, Franklin Brown, Jr. *André Tardieu, politician and statesman of the French Third Republic; a study of his ministries and policies, 1929-1932.* University of California, Berkeley, 1962.

HYDE, John Michael. *Pierre Laval: the illusions of a realist, 1939-1940.* Harvard University, 1963.

IRVINE, William Drummond. *The Republican Federation of France during the 1930's.* Princeton University, 1972. DAI 33/03-A, p. 1112. Order No. 72-24,684.

JONES, John Rison, Jr. *The foreign policy of Louis Barthou, 1933-1934.* The University of North Carolina at Chapel Hill, 1958. DAI 19/11, p. 2926. Order No. 58-5951.

KESERICH, Charles. *The Popular Front in France and the Rhineland crisis of 1936.* Washington State University, 1966. DAI 27/09-A, p. 2990. Order No. 67-1565.

KOMJATHY, Anthony T. *Three small pivotal states in the crucible: the foreign relations of Austria, Hungary, and Yugoslavia with France, 1934-1935.* Loyola University of Chicago, 1972. DAI 33/04-A, p. 1650. Order No. 72-25,100.

LARMOUR, Peter John Garnett. *The French Radical party and the decline of the Third Republic, 1932-1940.* Columbia University, 1963. DAI 25/01, p. 435. Order No. 64-7172.

LAURENS, Franklin Davenport. *France and the Italo-Ethiopian crisis, 1935-1936.* University of North Carolina, 1962. DAI 23/12, p. 4665. Order No. 63-3500.

LEFFLER, Melvyn Paul. *The struggle for stability: American policy toward France, 1921-1933.* The Ohio State University, 1972. DAI 33/02-A, p. 700. Order No. 72-20,979.

LENOIR, Nancy Ruth. *The Ruhr in Anglo-French diplomacy: from the beginning of the occupation until the end of passive resistance.* The University of Oklahoma, 1972. DAI 33/10-A, p. 5655. Order No. 73-9163.

MAVRINAC, Albert A. *The French Popular Democratic Party, 1924-1940: a study in social Catholic-Christian democratic political action.* Harvard University, 1955.

MICAUD, Charles A. *The French right and Nazi Germany, 1933-1939; a study of public opinion.* Columbia University, 1944.

MOWEN, Howard Alden. *Rhenish separatism, 1919-1923: a study in the Franco-German problem.* Case Western Reserve University, 1956.

NOBLE, George B. *Policies and opinions at Paris, 1919; Wilsonian diplomacy, the Versailles peace, and French public opinion.* Columbia University, 1935.

NORRIS, James Robert. *Anglo-French conflict and the failure of the Geneva protocol in 1924-25.* Washington State University, 1971. DAI 32/01-A, p. 364. Order No. 71-18,588.

OLIN, John Charles. *Christian Democrats and foreign policy in France, 1919-1950.* Columbia University, 1960. DAI 21/04, p. 867. Order No. 60-3124.

PHIPPS, Foster V., Jr. *The climax of appeasement: British and French policy toward the Axis, September, 1938 to March, 1939.* The University of Texas at Austin, 1950.

PRIEST, Lyman W. *The Cordon Sanitaire, 1918-22.* Stanford University, 1954. DAI 14/12, p. 2330. Order No. 10,385.

REDMAN, Margaret E. *Franco-American diplomatic relations, 1919-1926.* Stanford University, 1946.

RESOVICH, Thomas. *France in transition: pre-Vichy diplomatic and political realignments May 10-June 25, 1940.* The University of Wisconsin, 1966. DAI 28/02-A, p. 604. Order No. 66-5937.

SAMPAS, Dorothy Helen Myers. *The controversy over the major political causes of the French collapse in 1940.* Georgetown University, 1970. DAI 31/08-A, p. 4243. Order No. 70-26,665.

SCHLESINGER, Mildred Saks. *The French Radical party: its organization and parliamentary politics, 1914-1932.* Yale University, 1961.

SCHWEITZER, Thomas Adrian. *The French colonialist lobby in the 1930's: the economic foundations of imperialism.* The University of Wisconsin, 1971. DAI 32/09-A, p. 5164. Order No. 72-2661.

SCOTT, William E. *The origins of the Franco-Soviet Pact of 1935.* Yale University, 1954.

SILVESTRI, Gino Dominic. *Paul Reynaud and the fall of France.* Syracuse University, 1969. DAI 30/12-A, p. 5396. Order No. 70-10,397.

SMART, Terry Lee. *The French intervention in the Ukraine, 1918-1919.* University of Kansas, 1968. DAI 30/01-A, p. 259. Order No. 69-11,250.

SMITH, Brenton Hoyt. *The collapse of France in World War II and the armistice conventions of June 1940.* The University of Michigan, 1959. DAI 20/04, p. 1347. Order No. 59-3958.

STARK, Benton Charles. *A political history of the Maginot Line.* Columbia University, 1972. DAI 33/01-A, p. 262. Order No. 72-19,165.

STRAUSS, David. *Anti-Americanism and the defense of France: an analysis of French travel reports, 1917-1960.* Columbia University, 1968. DAI 30/02-A, p. 669. Order No. 69-13,005.

SZALUTA, Jacques. *Marshal Pétain between two wars, 1918-1940: the interplay of personality and circumstances.* Columbia University, 1969. DAI 33/01-A, p. 263. Order No. 72-19,091.

TRAFFORD, David W. *A study of the problem of French security and the British and French presses, 1919-1925, a study in public opinion.* Indiana University, 1948.

UTT, Walter C. *Decree-laws of the Third Republic 1916-1939: a study of the decline of the French parliamentary system.* University of California, Berkeley, 1952.

WATHEN, M. Antonia. *The policy of England and France toward the "Anschluss" of 1938.* Catholic University of America, 1954.

WELCH, Eileen Joseph. *France and her East European allies in the League of Nations, 1920-1926.* Fordham University, 1958.

WIT, Daniel. *Ideology and French foreign policy: 1919-1948.* Princeton University, 1951. DAI 13/04, p. 579. Order No. 5178.

WOLFF, George Elliott. *Executive-legislative relations in the Third French Republic, 1920-1938.* University of North Carolina at Chapel Hill, 1956.

WYLY, Theodore Dawson. *Foreign relations of the United States with France from 1919 to 1929.* Fletcher School of Law and Diplomacy (Tufts University), 1964.

YATES, Louis A. R. *The United States and French security, 1917-1921 — a study of the Treaty of Guarantee.* University of Southern California, 1951.

GOVERNMENT, ADMINISTRATION, EDUCATION, MILITARY

ACOMB, Evelyn M. *The French laic laws (1879-1889); the first anti-clerical campaign of the Third French Republic.* Columbia University, 1942.

BREWER, James Henry Fitzgerald. *Politics in the French army: the aftermath of the Dreyfus case, 1899-1905.* The George Washington University, 1967. DAI 28/05-A, p. 1754. Order No. 67-14,398.

BROGDEN, Neal H. *French military reform after the defeat of 1870-1871.* University of California, Los Angeles, 1961.

CHALLENER, Richard Delo. *French thought on the nation in arms; evolution and consequences of a military theory, 1866-1939.* Columbia University, 1952. DAI 12/05, p. 732. Order No. 4165.

CLARKE, Jeffrey Johnstone. *Military technology in republican France: the evolution of the French armored force, 1917-1940.* Duke University, 1969. DAI 30/08-A, p. 3390. Order No. 70-2147.

COOX, Alvin D. *French military doctrine 1919-1939: concepts of ground and aerial warfare.* Harvard University, 1951.

COYLE, Joanne Marie. *Indochinese administrative elites: French educational policy and practice, 1917-1945.* Fletcher School of Law and Diplomacy (Tufts University), 1963.

FREEDEMAN, Charles E. *A history of the Conseil d'État since 1872.* Columbia University, 1958. DAI 18/06, p. 2116. Order No. 58-1337.

GILPATRICK, Meredith Perry. *Military strategy on the western front, 1871-1914.* University of Chicago, 1958.

GOLDIN, Rosaline. *The chief of staff in diplomacy: a study of the conferences between the chiefs of staffs of the French and Russian armies, 1892-1914.* University of Pennsylvania, 1940.

GREENE, Fred. *French military leadership and security against Germany, 1919-1940.* Yale University, 1950. DAI 31/11-A, p. 5983. Order No. 71-12,506.

HARVEY, Donald Joseph. *French concepts of military strategy (1919-1939).* Columbia University, 1953. DAI 14/09, p. 1374. Order No. 8681.

HARVEY, James C. *The French security thesis and French foreign policy from Paris to Locarno, 1919-1925.* University of Texas at Austin, 1955.

HUGHES, Judith Markham. *To the Maginot Line: the politics of French military preparation in the 1920's.* Harvard University, 1970.

JACKSON, Brian Joseph. *The French Left and national education: 1919-1939.* The Catholic University of America, 1963.

DAI 24/04, p. 1591. Order No. 63-4464.

JUMPER, Roy E. *The recruitment and training of civil administrators for overseas France: a case study in French bureaucracy.* Duke University, 1955.

KATZENBACH, Edward Lawrence, Jr. *Charles-Louis de Saulces de Freycinet and the army of metropolitan France — 1870-1918: a study in the politics of military security.* Princeton University, 1953. DAI 14/02, p. 346. Order No. 6820.

KRAUSE, Michael Detlef. *Anglo-French military planning, 1905-1914, before the First World War: a study in military diplomacy.* Georgetown University, 1968. DAI 29/03-A, p. 853. Order No. 68-12,808.

KRAUSKOPF, Robert W. *French air power policy: 1919-1939.* Georgetown University, 1965. DAI 26/08, p. 4609. Order No. 65-6511.

LANEY, Frank Miller, Jr. *The military implementation of the Franco-Russian alliance, 1890-1914.* University of Virginia, 1954. DAI 14/10, p. 1695. Order No. 9653.

LEBERSTEIN, Stephen. *Revolutionary education: French libertarian theory and experiments, 1895-1915.* The University of Wisconsin, 1972. DAI 32/10-A, p. 5715. Order No. 72-9135.

LOOKS, Bernard Joseph. *National renaissance and educational reform in France, 1863-1914: normaliens, political change, and the schools.* Columbia University, 1968. DAI 29/06-A, p. 1659. Order No. 68-16,913.

MATTHEW, Virgil Lee, Jr. *Joseph Simon Gallieni (1849-1916): Marshal of France.* University of California, Los Angeles, 1967. DAI 28/04-A, p. 1375. Order No. 67-12,227.

MUNHOLLAND, John Kim. *The emergence of the colonial military in France, 1880-1905.* Princeton University, 1964. DAI 25/10, p. 5894. Order No. 65-56.

RALSTON, David Bird. *The army and the republic: the place of the military in the political and constitutional evolution of France, 1871-1914.* Columbia University,

1964. DAI 26/03, p. 1618. Order No. 65-7394.

ROPP, Theodore. *The development of a modern navy: French naval policy, 1871-1904.* Harvard University, 1937.

RYAN, Stephen. *Pétain and French military planning, 1900-1940.* Columbia University, 1961. DAI 22/08, p. 2777. Order No. 61-5480.

SINZER, Joseph. *The revival of nationalism as reflected in French military thinking from the Dreyfus affair to the Battle of the Marne.* St. John's University, 1950.

SMITH, Robert John. *The école normale supérieure in the Third Republic: a study of the classes of 1890-1904.* University of Pennsylvania, 1967. DAI 28/04-A, p. 1380. Order No. 67-12,808.

SMUCK, Thomas E. *Conscription in France, 1870-1914: a study in parliamentary action.* University of California, Berkeley, 1952.

SOCAS, Roberto Enrique. *France, naval armaments, and naval disarmament: 1918-1922.* Columbia University, 1965. DAI 29/07-A, p. 2334. Order No. 69-568.

STOCK, Phyllis Hartman. *New quarrel of ancients and moderns: the French university and its opponents, 1899-1914.* Yale University, 1965. DAI 27/02-A, p. 447. Order No. 66-1107.

STOLFI, Russel Henry. *Reality and myth: French and German preparations for war, 1933-1940.* Stanford University, 1966. DAI 27/07-A, p. 2125. Order No. 66-14,724.

TALBOTT, John Edwin. *Politics and educational reform in interwar France, 1919-1939.* Stanford University, 1966. DAI 27/10-A, p. 3385. Order No. 67-4437.

TODD, James Everett. *Charles de Gaulle: his role in the military controversies of the 1930's and in the formation of the Free French Movement in the summer of 1940.* University of Colorado, 1965. DAI 28/07-A, p. 2633. Order No. 65-4220.

WEIGOLD, Marilyn E. *National security versus collective security: the role of the couverture in shaping French military and foreign policy (1905-1934).* St. John's University, 1970. DAI 31/05-A, p. 2328. Order No. 70-22,259.

WILLIAMSON, Samuel Ruthven, Jr. *Anglo-French military and naval relations, 1904-1914.* Harvard University, 1966.

SOCIAL AND ECONOMIC

BJORK, Robert Marshall. *The Italian immigration into France, 1870-1954.* Syracuse University, 1955. DAI 15/12, p. 2520. Order No. 15,045.

FINE, Martin. *Toward corporatism: the movement for capital-labor collaboration in France, 1914-1936.* The University of Wisconsin, 1971. DAI 32/07-A, p. 3916. Order No. 71-28,987.

GOLDENBERG, Leon. *Income and savings in France, 1871-1914: a study of income and savings trends in a state with a relatively stationary population.* Northwestern University, 1941.

GOLOB, Eugene O. *The Méline Tariff: French agriculture and nationalist economic policy.* Columbia University, 1945.

HAMMOND, Charles, Jr. *Factors affecting economic growth in France: 1913-1938.* University of Illinois, 1958. DAI 19/01, p. 60. Order No. 58-1701.

HANNAFORD, John W. *French interwar monetary problems.* Harvard University, 1953.

JOHNSON, Harry M. *The fall of France: an essay on the social structure of France between two wars.* Harvard University, 1949.

KAPLAN, Robert Elliot. *France 1893-1898: the fear of revolution among the bourgeoisie.* Cornell University, 1971. DAI 32/04-A, p. 2032. Order No. 71-25,162.

KUISEL, Richard Francis. *The career of Ernest Mercier: politics and the business elite in twentieth-century France.* University of California, Berkeley, 1963. DAI 24/09, p. 3711. Order No. 64-2085.

LIEBOWITZ, Jonathan Joseph. *Strength and hostility: the French image of their nation's economic strength, 1871-1914.* University

of California, Berkeley, 1970. DAI
32/02-A, p. 889. Order No. 71-20,845.

LONG, James William. *The economics of
the Franco-Russian alliance, 1904-1906.*
The University of Wisconsin, 1968. DAI
29/08-A, p. 2644. Order No. 68-14,004.

McGRAW, Booker T. *French monetary
policy, 1927-1938.* Harvard University,
1939.

MAIER, Charles Steven. *The strategies of
bourgeois defense, 1918-1924: a study of
conservative politics and economics in
France, Germany, and Italy.* Harvard University, 1967.

MALLORY, Lester D. *Wheat valorization:
the French attempt.* University of California, Berkeley, 1936.

MARKER, Gordon Allan. *Internal migration
and economic opportunity: France, 1872-
1911.* University of Pennsylvania, 1964.
DAI 25/12, p. 7018. Order No. 65-5788.

MARRUS, Michael Robert. *The politics of
assimilation: a study of the French Jewish
community at the time of the Dreyfus
Affair.* University of California, Berkeley,
1968. DAI 29/12-A, p. 4432. Order No.
69-10,345.

MINNICH, Lawrence A. *Social problems
and political alignments in France, 1893-
1898; Léon Bourgeois and solidarity.*
Cornell University, 1949.

PITTS, Jesse Richard. *The bourgeois family
and French economic retardation.* Harvard
University, 1958.

POWELSON, John P. *French exports and
commercial policy, 1919-1949.* Harvard
University, 1950.

ROBISON, James T. *A historical study of
the Popular Front Movement in France
with emphasis on the social and economic
policies under Léon Blum, 1936-1937.*
University of Colorado, 1949.

ROGERS, David Arthur. *The campaign for
the French National Economic Council,
1918-1925.* The University of Wisconsin,
1957. DAI 17/10, p. 2255. Order No.
22,407.

ROGERS, George Arthur. *French agricultural developments, 1919-1939.* University of Illinois, 1950. DAI 11/01, p. 95.
Order No. 2222.

SANDS, Theodore. *Corporatism in French
agriculture.* The University of Wisconsin,
1951.

SCHMID, Gregory Carl. *The politics of
financial instability: France, 1924-1926.*
Columbia University, 1968. DAI 30/02-A,
p. 475. Order No. 69-9215.

SCHUKER, Stephen Alan. *The French financial crisis and the adoption of the Dawes
Plan—1924.* Harvard University, 1969.

SHARPE, Willard D. *The economic policies
of the Popular Front governments of
France, 1936-1938.* Harvard University,
1955.

SMITH, Michael Stephen. *Free trade, pro-
tection, and tariff reform: commerce and
industry in French politics, 1868-1882.*
Cornell University, 1972. DAI 33/09-A,
p. 5105. Order No. 73-7152.

SPRINGER, Annemarie. *Woman in French
fin-de-siècle posters.* Indiana University,
1971. DAI 32/03-A, p. 1416. Order No.
71-23,279.

VALASKAKIS, Kimon Platon. *The influence
of French nationalism on the balance of
payments and balance of indebtedness of
France, 1870-1914.* Cornell University,
1967. DAI 28/06-A, p. 1973. Order No.
67-16,375.

WARNER, Charles K. *The government and
the wine-growers in France, 1875-1953.*
Columbia University, 1958.

WHITLOW, Charles M. *Prices and returns of
securities in France, 1914-1930.* University of Illinois, 1937.

WOLFE, Martin B. *The French franc between the wars, 1919-1939.* Columbia
University, 1951.

SOCIALISM AND THE LABOR MOVEMENT

ALLARDYCE, Gil Daniel. *The political
transition of Jacques Doriot, 1926-1936.*

University of Iowa, 1966. DAI 27/05-A, p. 1311. Order No. 66-11,636.

ARUM, Peter Marshall. *Georges Dumoulin: biography of a revolutionary syndicalist, 1877-1923.* University of Wisconsin, 1971. DAI 32/06-A, p. 3190. Order No. 71-23,288.

BAKER, Donald Noel. *Revolutionism in the French Socialist party between the World Wars: the revolutionary* tendances. Stanford University, 1965. DAI 26/07, p. 3894. Order No. 65-12,740.

BAKER, Robert Parsons. *A regional study of working-class organization in France: socialism in the Nord, 1870-1924.* Stanford University, 1967. DAI 28/01-A, p. 172. Order No. 67-7894.

BOWDITCH, John, III. *A history of the General Confederation of Labor in France from the beginnings to 1914.* Harvard University, 1948.

BROWER, Daniel Roberts, Jr. *The French Communist party and the Popular Front, 1934 to 1938.* Columbia University, 1963. DAI 25/11, p. 6560. Order No. 64-2739.

BUTLER, James Charles. *Fernand Pelloutier and the emergence of the French syndicalist movement, 1880-1906.* The Ohio State University, 1960. DAI 21/01, p. 178. Order No. 60-2112.

COHN, William Henry. *Paul LaFargue: Marxist disciple and French revolutionary socialist.* University of Wisconsin, 1972. DAI 32/12-A, p. 6883. Order No. 72-13,077.

COLTON, Joel G. *Compulsory labor arbitration in France 1936-1939.* Columbia University, 1950. DAI 10/03, p. 196. Order No. 1839.

DALBY, Louise Elliott. *The ideas of Léon Blum.* Radcliffe College, 1956.

DALE, Leon A. *A genetic study of the French labor movement and its doctrines with emphasis on contemporary trends.* University of Wisconsin, 1949.

DeLUCIA, Michael Sabatino. *The remaking of French syndicalism, 1911-1918: the growth of the reformist philosophy.* Brown

University, 1971. DAI 32/09-A, p. 5145. Order No. 72-8105.

DERFLER, A. Leslie. *Reformism: the socialist years of Alexandre Millerand.* Columbia University, 1962.

ELLIS, Jack Don. *French socialist and syndicalist approaches to peace, 1904-1914.* Tulane University, 1967. DAI 28/10-A, p. 4072. Order No. 68-4034.

FRY, Nenah Elinor. *Integral socialism and the Third Republic, 1883 to 1914.* Yale University, 1964. DAI 25/11, p. 6567. Order No. 65-1930.

GARDNER, Vivian Pauline. *Maurice Thorez: policies and practices of the French Communist leader.* University of Southern California, 1966. DAI 27/09-A, p. 2985. Order No. 67-2108.

GOLDSMITH, Susan Jane. *Schism and decline: a study of the French Socialist party.* University of Chicago, 1963.

GOSCH, Stephen S. *Socialism and the intellectuals in France, 1890-1914.* Rutgers University The State University of New Jersey, 1972. DAI 33/09-A, p. 5067. Order No. 73-4747.

GREENE, Nathanael. *French socialism and the international crisis, 1936-1939.* Harvard University, 1964.

GREENE, Thomas Hiatt. *The French Communist party: Marxism, communism, and politics.* Cornell University, 1965. DAI 26/10, p. 6138. Order No. 66-59.

HOSTETTER, Richard J. *The anti-war policy of the French Socialist party (S.F.I.O.), 1905-1914: a study of patriotism expressed through the ideas of the general strike and insurrection.* University of California, Berkeley, 1947.

HOVDE, Brynjolf Jakob. *Studies in the attitude of the French socialists toward imperialism, 1893-1914.* University of Iowa, 1924.

JOUGHIN, Jean A. T. *The labor movement in France, 1876-1884.* University of Texas, 1947.

LAURIDSEN, Kurt Victor. *Revolution in Russia and response in France contemporary views from the French Far Left, 1905-1907.* New York University, 1971. DAI 32/07-A, p. 3926. Order No. 72-3090.

LEHMANN, Shirley Jeanne. *The French Socialist party, 1905-1914: a socio-political analysis.* Radcliffe Colleges, 1961.

LEVEY, Jules. *The Sorelian syndicalists: Édouard Berth, Georges Valois, and Hubert Lagardelle.* Columbia University, 1967. DAI 30/10-A, p. 4376. Order No. 70-7016.

LOCKWOOD, Theodore Davidge. *French Socialists and political responsibilities, 1898-1905.* Princeton University, 1952. DAI 15/04, p. 570. Order No. 10,951.

LOGUE, William H. *The career of Léon Blum to 1914.* University of Chicago, 1965.

LORWIN, Val R. *Trade unions in France.* Cornell University, 1953.

MARCUS, John Theodor. *French Socialism: its response to the growing threats of fascism and war, 1933-1936.* Cornell University, 1954. DAI 14/11, p. 2050. Order No. 9765.

MEAD, Robert Osborn. *The struggle for power: reformism in the French Socialist party (S.F.I.O.), 1919-1939.* Columbia University, 1952. DAI 12/05, p. 738. Order No. 4221.

MOODIE, Thomas. *The Parti Ouvrier Français, 1879-1893: the formation of a political sect.* Columbia University, 1966. DAI 30/04-A, p. 1507. Order No. 69-15,574.

MURPHY, Francis J. *Maurice Thorez and "La Main Tendue": French communists and Catholics, 1936-1939.* The Catholic University of America, 1971. DAI 32/05-A, p. 2613. Order No. 71-29,237.

NOLAND, Aaron. *The founding of the French Socialist party, 1893-1905.* Harvard University, 1948.

NOONAN, Lowell G. *Study of the theory and tactical policy of the French Socialist party (S.F.I.O.), 1920-1937; an evaluation of French reformist socialism.* University of California, Berkeley, 1952.

PAPAYANIS, Nicholas Christopher. *Alphonse Merrheim and revolutionary syndicalism, 1871-1917.* The University of Wisconsin, 1969. DAI 31/02-A, p. 716. Order No. 70-3655.

PATSOURAS, Louis. *Jean Grave: French intellectual and anarchist, 1854-1939.* The Ohio State University, 1966. DAI 27/09-A, p. 2997. Order No. 67-2512.

PENN, Donald R. *The Dreyfus and Millerand crises and the French Socialist party.* The University of Wisconsin, 1950.

ROBINSON, Genevieve L. *The public career of Jean Léon Jaurès.* University of Southern California, 1935.

ROTSTEIN, Maurice. *The public life of Gustave Hervé.* New York University, 1956. DAI 16/10, p. 1894. Order No. 18,064.

SANDERS, Richard Wayne. *The labor policies of the French Radical party, 1901-1909.* Duke University, 1972. DAI 33/03-A, p. 1127. Order No. 72-23,254.

SAVAGE, William Rex, Jr. *The cult of Jean Jaurès, 1914-1924.* University of Chicago, 1963.

THORMANN, Gerard Charles. *Christian trade unionism in France: a history of the French Confederation of Christian Workers.* Columbia University, 1952. DAI 12/01, p. 50. Order No. 3386.

WALL, Irwin Myron. *French socialism and the Popular Front.* Columbia University, 1968. DAI 30/02-A, p. 672. Order No. 69-9226.

WEINSTEIN, Harold R. *Jean Jaurès; a study of patriotism in the French socialist movement.* Columbia University, 1937.

WOHL, Robert Albert. *The road to Tours; the origins of the French Communist party, 1914-1920.* Princeton University, 1965. DAI 24/09, p. 3725. Order No. 64-3580.

REGIONAL STUDIES

CRAFT, George Springer, Jr. *The emergence of national sentiment in French Lorraine, 1871-1889.* Stanford University, 1971. DAI 32/02-A, p. 876. Order No. 71-19,667.

GALLUP, Stephen Vincent. *Communists and Socialists in the Vaucluse, 1920-1939.* University of California, Los Angeles, 1972. DAI 32/11-A, p. 6338. Order No. 72-13,607.

GLASER, William. *Local government and life in Paris, 1914-1918.* University of Missouri, 1962. DAI 23/09, p. 3333. Order No. 63-1552.

GREENBERG, Louis Morris. *Marseille, Lyon and the Paris Commune: the search for local liberties 1868-1871.* Harvard University, 1963.

HUTTON, Patrick Henry. *The Boulangist movement in Bordeaux politics.* University of Wisconsin, 1970. DAI 31/02-A, p. 708. Order No. 70-3564.

REECE, Jack Eugene. *Anti-France: the search for the Breton nation, (1898-1948.)* Stanford University, 1971. DAI 32/10-A, p. 5719. Order No. 72-11,643.

SCHEIFLEY, William H. *Brieux and contemporary French society.* University of Pennsylvania, 1914.

WOLF, Peter Michael. *Eugène Hénard and city planning of Paris 1900-1914.* New York University, 1968. DAI 30/11-A, p. 4894. Order No. 70-7398.

INTELLECTUAL AND CULTURAL

ADAMS, David Kenneth. *The voyage to Sparta: political ideas in selected writings of Maurice Barrès.* Indiana University, 1962. DAI 23/11, p. 4329. Order No. 63-3797.

ALLEN, Donald Roy. *French views of America in the nineteen-thirties.* Boston University, 1970. DAI 31/05-A, p. 2292. Order No. 70-22,359.

ALPERT, Harry. *Émile Durkheim and his sociology.* Columbia University, 1940.

ALZONA, Encarnación. *Some French contemporary opinions of the Russian Revolution of 1905.* Columbia University, 1922.

ANDERSON, Thomas Patrick. *The French intelligentsia and the Spanish civil war, 1936-1939.* Loyola University of Chicago, 1965.

BJELLAND, Andrew George. *The foundations of Bergson's metaphysics: an essay on Henri Bergson's early metaphysical dualism.* St. Louis University, 1970. DAI 31/08-A, p. 4212. Order No. 71-3250.

BOHLMANN, Wilmer L. *Some aspects of the legal and political theories of Léon Duguit: a study in constitutionalism.* University of Washington, 1960. DAI 20/12, p. 4700. Order No. 60-1860.

BURNS, M. François, Sister. *Maurice Barrès: myth-maker of modern French nationalism.* The Catholic University of America, 1968. DAI 29/12-A, p. 4415. Order No. 69-9161.

BUTHMAN, William C. *The rise of integral nationalism in France, with special reference to the ideas and activities of Charles Maurras.* Columbia University, 1940.

CIEPLAK, Tadeusz Nowak. *Sorel and French radicalism.* McGill University, 1962.

CLARK, Terry Nichols. *Empirical social research in France, 1850-1914.* Columbia University, 1967. DAI 28/02-A, p. 798. Order No. 67-10,572.

CURTIS, Michael Raymond. *Counter-revolution in France 1885-1914: a study of Sorel, Barrès, and Maurras.* Cornell University, 1958. DAI 19/07, p. 1806. Order No. 59-22.

DAVIES, David Cyril. *Ideology and myth in the philosophy of Georges Sorel.* University of Toronto, 1970. DAI 32/09-A, p. 5299.

DICK, Mechtraud, Sister. *A comparative study of the concept of solidarity as viewed in the teachings of Heinrich Pesch, S.J., and Émile Durkheim.* St. Louis University, 1954.

D'OUAKIL, Basile G. *French individualism and American individualism compared.* Fordham University, 1934.

DUNBAR, Harry B. *The impact of the École Normale Supérieure on selected men of letters of France, 1875-1902. (Parts I and II).* New York University, 1961. DAI 23/02, p. 630. Order No. 62-1413.

ELTON, Maurice George Anthony. *The returning soldier in French literature.* University of Cincinnati, 1969. DAI 30/07-A, p. 2965. Order No. 70-483.

ERCHUL, Ellen Z. *A comparative analysis of the sociological methods of Frédéric LePlay and Émile Durkheim.* University of Southern California, 1953.

FARMER, Paul. *France reviews its revolutionary origins; social politics and historical opinion in the Third Republic.* Columbia University, 1944.

FISCHER, Philip S. *The French theatre and French attitudes toward war, 1919-1939.* University of Connecticut, 1970. DAI 31/12-A, p. 6515. Order No. 71-15,981.

FOSKETT, John McK. *Émile Durkheim and the problem of social order.* University of California, Berkeley, 1940.

FOX, Edward Whiting. *An estimate of the character and extent of antiparliamentary thought in France, 1887-1914.* Harvard University, 1942.

GAGNON, Paul Abelard. *French views of post-war America, 1919-1932.* Harvard University, 1960.

GEIGER, Roger Lewis. *The development of French sociology, 1871-1905.* The University of Michigan, 1972. DAI 33/09-A, p. 5084. Order No. 73-6835.

GOLDBERGER, Avriel Horwitz. *Silhouette of the twentieth century hero in France.* Bryn Mawr College, 1960. DAI 22/12, p. 4350. Order No. 62-2112.

GROGIN, Robert Charles. *The French intellectuals: reactions to Henri Bergson, 1900-1914.* New York University, 1969. DAI 30/06-A, p. 2459. Order No. 69-21,250.

HARRISON, Benjamin. *Gabriel Monod and the professionalization of history in France,* 1844-1912. The University of Wisconsin, 1972. DAI 33/09-A, p. 5090. Order No. 72-31,679.

HELLMAN, John William. *Emmanuel Mounier and esprit: personalist dialogue with existentialism, Marxism and Christianity.* Harvard University, 1969.

HENNESSY, Joseph Howard. *Maurice Barrès: aesthetics and politics of national enthusiasms (1884-1914).* University of Notre Dame, 1967. DAI 28/12-A, p. 5116. Order No. 68-5103.

HERBERT, Eugenia Warren. *The artist and social reform in France and Belgium, 1885-1898.* Yale University, 1957.

HERRICK, Jane. *The historical thought of Fustel de Coulanges.* Catholic University of America, 1955.

HOLDHEIM, William Wolfgang. *Gide and Nietzsche.* Yale University, 1955. DAI 31/03-A, p. 1279. Order No. 69-18,548.

HUMPHREY, Richard D. *The thought of Georges Sorel as an anti-intellectualist interpretation of history.* Harvard University, 1937.

HUNTINGTON, Frank C. *The ideology of the Action Française.* Yale University, 1954. DAI 31/03-A, p. 1195. Order No. 70-16,655.

JEFFERSON, Alfred Carter. *The political attitudes and activities of Anatole France, 1897-1924.* University of Chicago, 1960.

KEYLOR, William Robert. *Clio and the King: Jacques Bainville and the renaissance of royalist history in modern France.* Columbia University, 1972.

Le BLANC, Emile N. *L'Action Française interpreted in the light of French positivism.* Fordham University, 1937.

LEWIS, Helena Fales. *The politics of the French surrealists, 1919-1945.* New York University, 1971. DAI 32/10-A, p. 5716. Order No. 72-13,384.

LINVILLE, Lyle E. *Jacques Bainville: his political life and thought in the era of the Great War.* Kent State University, 1972. DAI 32/11-A, p. 6345. Order No. 72-16,262.

LYTLE, Scott H. *Historical materialism and the social myth: a study of Georges Sorel's conception of history.* Cornell University, 1949.

MANDELL, Richard Donald. *Politicians, intellectuals, and the Universal Exposition of 1900 in Paris.* University of California, Berkeley, 1965. DAI 26/08, p. 4610. Order No. 65-13,537.

MILLER, B. Jaye. *French personalism and the search for community: the social and political philosophy of the pre-war esprit.* Yale University, 1972. DAI 33/07-A, p. 3550. Order No. 72-33,026.

MORTON, Jacqueline. *André Gide and François Mauriac: counter-currents of our time.* Columbia University, 1969. DAI 32/11-A, p. 6444. Order No. 72-15,588.

NICHOLS, Raymond Lindley. *The intellectual and modern politics: Julien Benda and the case of France.* Princeton University, 1965. DAI 26/12, p. 7424. Order No. 66-5005.

NYBAKKEN, Ruth Elaine. *Anatole France: the artist as historian.* Columbia University, 1967. DAI 28/02-A, p. 688. Order No. 67-9362.

O'DONNELL, Charles Peter. *The cultural and political philosophy of Jacques Maritain.* Harvard University, 1940.

ROBERTSON, Nancy Susan. *L'Action Française: "L'appel à la race".* Université Laval (Canada), 1971.

SIEGEL, Martin. *Science and the historical imagination: patterns in French historiographical thought, 1866-1914.* Columbia University, 1965. DAI 27/02-A, p. 446. Order No. 66-6961.

SILVERA, Alan David. *Daniel Halévy and his times: a gentleman-commoner in the Third Republic.* Harvard University, 1963.

SLOTNICK, Herman Edward. *The French Academy and the Third Republic, 1897-1914.* University of Washington, 1958. DAI 19/11, p. 2932. Order No. 59-1237.

SMITH, Clark Cavanaugh. *The culture and politics of Dryfusisme: a history of Charles Péguy's Cahiers de la Quinzaine, 1900-1905.* University of California, Berkeley, 1972.

SOUCY, Robert Joseph. *The image of the hero in the works of Maurice Barrès and Pierre Drieu La Rochelle.* The University of Wisconsin, 1963. DAI 24/06, p. 2452. Order No. 64-674.

SUSMAN, Warren Irving. *Pilgrimage to Paris: the backgrounds of American expatriation, 1920-1934.* University of Wisconsin, 1958. DAI 18/03, p. 1032. Order No. 58-833.

TROTTMAN, Paul Miller. *French criticism of Charles Baudelaire, themes and ideas— 1918-1940.* University of Georgia, 1971. DAI 32/09-A, p. 5247. Order No. 72-11,053.

WARSHAW, Daniel. *Paul Leroy-Beaulieu, bourgeois ideologist: a study of the social, intellectual and economic sources of late nineteenth century imperialism.* University of Rochester, 1966. DAI 27/05-A, p. 1328. Order No. 66-10,830.

WUSSOW, Walter Jack. *French freemasonry and the threat of war, 1917-1939.* University of Colorado, 1966. DAI 28/03-A, p. 1043. Order No. 67-10,095.

YASHINSKY, Palomba. *Le type juif sur la scène française de 1870 à 1914.* Wayne State University, 1969. DAI 32/05-A, p. 2715. Order No. 71-29,991.

YATES, Stanley Martin. *The Commune in French historical writing.* University of Illinois, 1961. DAI 21/12, p. 3764. Order No. 61-1683.

RELIGION

AMATO, Joseph Anthony. *Emmanuel Mounier and Jacques Maritain: a French Catholic understanding of the modern world.* The University of Rochester, 1970. DAI 31/07-A, p. 3458. Order No. 71-1365.

BREUNIG, Charles. *The Sillon of Marc Sangnier: Christian-Democracy in France (1894-1910).* Harvard University, 1953.

DARROW, Robert M. *Catholic political power — a study of the American Catholic Church on behalf of France, 1936-1939.* Columbia University, 1953. DAI 22/10, p. 3721. Order No. 62-86.

DETERT, Mary Xavier. *Catholic political activity in France, 1892-1914.* The Catholic University of America, 1963. DAI 24/02, p. 714. Order No. 63-6339.

GIMPL, M. Caroline Ann. *The* Correspondent *and the founding of the French Third Republic.* Catholic University of America, 1959.

HOLLEY, John Bostwick. *The religious ideas of Prosper Mérimée.* Catholic University of America, 1971. DAI 32/03-A, p. 1442. Order No. 71-22,764.

JUNG, Hwa Yol. *God, man and politics: the political philosophy and theology of Jacques Maritain.* University of Florida, 1962. DAI 24/01, p. 371. Order No. 62-3949.

KESSLER, Mary Verona. *The effects of the Laic Laws of 1901 and 1904 on the Benedictines in France.* University of Notre Dame, 1963. DAI 24/03, p. 1152. Order No. 63-6763.

MARION, Raymond Joseph. La Croix *and the ralliement.* Clark University, 1957. DAI 18/01, p. 217. Order No. 23,901.

MATHER, Judson Irving. La Croix *and the assumptionist response to secularization in France: 1870-1900.* The University of Michigan, 1971. DAI 32/07-A, p. 3926. Order No. 72-4930.

PAUL, Harry Wilmore. *The second ralliement: church-state relations in France, 1919-1928.* Columbia University, 1962. DAI 24/12, p. 5364. Order No. 63-5959.

POIRIER, Rene. *Un abbé démocrate picard: Charles Calippe. Sa pensée sociale, 1893-1914.* The Catholic University of America, 1972. DAI 33/02-A, p. 7040. Order No. 72-22,680.

RAUCH, Rufus William, Jr. *Politics and belief in modern France: Emmanuel Mounier and the Christian Democratic movement, 1932-1950.* Columbia University, 1964. DAI 25/12, p. 7231. Order No. 64-11,314.

RUMMELL, Leo Leonard. *The Third French Republic and the religious associations.* The University of Wisconsin, 1945.

RYAN, William Francis. La Croix *and the development of rightist nationalism in France: 1883-1889.* The University of Connecticut, 1970. DAI 31/12-A, p. 6530. Order No. 71-16,034.

FRANCE SINCE 1940

GENERAL AND MISCELLANEOUS

ADJEMIAN, George Roopen. *NATO without France.* Claremont Graduate School and University Center, 1971. DAI 32/02-A, p. 1046. Order No. 71-21,675.

AMBLER, John Steward. *French civil-military relations: the problem of civilian control, 1940-1961.* University of California, Berkeley, 1964. DAI 25/03, p. 2012. Order No. 64-8979.

ANDREWS, William George. *Pierre Mendès-France: a study of political ideas in action.* Cornell University, 1959. DAI 20/09, p. 3808. Order No. 60-297.

BATCHELDER, John Thayer. *Parliament, planning, and politics in post-war France: a study of plan-parliamentary relations from 1945-1965.* The University of Michigan, 1967. DAI 28/07-A, p. 2743. Order No. 67-17,723.

CARASSO, Roger Claude Andrew. *Ideological considerations in the French rejection of the European defense community.* Princeton University, 1964. DAI 25/11, p. 6733. Order No. 64-12,113.

CHARLTON, Sue Ellen M. *The attitudes and policies of the French Socialist Party (SFIO) regarding European integration (1946-1966).* University of Denver, 1966. DAI 30/05-A, p. 2102. Order No. 69-19,348.

CODEVILLA, Angelo M. *Modern democracy in France.* Claremont Graduate School, 1973. DAI 33/09-A, p. 5246. Order No. 73-6167.

COLE, Robert Reed. *Gaullism and French youth.* Duke University, 1971. DAI 32/03-A, p. 1578. Order No. 71-24,181.

CROCKER, Chester Arthur. *The military transfer of power in Africa: a comparative study of change in the British and French systems of order.* The Johns Hopkins University, 1969. DAI 32/12-A, p. 7066. Order No. 72-16,834.

DAVIS, Edward Braxton, III. *Relations between France and Senegal: 1960-1969.* University of Virginia, 1970. DAI 31/09-A, p. 4865. Order No. 70-26,579.

GARDINIER, David Elmer. *French policy in the Cameroons, 1945-1959.* Yale University, 1960.

GEISMAR, Peter Maxwell. *De Gaulle, the army, and Algeria: the civil-military conflict over decolonization, 1958-1962.* Columbia University, 1967. DAI 31/03-A, p. 1189. Order No. 70-17,010.

GIRARD, Rene N. *American opinion of France, 1940-1943.* Indiana University, 1950.

GORLIN, Jacques J. *National security and the claims of democracy: a comparative study of the conflict in the United States and France.* The Johns Hopkins University, 1971. DAI 32/05-A, p. 2771. Order No. 71-29,147.

HAMBURGER, Robert Lee. *Franco-American relations, 1940-1962: the role of United States anticolonialism and anticommunism in the formulation of United States policy on the Algerian question.* University of Notre Dame, 1970. DAI 32/01-A, p. 519. Order No. 71-19,080.

HAMILTON, Margaret L. *French policy toward Morocco: 1944-1956.* Columbia University, 1959. DAI 20/09, p. 3812. Order No. 60-16.

HUNT, William Harrison. *Careers and perspectives of French politicians.* Vanderbilt University, 1966. DAI 27/10-A, p. 3496. Order No. 67-4089.

JOSHUA, Wynfred. *French attitudes toward NATO.* University of Pittsburgh, 1964. DAI 25/06, p. 3670. Order No. 64-10,339.

KING, Francis Paul. *The third force in French politics.* Stanford University, 1953. DAI 13/02, p. 252. Order No. 4674.

McNUTT, Dennis Melvin. *Independent West Africa: an examination of British and French colonial policies.* The Claremont Colleges, 1966. DAI 28/02-A, p. 742. Order No. 67-9551.

MARCUM, John Arthur. *French North Africa in the Atlantic community.* Stanford University, 1955. DAI 15/06, p. 1105. Order No. 12,270.

MORSE, Edward Lewis. *France and the politics of interdependence.* Princeton University, 1969. DAI 31/03-A, p. 1349. Order No. 70-14,227.

MURCH, Arvin Wayne. *Political integration as an alternative to independence in the French Antilles.* Yale University, 1968. DAI 29/03-A, p. 976. Order No. 68-13,183.

PIERCE, Roy. *The Rassemblement du Peuple Française.* Cornell University, 1951.

PITTS, Ruth Ann. *De Gaulle and the parties: a study in political legitimacy.* University of Washington, 1968. DAI 29/08-A, p. 2823. Order No. 68-17,201.

PRUD'HOMME, Lawrence Haviland. *The second career of Paul Reynaud: 1946-1966.* University of California, Davis, 1971. DAI 32/09-A, p. 5161. Order No. 72-9909.

RICHTER, Robert Charles. *French policy and attitudes toward Poland, 1944-1964.* New York University, 1965. DAI 27/03-A, p. 808. Order No. 66-5694.

RINGQUIST, Delbert Joseph. *Cross-national patterns of development and political violence in countries formerly under French rule.* The University of Oklahoma, 1971. DAI 32/11-A, p. 6515. Order No. 72-14,119.

ROSENTHAL, Howard Lewis. *Contemporary French politics and sub-strata analysis.*

106

Massachusetts Institute of Technology, 1965.

SCHECHTER, Stephen L. *International dependence relations: a study of the transactional ties of the former British and French dependencies.* University of Pittsburgh, 1972. DAI 33/11-A, p. 6430. Order No. 73-12,363.

SCHONFELD, William Rost. *Authority in France: a model of political behavior drawn from case studies in education.* Princeton University, 1970. DAI 31/06-A, p. 2997. Order No. 70-23,636.

SERFATY, Simon Henry. *An ascendant France: French policy toward Europe since World War II.* The Johns Hopkins University, 1967. DAI 28/05-A, p. 1880. Order No. 67-13,828.

SILVER, Jacob. *France and European integration: an inquiry into the elements of political loyalty.* The Ohio State University, 1971. DAI 32/05-A, p. 2764. Order No. 71-27,559.

SLOTTA, Peter Luis. *France, Germany, and European unification: a formal analysis.* University of Pennsylvania, 1968. DAI 29/10-A, p. 3661. Order No. 69-5669.

SMITH, Peter Damian, Sister. *Politique: a current of French Christian democracy.* The Catholic University of America, 1967. DAI 29/01-A, p. 217. Order No. 68-9256.

SPRINZAK, Ehud Zelig. *Democracy and illegitimacy: a study of the American and the French student protest movements and some theoretical implications.* Yale University, 1971. DAI 33/02-A, p. 804. Order No. 72-22,522.

STRONG, Edwin B., Jr. *The disarray of NATO: a study of the American and French designs for the Atlantic alliance and an appraisal of the resulting crisis they have created for the North Atlantic Treaty adherents.* University of Kansas, 1967. DAI 28/11-A, p. 4687. Order No. 68-6945.

THORSEN, Laurence Conger. *French medical syndicates as political pressure groups.* University of Illinois at Urbana-Champaign, 1970. DAI 31/05-A, p. 2465. Order No. 70-21,074.

TRAINER, Edwin Hudson. *The dilemma of the center: the Mouvement Republicain Populaire and the Radical Socialists face the Rassemblement du Peuple Français.* Emory University, 1964. DAI 25/04, p. 2478. Order No. 64-11,222.

WERMUTH, Anthony Lewis. *France, alliance partner.* Boston University Graduate School, 1972. DAI 33/04-A, p. 1808. Order No. 72-25,351.

WILLS, George Robert. *The European policies of General de Gaulle.* Duke University, 1967. DAI 28/09-A, p. 3739. Order No. 68-2752.

WOSHINSKY, Oliver Hanson. *The political incentives of French deputies.* Yale University, 1971. DAI 32/12-A, p. 7065. Order No. 72-17,199.

ZARTMAN, I. William. *De la résistance à la révolution: postwar French neutralism.* Yale University, 1956.

THE OCCUPATION AND THE LIBERATION, 1940-1945

COPELAND, Henry Jefferson, Jr. *The resistance and post-liberation French politics, 1940-1946.* Cornell University, 1966. DAI 27/03-A, p. 724. Order No. 66-7860.

FLETCHER, Harold Augustus, Jr. *The nationalization debate in France (1942-1946).* Harvard University, 1957.

GIRARD, Charlotte Sylvia Marie. *The effects of Western Hemispheric issues upon Franco-American relations during the Second World War.* Bryn Mawr College, 1968. DAI 18/24-A, p. 4424. Order No. 69-9049.

HYTIER, Adrienne D. *Two years of French foreign policy 1940-1942.* Columbia University, 1958.

JASPERSON, Michael. *Laval and the Nazis: a study of Franco-German relations.* Georgetown University, 1967. DAI 28/08-A, p. 3112. Order No. 68-1907.

KRAMER, Steven Philip. *The provisional republic, the collapse of the French resistance front and the origins of post-war politics: 1944-1946.* Princeton University,

1971. DAI 32/11-A, p. 6344. Order No. 72-14,152.

MATHIEU, Gilbert. *The strategy and tactics of the French and Belgian Communist parties in relation to Soviet objectives towards Western Europe in 1940 and 1944.* The University of Wisconsin, 1970. DAI 31/11-A, p. 6137. Order No. 71-3142.

MELTON, George Edward. *Admiral Darlan and the diplomacy of Vichy, 1940-1942.* University of North Carolina at Chapel Hill, 1966. DAI 27/08-A, p. 2482. Order No. 67-1033.

PETERSEN, Neal H. *Nor call too loud on freedom: the Department of State, General de Gaulle and the Levant crisis of 1945.* Georgetown University, 1970. DAI 31/06-A, p. 2854. Order No. 70-26,664.

REBHORN, Marlette Diane Olsen. *De Gaulle's rise to power: the failure of American diplomacy, 1942-1944.* The University of Texas at Austin, 1971. DAI 32/11-A, p. 6350. Order No. 72-15,819.

STEINMANN, M. Evangeline. *The Vichy state and French national unity.* St. John's University, 1950.

SWEETS, John Frank. *The Mouvements Unis de la Résistance (M. U. R.), a study of noncommunist resistance movements in France, 1940-1944.* Duke University, 1972. DAI 33/03-A, p. 1132. Order No. 72-23,257.

WACHTEL, Dennis Fay. *De Gaulle and the invasion of North Africa.* St. Louis University, 1964. DAI 25/08, p. 4678. Order No. 64-13,485.

WAHL, Anthony Nicholas. *De Gaulle and the resistance: the rise of reform politics in France.* Harvard University, 1956.

WAINWRIGHT, William Harvey. *De Gaulle and Indochina, 1940-1945.* Fletcher School of Law and Diplomacy (Tufts University), 1972.

THE FOURTH REPUBLIC

AN, Nack Young. *A study of the French presidency under the Fourth Republic.* University of Virginia, 1965. DAI 26/11, p. 6820. Order No. 66-3161.

AUGE, Thomas Edward. *Justice and injustice: the French collaboration trials 1944-1949.* State University of Iowa, 1957. DAI 17/12, p. 2986. Order No. 23,713.

BARRON, Richard William. *The political parties and politics of the Fourth Republic in France: 1944-1948.* University of Virginia, 1956. DAI 17/04, p. 884. Order No. 20,348.

BENYAMIN, Mary Mayflower. *Fluctuations in the prestige of the United States in France: a description of French attitudes toward the United States and its policies, 1945-1955.* Columbia University, 1960. DAI 20/10, p. 4157. Order No. 60-1131.

CAPELLE, Russell Beckett. *The role of the M.R.P. in French foreign policy, 1944-1954.* Boston University, 1958. DAI 19/11, p. 3004. Order No. 58-3092.

CRADDOCK, Walter Randall. *The Saar problem in Franco-German relations, 1945-57.* University of North Carolina at Chapel Hill, 1960. DAI 21/09, p. 2686. Order No. 60-4834.

DOBRICH, John Richard Joseph. *West German rearmament and European integration: the European Defense Community Treaty in France and Western Germany.* New School for Social Research, 1958.

EL-AFANDI, Ahmed Hamed. *Roll call analysis of the input of support: the case of the French political system under stress, 1954-1962.* University of Missouri, Columbia, 1970. DAI 31/05-A, p. 2455. Order No. 70-20,776.

ESTERLINE, John H. *Executive power in France and the United Kingdom, 1945-1949.* University of California, Los Angeles, 1950.

HÉBERT, Robert Dale. *France and the United Nations: 1946-1958.* The Florida State University, 1966. DAI 33/02-A, p. 696. Order No. 72-21,315.

HUDSON, Robert Bowman, III. *Public policy formation in France: application of a policy typology to roll call voting in the National Assembly of the Fourth Republic.* University of North Carolina at Chapel Hill, 1972. DAI 33/04-A, p. 1795. Order No. 72-24,803.

LAFORE, Laurence D. *Press and diplomacy in liberated France: a study of French attitudes toward international affairs as revealed in Paris newspapers, 1944-1947.* Fletcher School of Law and Diplomacy (Tufts University), 1950.

LAUBACH, John Herbert. *The Franco-German Saar Statute; factors contributing to its rejection in the 1955 referendum.* Harvard University, 1958.

LYNE, Stephen Richard. *The French Socialist Party and the Indochina War, 1944-1954.* Stanford University, 1965. DAI 26/07, p. 3908. Order No. 65-12,814.

MACKIE, Norman Story, Jr. *French national security and the postwar treatment of Germany, 1944-1948.* Columbia University, 1960. DAI 21/01, p. 229. Order No. 60-2456.

MARSHALL, Donald Bruce. *The French colonial myth and constitution making in the Fourth Republic.* Yale University, 1968. DAI 30/02-A, p. 662. Order No. 69-13,358.

MOORE, Anne Tucker. *France and the Schuman Plan, 1948-1953.* University of North Carolina at Chapel Hill, 1964. DAI 26/03, p. 1616. Order No. 65-9039.

NIEMI, Donald. *French conservatives and the 1951 electoral reform.* University of Chicago, 1963.

NOVICK, Peter. *The purge in liberated France: 1944-1946.* Columbia University, 1965. DAI 28/12-A, p. 4998. Order No. 68-8550.

OLSON, Charles William. *Decolonization in French politics (1950-1956): Indo-China, Tunisia, Morocco.* Northern Illinois University, 1966. DAI 27/09-A, p. 2996. Order No. 67-1338.

PLANCK, Russell Everett Francis. *Public opinion and political development in the Fourth French Republic, 1944-1949.* Columbia University, 1953. DAI 14/01, p. 101. Order No. 6684.

RITSCH, Frederick Field, Jr. *The French political parties of the left and European integration, 1947-1949.* University of Virginia, 1962. DAI 23/08, p. 2897. Order No. 62-5945.

ROBERTS, Owen Winthrop. *The French Socialist Party and its Indochina policy, 1946-1951.* Columbia University, 1955. DAI 15/07, p. 1249. Order No. 12,318.

SCHEINMAN, Lawrence. *The formulation of atomic energy policy in France under the Fourth Republic.* The University of Michigan, 1963. DAI 24/12, p. 5518. Order No. 64-6744.

SEIGEL, Janet S. *An introduction to the study of the constitution of the Fourth French Republic.* New School for Social Research, 1950.

SHAHEEN, Rafik A. *The evolution of French policy toward Germany, 1945-1950.* University of Southern California, 1952.

STREET, Roberta. *The origins of the Mouvement Republicain Populaire.* Bryn Mawr College, 1953.

TOUSSAINT, Donald Ray. *French policy toward the political unification of Europe: 1944-1954.* Stanford University, 1956. DAI 16/12, p. 2508. Order No. 17,744.

TUCKER, Spencer Coakley. *The Fourth Republic and Algeria.* The University of North Carolina at Chapel Hill, 1966. DAI 27/09-A, p. 3000. Order No. 67-1058.

WILLIS, Frank Roy. *The French zone of occupation in Germany, 1945-49.* Stanford University, 1959. DAI 20/04, p. 1350. Order No. 59-3728.

YATES, Willard Ross. *The doctrine of the Mouvement Republicain Populaire, 1944-1947.* Yale University, 1956. DAI 17/12, p. 3079.

THE FIFTH REPUBLIC

DAWES, De Ann Oborn. *The rhetoric of Charles de Gaulle during the Fifth Republic.* University of Illinois at Urbana-Champaign, 1972. DAI 33/10-A, p. 5866. Order No. 73-9915.

DePORTE, Anton W. *The foreign policy of France under Charles de Gaulle.* University of Chicago, 1957.

FARKAS, Tibor. *The French presidential elections of 1965.* New School for Social Research, 1968. DAI 30/11-A, p. 5040. Order No. 70-7655.

KAIROUZ, Akl. *Franco-German relations between 1958-1968.* University of Utah, 1968. DAI 29/09-A, p. 3195. Order No. 69-3862.

KOHL, Wilfrid Lenard. *The French nuclear force and alliance diplomacy, 1958-1967.* Columbia University, 1968. DAI 31/06-A, p. 3002. Order No. 70-23,449.

KOWITT, Sylvia. *The politics of a tacit alliance: France-Israel relations 1956-1967.* Columbia University, 1970. DAI 33/10-A, p. 5793. Order No. 73-8962.

McHALE, Vincent Edward. *Political aggregation and the French party system: the politics of left-wing unity under the Fifth Republic, 1958-1968.* The Pennsylvania State University, 1969. DAI 31/04-A, p. 1859. Order No. 70-19,436.

MENARD, Orville Duane. *The army and the Fifth Republic: the role of the army in French politics.* University of Nebraska, 1964. DAI 25/05, p. 3086. Order No. 64-11,939.

STRATMAN, David Volodia. *The 1968 French student revolt: a study of modern political delinquency.* Boston University Graduate School, 1970. DAI 31/08-A, p. 4294. Order No. 70-22,426.

SULLIVAN, Alfred Burke. *Franco-American relations: aspects of French politics under Charles de Gaulle.* University of Utah, 1967. DAI 28/04-A, p. 1492. Order No. 67-12,361.

SULLIVAN, Marianna Pulaski. *De Gaulle's policy toward the conflict in Vietnam, 1963-1969.* University of Virginia, 1971. DAI 32/08-A, p. 4696. Order No. 72-7179.

TAYLOR, Patricia. *French voting behavior in 1962: the role of the electorate in the consolidation of the Fifth Republic.* The University of Connecticut, 1970. DAI 31/12-A, p. 6686. Order No. 71-16,048.

WILSON, Franklin Leondus, III. *The attempted unification of the French democratic left, 1963-1968.* University of California, Los Angeles, 1969. DAI 30/11-A, p. 5048. Order No. 70-8225.

GOVERNMENT, ADMINISTRATION, EDUCATION, MILITARY

BENTLEY, Freddie Blake. *An analysis of French higher education.* Indiana University, 1962. DAI 23/10, p. 3711. Order No. 63-2584.

BOLIBAUGH, Jerry Bevoly. *French educational strategies for sub-saharan Africa: their intent, derivation, and development.* Stanford University, 1964. DAI 25/07, p. 3910. Order No. 64-13,563.

CARPENTER, John Anton. *Education in France: decade of reform, 1959-1969: a descriptive analysis of educational reform.* University of Southern California, 1968. DAI 29/07-A, p. 2143. Order No. 69-607.

CLARK, James Milford. *Teachers and politics: a pressure group study of the Fédération de l'Éducation Nationale.* University of Michigan, 1962. DAI 23/02, p. 679. Order No. 62-3228.

FIELDS, Adolph Belden. *Students in politics: L'Union Nationale des Étudiants de France.* Yale University, 1968. DAI 29/11-A, p. 4064. Order No. 69-8346.

FRANKLIN, Joseph Ross. *An examination of the army's role in French military strategy.* The American University, 1968. DAI 28/07-A, p. 2744. Order No. 67-16,532.

GALANT, Henry C. *The French social security system: the politics of administration.* Harvard University, 1953.

IANNUZZELLI, Robert D. *Education for the disadvantaged in France and the United States.* Miami University, 1972. DAI 33/07-A, p. 3481. Order No. 73-1316.

KAMINSKY, Elijah Ben-Zion. *An anti-subversive program in the French public service: the Epuration Administrative of 1944-1953.* Harvard University, 1962.

KING, Jerome Babcock. *Executive organization and administrative practice in the Fourth Republic of France.* Stanford University, 1958. DAI 19/09, p. 2380. Order No. 59-272.

KOBAN, Marie-Pierre. *L'étudiant français tel qu'il apparaît dans l'enquête sociologique et le roman français, 1953/1963.* University

of Washington, 1971. DAI 32/03-A,
p. 1477. Order No. 71-24,050.

LUDWIG, Richard Lowell. *Administrative
systems for urban development and renewal: the case of urban renewal in France.*
University of Pittsburgh, 1971. DAI
32/04-A, p. 2225. Order No. 71-23,940.

MARTIN, William Ryall. *Crisis institutions
and the law in France.* University of
Oklahoma, 1965. DAI 25/06, p. 3655.
Order No. 64-13,330.

PAXTON, Robert Owen. *Army officers in
Vichy France: "The Armistice Army,"
1940-42.* Harvard University, 1963.

SMITH, Anthony Alan. *Concepts of military strategy in the Fifth Republic of
France.* The American University, 1970.
DAI 32/03-A, p. 1456. Order No.
71-22,119.

SOCIAL AND ECONOMIC

ARGERIOU, Milton. *Consequences of up-
ward social mobility among French
workers: a test of the Lipset and Bendix
hypothesis.* University of California, Los
Angeles, 1972. DAI 33/09-A, p. 5295.
Order No. 73-6374.

BAME, Jack. *The Paris money market —
changing patterns in French money and
finance.* New York University, 1961.

BARZANTI, Sergio. *The economic impact
of European integration and particularly
of the European Economic Community
upon certain underdeveloped areas in Italy
and France.* New York University, 1963.
DAI 24/10, p. 4018. Order No. 63-7180.

BOSWORTH, William Arthur. *French
Catholicism on the threshold of the Fifth
Republic: a survey of politically significant Catholic groups at a turning point in
French history.* Princeton University,
1960. DAI 21/05, p. 1237. Order No.
60-4965.

BOUHOUCHE, Ammar. *Conditions and
attitudes of migrant Algerian workers in
France: a survey analysis.* University of
Missouri-Columbia, 1971. DAI 32/03-A,
p. 1576. Order No. 71-22,896.

BUTTIMER, Anne. *Some contemporary
interpretations and historical precedents
of social geography: with particular emphasis on the French contributions to the
field.* University of Washington, 1965.
DAI 27/02-B, p. 514. Order No. 65-5411.

DYAS, Gareth Pooley. *The strategy and
structure of French industrial enterprise.*
Harvard University, 1972. DAI 33/11-A,
p. 5893. Order No. 73-10,498.

FRANCO, Giuseppe Roberto. *Studies of
French post-war inflation.* University of
California, Riverside, 1971. DAI 32/12-A,
p. 6664. Order No. 72-17,057.

FROOMKIN, Joseph N. *French fiscal and
monetary policy in the aftermath of World
War II.* University of Chicago, 1950.

GODT, Paul Jay. *Regionalization and interest groups in France.* New School for
Social Research, 1972. DAI 33/05-A,
p. 2473. Order No. 72-27,873.

HARBOLD, William H. *The Monnet Plan:
the French experiment in national economic planning.* Harvard University, 1953.

HERVÉ, Michel Émile Auguste. *Counter-
inflationary factors in the French economy,
1952-1958.* Harvard University, 1963.

KARSCH, Robert Frederick. *French constitutionalism and the social question.*
University of Missouri, 1948. DAI 9/02,
p. 148. Order No. 1279.

KEARE, Douglas Hamilton. *Planning and
French economic policy: 1958-1965.*
Princeton University, 1966. DAI 27/12-A,
p. 4018. Order No. 67-5730.

LAUX, James Michael. *French economic
policy since the liberation, 1944-1954.*
Northwestern University, 1957. DAI
17/12, p. 2994. Order No. 23,520.

LAWRENCE, Roger Carr. *Tariff preference
and welfare: a study of the EEC and its
French overseas associates.* Columbia University, 1966. DAI 27/11-A, p. 3560.
Order No. 67-5790.

LUBELL, Harold. *The French investment
program: a defense of the Monnet Plan.*
Harvard University, 1953.

MILDER, Nathaniel David. *The political culture of the French business community.* Cornell University, 1970. DAI 31/06-A, p. 2995. Order No. 70-24,902.

MILLER, Seymour Harold. *Inflation in France, 1939-1952.* Columbia University, 1957. DAI 18/04, p. 1296. Order No. 58-1351.

PETERSON, Wallace C. *Economic reconstruction in France: 1946-1952.* The University of Nebraska-Lincoln, 1954.

PRICE, Homer Smith, Jr. *Position and prospects of agriculture in French Mediterranea: a regional case study.* Columbia University, 1964. DAI 26/07, p. 3856. Order No. 65-7392.

SATRA, John Ctirad. *The fate of Jean Monnet's concept of European integration in the light of cross pressures on the European Coal and Steel Community.* The University of Florida, 1961. DAI 22/10, p. 3730. Order No. 62-726.

SCHOLLHAMMER, Hans. *French economic planning and its impact on business decisions.* Indiana University, 1967. DAI 28/12-A, p. 4768. Order No. 68-8786.

SELIGSON, Harry. *The Economic Council of the Fourth French Republic.* University of Colorado, 1954.

STIGUM, Marcia Lee. *Impact of the European Economic Community on the French cotton and electrical engineering industries.* Massachusetts Institute of Technology, 1961.

Van NIMMEN, Armand Marie Jean. *French planning: an essay in evaluation.* Columbia University, 1967. DAI 31/03-A, p. 891. Order No. 70-17,053.

VASCONCELLOS, Antonio Serafim Vale E. *Toward the systematization of economic policy: the French experience in economic planning.* Tulane University, 1968. DAI 29/05-A, p. 1334. Order No. 68-15,277.

WOOD, David Michael. *Political issues and the nationalized coal industry in France: 1946-1947.* University of Illinois at Urbana-Champaign, 1961. DAI 21/10, p. 3150. Order No. 61-219.

SOCIALISM AND THE LABOR MOVEMENT

CLARKE, Robert Hamilton. *The politics of French agricultural syndicalism.* Princeton University, 1965. DAI 26/07, p. 4046. Order No. 65-13,131.

DECKER, Jane Elizabeth. *A study in revolutionary theory: the French student-worker revolt of May 1968.* Washington University, 1971. DAI 32/12-A, p. 7053. Order No. 72-17,948.

GODFREY, Edwin Drexel, Jr. *The non-communist left in post war France: an interpretive study in doctrinal intransigence and inflexibility as exemplified by the Socialist Party and non-communist syndicalism.* Princeton University, 1952. DAI 14/02, p. 389. Order No. 6809.

HAMILTON, Richard Frederick. *The social bases of French working-class politics.* Columbia University, 1963. DAI 27/06-A, p. 1947. Order No. 65-7453.

RIEBER, Alfred Joseph. *Stalin and the French Communist Party 1941-1947.* Columbia University, 1959. DAI 20/10, p. 4090. Order No. 60-1160.

SCHAIN, Martin A. *The French trade union movement: mass action, organization and politics.* Cornell University, 1971. DAI 32/04-A, p. 2161. Order No. 71-27,398.

SHULMAN, Marshall Darrow. *Soviet policy in Western Europe and the French Communist party, 1949-1952.* Columbia University, 1959. DAI 20/02, p. 727. Order No. 59-3056.

SIMMONS, Harvey Gerald. *The French Socialist party from 1956 to 1966.* Cornell University, 1967. DAI 28/08-A, p. 3240. Order No. 67-13,925.

INTELLECTUAL AND CULTURAL

BETTLER, Alan Raymond. *A chronicle of the beginnings of French existentialism.* Indiana University, 1970. DAI 31/05-A, p. 2432. Order No. 70-22,825.

DELUE, Steven Muller. *On the Marxism of Jean-Paul Sartre in the light of Jean*

Jacques Rousseau: an analysis of the Critique de la Raison Dialectique. University of Washington, 1971. DAI 32/08-A, p. 4674. Order No. 72-7336.

GREENE, Norman Nathaniel. *Jean-Paul Sartre as critic of political ideologies.* University of Michigan, 1959. DAI 20/05, p. 1847. Order No. 59-4918.

HAMPTON, Joseph B. *The political theory of Jean-Paul Sartre.* Rutgers University The State University of New Jersey, 1959. DAI 20/04, p. 1420. Order No. 59-3579.

ROSENBERG, Merrill Alan. *The French theater during the German occupation.* Harvard University, 1963.

SORUM, Paul Clay. *French intellectuals and decolonization: the search for an ideology of colonial emancipation, 1945-1962.* Harvard University, 1972.

AUTHOR INDEX

Abarca, Ramón Eugenio, 62
Abbiateci, A., 3
Abercrombie, Nigel, 12
Abetz, Otto Friedrich, 49
Acomb, Evelyn M., 43, 95
Acomb, Frances D., 17, 62
Acton, John Emrich, baron, 20
Adam, Antoine, 11
Adam, Gerard, 1, 55
Adams, David Kenneth, 101
Adams, Derrik Brian, 92
Adams, Francis G.W., 70
Adams, Henry M., 80
Adams, Paul Vauthier, 83
Adams, Thomas McStay, 64
Adams, Wallace Earl, 91
Ade, Walter Frank Charles, 68
Adjemian, George Roopen, 104
Adriance, Thomas James, 82
Agoult, Marie Catherine, comtesse d', 32
Aguet, J.-P., 36
Agulhon, Maurice, 16, 36
Alasseur, Claude, 17
Albertini, Rudolf von, 11
Aldridge, A.O., 17
Allardyce, Gil Daniel. 98
Allem, Maurice, 34
Allen, Donald Roy, 101
Allen, Luther, 93
Allen, Mary Kibbe, 86
Allen, Turner Wharton, 65
Allison, John M.S., 31, 86
Alpert, Harry, 101
Alroy, Gil Carl, 86
Althusser, Louis, 18
Alton-Shée, Edmond de Le Lignères, comte d', 39
Alzona, Encarnación, 101
Amann, Peter, 79
Amato, Joseph Anthony, 103
Ambler, John Steward, 54, 104
Amouroux, Henri, 52
An, Nack Young, 107
Anchel, Robert, 14
Anderson, Frank Maloy, 1

Anderson, Jane Jaspersen, 68
Anderson, Thomas Patrick, 101
Andler, Charles P.T., 48
André, Louis, 8
André, Louis Joseph, Général, 49
Andrew, Christopher, 44
Andrews, William George, 104
Ansart, Pierre, 36
Antoine, Michel, 14
Applewhite, Harriet Verdier Branson, 71
Apt, Leon Jerome, 75
Archer, Julian Pratt Waterman, 84
Ardagh, John, 54
Ardashev, Pavel Nikolaevich, 14
Argenson, René Louis de Voyer, 12
Argeriou, Milton, 110
Ariès, Philippe, 3
Armand, Felix, 36
Armand, Laura Maslow, 70
Armengaud, André, 32, 34, 37
Armstrong, Brian G., 12
Arnold, Eric A., Jr., 73
Aron, Raymond, 50, 53, 55
Aron, Robert, 52, 53
Artz, Frederick B., 3, 30
Arum, Peter Marshall, 99
Ascoli, Georges, 11
Asher, Eugene Leon, 60
Atkinson, Geoffrey, 17
Atkinson, John L.B., 86
Auge, Thomas Edward, 107
Augé-Laribé, Michel, 46
Augustine, Flavia, 86
Aulard, François Victor Alphonse, 20, 22, 26, 28, 29
Avenel, George, vicomte d', 7
Avril, Pierre, 53, 54

Baehrel, René, 10
Bagge, Dominique, 37
Bailey, Charles Randall, 64
Bain, Chester Arthur, 86
Bainville, Jacques, 24, 41

Baird, Thomas Reynolds, 73
Baker, Donald Noel, 99
Baker, Robert Parsons, 99
Baldensperger, Fernand, 28
Ball, Rex Harrison, 84
Ballot, Charles, 26
Bame, Jack, 110
Bamford, Paul Walden, 8, 60
Bankwitz, Philip Charles Farwell, 44, 93
Barber, Elinor G., 15, 65
Barbier, Edmund Jean François, 19
Bardoux, Jacques, 49
Barère de Vieuzac, Bertrand, 29
Barker, Nancy N., 80
Barker, Richard John, 83
Barnard, Howard Clive, 25
Barnett, Gary Lew, 66
Barnwell, Stephen B., 77
Barral, Pierre, 47
Barras, Paul Francois Jean Nicolas, 29
Barrière, Pierre, 5
Barron, Richard William, 107
Barrot, Odilon, 39
Barzanti, Sergio, 110
Barzun, Jacques, 66
Bastid, Paul, 30, 32, 37
Batchelder, John Thayer, 104
Batiffol, Louis, 6, 7
Bauchet, Pierre, 54
Baughman, John Joseph, 79
Baum, Warren C., 54
Baumont, Maurice, 41, 44
Baxter, Douglas Clark, 60
Bayet, C., 2
Bayle, Francis, 37
Beach, Vincent W., 30, 78
Beatty, John Louis, 73
Beau de Loménie, Emmanuel, 30, 37
Beaufre, André, 44
Beck, Thomas Davis, 73
Becker, Carl L., 18
Becker, Jean-Jacques, 47
Becker, Michael Kelleher, 58

SE-3091-CA

DATE DUE